irrational security

Irrational Security

The Politics of Defense from Reagan to Obama

Daniel Wirls

The Johns Hopkins University Press
Baltimore

© 2010 The Johns Hopkins University Press
All rights reserved. Published 2010
Printed in the United States of America on acid-free paper
9 8 7 6 5 4 3 2 1

The Johns Hopkins University Press
2715 North Charles Street
Baltimore, Maryland 21218-4363
www.press.jhu.edu

Library of Congress Cataloging-in-Publication Data
Wirls, Daniel, 1960–
    Irrational security : the politics of defense from Reagan to Obama /
    Daniel Wirls.
        p. cm.
    Includes bibliographical references and index.
    ISBN-13: 978-0-8018-9438-1 (hardcover : alk. paper)
    ISBN-10: 0-8018-9438-7 (hardcover : alk. paper)
    ISBN-13: 978-0-8018-9439-8 (pbk. : alk. paper)
    ISBN-10: 0-8018-9439-5 (pbk. : alk. paper)
    1. National security — United States — History — 20th century.
2. National security — United States — History — 21st century.
3. Military spending. 4. United States — Military policy. 5. United
States. Dept. of Defense — Appropriations and expenditures. 6. United
States — Armed Forces — Appropriations and expenditures. 7. United
States — Appropriations and expenditures. 8. United States — Politics
and government. I. Title.
UA23.W49 2010
355'.033073 — dc22   2009026917

A catalog record for this book is available from the British Library.

*Special discounts are available for bulk purchases of this book. For more
information, please contact Special Sales at 410-516-6936 or
specialsales@press.jhu.edu.*

The Johns Hopkins University Press uses environmentally friendly
book materials, including recycled text paper that is composed of at
least 30 percent post-consumer waste, whenever possible. All of our
book papers are acid-free, and our jackets and covers are printed on
paper with recycled content.

contents

Figures

preface

The end of the Cold War prompted social scientists and politicians to probe the forces behind this surprising and historic upheaval in global politics. The same transformation, however, provided a rare natural experiment to investigate the effects of such a seismic shift not only on world politics but also on U.S. politics and policies. Many elements of the American system had been at least in part structured by the Cold War, including presidential power and the role of government in the economy. How would the system respond to this rapid and profound change? In particular, would the end of the threat, which supposedly justified the warfare state, produce commensurate changes in military policy and programs?

I published a book on the politics of the Reagan military buildup in 1992, just as some of the contours of the new era were taking shape. I knew that I wanted to investigate the adjustment by the United States to the end of the Cold War. But it was too soon, much too soon, and I turned my attention to other subjects and projects. Nevertheless, as the 1990s progressed, I collected and drafted material on the developments in defense policy. I was nearly ready to return to this project in earnest, thinking enough time had passed to say something meaningful about the post–Cold War era, when along came September 11, 2001. The Bush defense buildup and the other manifestations of war and militarization demanded that the project incorporate this sea change. What had been a book about the first decade after the Cold War became one about the first two decades and the rollercoaster ride of national security that took the United States from the peak of the Reagan military buildup to the efforts by George H. W. Bush and Bill Clinton to manage the changes following the Cold War, to 9/11 and George W. Bush's massive expansion of military spending and militaristic policies. The result is a purposefully compact critical history of the relationship between military policy and national politics from 1989 to 2009.

The protracted genesis of this book meant that a few generations of students made vital contributions as research assistants, spanning most of my entire career at the University of California, Santa Cruz (UCSC). I express my profound gratitude to Eric Crane, Matt Green (now an assistant professor of political science at Catholic University), Laurie Hauf, Annalisse Leekley, Brandon Neustader, Annie Oliveto, Coby Rudolph — all UCSC undergraduate politics majors. I also had the pleasure of working with several graduate students — Sara Benson, Alex Hirsch, Shawn Nichols, and Lydia Osolinsky — who provided excellent research and assistance. It is a pleasure to single out Corina McKendry, also a Santa Cruz politics graduate student, who not only did superb research but also, when the time came, read the entire manuscript and provided substantive feedback and expert editing. I could not have finished in a timely fashion without her skill and efficiency. Although I remain fully responsible for whatever flaws remain, it is a much better book for her efforts. Finally, Santa Cruz students in my undergraduate course on the politics of military policy listened to and refined my ideas. I had the privilege as well of reading some excellent research papers on a variety of subjects related to this volume.

Aspects of this work, especially on the theoretical debates and approaches (that, it should be noted, are given relatively light treatment in this text), were presented at the Western Political Science Association meetings in 2005 (Oakland, California), 2006 (Albuquerque, New Mexico), and 2008 (San Diego, California) and at the 2006 American Political Science Association annual meeting in Philadelphia, Pennsylvania. I presented some of the empirical research as a "Class of 1960" visitor at Williams College (many thanks to Professors Cathy Johnson and Cheryl Shanks) and during two talks in Washington, D.C., including one to congressional staff, sponsored by the University of California's Institute for the Study of Global Conflict and Cooperation.

I thank the following friends and colleagues for providing along the way data, advice, comments, and criticisms: Amy Belasco, Eva Bertram, Michael Brown, Russell Burgos, Isebill Gruhn, Christopher Kirkey, Jeffrey Knopf, Ronnie Lipschutz, Dina Rasor, Derek Reveron, Elizabeth Sanders, Bartholomew H. Sparrow, Judith Stiehm, Sean Theriault, and Winslow Wheeler. Peter Trubowitz provided vital critical feedback on the draft manuscript. A truncated version of chapter 5 was published in *Inside Defense: Understanding U.S. Military Policy in the 21st Century*, edited by Derek Reveron and Judith Stiehm (New York: Palgrave Macmillan, 2008), 99–114. A small portion of the argument in chapter 2 draws on "Busted: Government and Elections in the Era of Deficit Politics," in *Do Elections Matter?* edited by Benjamin Ginsberg and Alan Stone, 3d ed. (Armonk, N.Y.: M. E. Sharpe), 65–85.

Although now a distant memory, some of the initial research on this project was done participant-observation style when I served as an American Political Science Congressional Fellow in 1993 and 1994. Working for both Representative Lee Hamilton and Senator Christopher Dodd, I provided analysis to both offices, particularly Hamilton's, on the nature and impact of the defense drawdown, and was able to observe the politics of defense as Congress and the Clinton administration reacted to and produced historic change. It was a great pleasure to work again with the staff of Johns Hopkins University Press. I thank Executive Editor Henry Tom for his early interest in and support of this project and Kay Kodner for her astute editing of the manuscript.

Everything is dedicated to my family—Alice, Steven, and Ruth—and so by implication is this book. But I think they will not mind sharing that wonderfully ineluctable recognition this time with two other members of the family. My father passed away while this book and the administration he so opposed were coming to their respective and related finishes. Among other things I owe a great deal of my sense of intellectual curiosity and love of American history to him. This, then, is for my parents, Charles and Ruth Wirls, now both departed but never forgotten.

irrational security

Irrational security

In early 2008, as Americans began the protracted process of picking their next president and the Iraq War entered its sixth year, few would have been shocked to learn that military spending had increased by about 70 percent during the presidency of George W. Bush. That might not seem like a lot for a nation at war. Just as they had accommodated themselves to the fact that the war of choice in Iraq had gone on longer than the war of necessity against Germany and Japan, most Americans might not have been surprised to know that the United States accounted for nearly half of the world's military expenditures. Americans might have been puzzled to learn, however, that the 70 percent increase (and the portion of the world total defense spending) did not include the more than $700 billion separately appropriated since 2001 to cover the costs of the wars in Iraq and Afghanistan. Adjusted for inflation, the U.S. military budget — without counting the war funding — was well above the average for the years of the Cold War. With this expanded budget, the United States was waging an arms race with itself, developing and buying a vast array of weapons — such as F-22 fighters for the air force, the Future Combat System for the army, and ballistic missile defense systems. At $76 billion, the Pentagon's 2007 budget for research and development alone was more than double the entire budget for the Department of Homeland Security and was about half again as big as the entire military budget of Great Britain.

The attacks of September 11, 2001 not only triggered a declaration by the

Bush administration of a "global war on terror," they also facilitated, under the cover of that conflict, a military buildup separate from funding the war on terror — one of the largest increases in military spending in the country's history. This buildup is one of the most important legacies of the Bush presidency. Yet it is not well understood, because the politics of war protected and obscured its size and significance. It was also less controversial than one would expect. The Iraq War was the single most important and contentious policy of the Bush presidency — dominating and dogging the administration until the day Bush left office. The military buildup, by contrast, proceeded quietly and without controversy; indeed most Americans had no idea that it was even happening.

In one of the most ironic consequences of the dysfunctional politics of national security, many of the presidential candidates seeking to replace Bush, including a few Democrats, called for an even stronger military and greater defense spending. Most Americans, even those otherwise well informed, heard next to nothing about the vast military buildup that had taken place alongside the wars. The majority of Americans came to regret the Iraq War. A small minority knew enough to comprehend, and possibly lament, the vast commitment of resources that extended beyond the war to a military buildup that exceeded any during the Cold War, that epochal contest, the ending of which not so many years earlier had augured a more peaceful world.

No single day denotes the end of the Cold War, but the fall of the Berlin Wall in November 1989 was for most Americans the signal that the forty-odd-year conflict was all but over. The United States entered the last decade of the twentieth century as the globe's undisputed and unchallenged superpower, preeminent among a group of allied nations that controlled most of the world's economic and military resources. While the Gulf War and multinational interventions from Haiti to Kosovo might disturb the overall sense of peace and prosperity, the prospect of a global conventional or nuclear conflict seemed remote. The United States would have international burdens and responsibilities but nothing like those of the Cold War.

A single day, September 11, 2001, changed all that; or to be more accurate, allowed all that to be changed. First President Bush declared a global war on terrorism; then, following a nearly inevitable military intervention in Afghanistan, he pushed the nation and world into a war against Iraq. In a few years, the U.S. military budget reached and exceeded Cold War levels. The U.S. military stretched round the globe as the "war" was extended far and wide to places many Americans had never heard of and, perhaps in some cases, would never hear about. In a matter of months, the United States had become a nation-builder of imperial proportions at war with a nebulous enemy of uncertain size and motives. Suddenly the relative peace and quiet of the fin de siécle interlude seemed as quaint as the Cold War itself.

In a decade the United States had buried one Cold War only to create the ideological, political, and fiscal equivalent of another. Just as the Cold War was not all that "cold" (that is, without armed conflict), the so-called war on terror was not entirely or even mostly a war on terror. Millions of lives were lost in the very real conflicts of the Cold War. During that contest, the United States fought wars that were at best marginally related to the struggle between East and West. Even more so the Global War on Terrorism (or GWOT) was defined by a conflict in Iraq that was unrelated to terrorism, let alone the crimes and punishments of September 11, 2001 (or 9/11, as it came to be known). As or more misguided than any hot war of the Cold War era, Iraq was less relevant to a war on terror than Vietnam was to a war against communism. In this way, GWOT was the functional equivalent of a new cold war insofar as it committed the United States politically and economically to an undeclared war to be fought by a variety of means around the globe over an indefinite period. Likewise echoing the Cold War, familiar social and political effects followed, including an empowered presidency, a supine Congress, a largely deferential Supreme Court, and, at least for a time, partisan competition based around jingoistic politics.

This book describes and critiques the politics of military policy that took us from the end of the Cold War to the Iraq War and the largest military buildup since World War II. The focus is on the national politics of choice in the grand strategy and resource commitment for the employment of military force (what I will henceforth call "military policy"). By "national politics of choice" I mean the efforts by elite actors — candidates, office-holders, bureaucrats, interest groups, party leaders — to use and shape military policy to serve their purposes at home and abroad. The politics of military policy involves the interplay of ideas and convictions about the best policies with the political goals and calculations of politicians as they seek to gain and maintain power for various reasons and objectives. Military policy itself is *sometimes* not the goal; it is a tool that can be used or an obstacle that must be dealt with to achieve other ends. Both the end of the Cold War and the events of 9/11 created a scramble to rethink the means and ends of U.S. military policy. A large part of this effort was among national security elite in the military and private sectors, including secretaries of defense, military officers, and academics in think tanks and universities. But politicians and political parties had to adjust as well and redefine their positions on national security issues.

I examine their efforts in this book, with an emphasis on the constraints and opportunities facing Republican and Democratic elites trying to win or retain power. An important component of this political process involves the ways in which changes in the national security environment and military policy affected domestic priorities whether liberal or conservative in the realms of taxes, social security, healthcare, and so forth. My discussion will emphasize the reciprocal relationship between domestic politics and military policy and also the dynamic and interactive relationship between national security policy and national politics. Changes in national security policy, whether or not in response to something as monumental as the end of the Cold War, must have support from the political system. This is obvious enough; indeed, at times changes in national security policy might emerge from the political process rather than from national security elites in the public and private sectors. But the relationship is often complex. Change or lack of change stems from the interactive process between policy ideas and politics. The dynamics of the political system (parties, elections, other policy priorities) can often determine the extent to which potential changes in national security policy can take hold and endure. Indeed, these dynamics can determine which potential changes even have a chance.

This book, then, tells the story of the U.S. military policy during these years largely from the perspective of American politics and for the sake of American politics, or to be more precise, for the sake of our comprehension of American politics and its consequences. The ongoing dominance of studies of military policy by specialists in international relations continues to frustrate the integration of military issues into the study of American political development and contemporary politics.[1] Too often studies of national security, insofar as they incorporate domestic politics, still do so as part of a longstanding debate over the relative influence of international versus domestic causes in the formation of military or foreign policy.[2] That is an important debate but it is not the puzzle for this book, in part because I think it is undeniable that domestic politics often do matter. Instead, this volume makes an argument about *how* domestic forces matter, not so much that they often influence military policy but that they tend to do so in a particular way. There is, as we shall see, a bias to the domestic politics of defense policy. Without denying the international sources and ramifications of these transformations in U.S. foreign and security policy, my goal is to tell this story from the perspective of American politics in terms of its causes and consequences.

In short, this study maps the political construction of U.S. military policy across two periods of significant change and thus provides a unified, but by no means comprehensive, history and analysis of the politics of military policy from the end of the Cold War through the presidency of George W. Bush. The resulting narrative layers three arguments — one historical, one analytic, and one normative. First, the events of September 2001 threaten to eclipse the era between about 1990 and 2000 and draw our attention to crucial but particular aspects of the United States and the world after 9/11. The attacks tempted many, but not all, journalists, historians, and political scientists interested in foreign and security policy to leap from the end of the Cold War to the war on terror.[3] Journalists have provided outstanding accounts of the wars, decision-making in the Bush White House and Pentagon, and the rise and abuse of presidential power.[4] The academic literature has comprehended 9/11 and its aftermath mostly through the ideas and terminology of international relations and security studies: empire and imperialism, unipolarity and hegemony, terrorism and asymmetrical conflict, nation-building and insurgencies, strategic doctrines.[5] Such studies understandably tend to overlook or underrepresent the domestic process of adjustment and the connections to national politics and partisan competition. Some scholarship has involved a reading backward to the 1990s to see, from a policy perspective, whether the United States foresaw or did anything about the danger of terrorism, especially later in the Clinton administration, or to see from the perspective of international politics indications pointing to the temptations of unipolar power. In this way, there is a gap between the literature on the end of the Cold War and the commencement of the war on terror. This problem is augmented by the fact that the scholarship on the 1990s and accounts of the Clinton era are dominated by domestic issues and ultimately by the scandal resulting in impeachment. These accounts tend to overwhelm our comprehension of this period in relation to the end of the Cold War and the nation's adjustment to that historic change in world politics. What is written about military or security policy in the 1990s tends to focus on Clinton's wars in Somalia, Bosnia, and Kosovo.[6]

Second, the gap or lack of continuity in historical coverage is compounded by the conventional understanding of the era from 1990 to 2002, which took shape as history was written by the political victors. The conventional narrative or accepted wisdom of the period from the end of the Cold War to the Bush wars following 9/11 runs something like the following: Ronald Reagan won the Cold War by confronting and bankrupting the Soviet Union. The first Bush presidency adjusted to the end of the Cold War by reducing force structure and military budgets, while fighting the first war as the sole international superpower. The Clinton presidency witnessed a lack of direction in foreign and national security policy, which compromised American prestige and security. September 11 forced the second Bush president to take U.S. military and foreign policy into a new era of preemption and nation-building. This conventional narrative is politically conservative as well. It is the basic outline of the Republican perspective on this era, especially Reagan's personal victory over communism and Clinton's squandering of American power.

The conventional and conservative narrative, even if spun out in considerable detail, is woefully inadequate and, in some cases, simply wrong. It is superficially persuasive because it roughly fits the overall facts: the Cold War ended as the Reagan presidency was coming to a close; defense spending fell dramatically under Reagan's successor; the 1990s did not produce a definite cast to post–Cold War national security policy; everything changed soon after 9/11. But Reagan's role in the end of the Cold War has been less an analytic conclusion than a political slogan, as we shall see in chapter 2. It was used at the time to justify what could have been seen as an unprecedented waste of national resources. Later, with Reagan's demise, it was resurrected with greater verve and panache because the passage of time had dimmed any public sense of nuance and detail, and it helped to enhance the impression of Republicans as the party of national security, especially during the reelection campaign of George W. Bush. Likewise the understanding of Clinton's putative failures is equally simplistic. This study will show the flow of politics and policy from George H. W. Bush to Clinton and George W. Bush to reveal both continuity and change from the attempts to adjust to the end of the Cold War to the war on terror.

Finally, in countering the conventional or conservative wisdom, I make no claim that mine is a disinterested or dispassionate history. The conservative or conventional view is a normative characterization of the era, whether explicit or implicit. As there is no purely objective measure of the options, decisions, and policies during these years, a normative slant is ineluctable, however one might wish or pretend otherwise. Depending on one's point of view, one's metrics, the changes in U.S. policy can be seen as profound or puny, prudent or perverse. My argument will reflect this ambiguity, but I approach this study from a critical perspective. I will argue that the politics of national security are systematically dysfunctional, and that as a result the United States failed to adjust military spending and policy in a rational manner to the end of the Cold War, which in turn did significant damage to itself and its national security with the military policies and budgets that a "global war on terrorism" made possible. The term "dysfunctional" in this case means a pronounced bias toward a particularly circumscribed or bounded rationality favoring, but not always resulting in, a politics tilted toward hawkish policies. In short, despite the dramatic cuts at the end of the Cold War, the United States perpetuated and maintained as much as possible a Cold War national security state in style and size for reasons that have as much or more to do with domestic politics than international imperatives. When 9/11 came along, similar political dynamics essentially recreated the politics of the early Cold War and rejuvenated an extravagant national security state with profound consequences for U.S. domestic and international politics. In many ways the period from 1998 to 2008 should be remembered as a true decade of neglect, as the United States undermined its own long-term security through profligate and often counterproductive military policies while critical national problems went unmitigated and unsolved.

United States policy changed after the Cold War, and significant reductions in force structure were inevitable, but some of the changes were nominal, symbolic, and short-lived. In more important ways, U.S. policy was adjusted well before September 2001 to maximize the continuities between the Cold War and the world thereafter. Thus U.S. national politics played out in such a way that fundamental changes were minimized as the dynamics of Cold War politics reemerged in party conflict years before the events of 2001. This failed adjustment had significant consequences for the U.S. response to 9/11. In some ways the United States was poorly prepared for the new century because it had not made the tough choices to compensate for the boom and bust weapons procurement cycle following the Reagan buildup, cut holdover Cold War systems, or promoted greater military burden-sharing by our rich and well-armed allies. In other ways the United States was too prepared; that is, it was predisposed by its lingering Cold War military apparatus and foreign policies to undertake something like the invasion of Iraq. Into this situation stepped George W. Bush, ready to use the crisis of 9/11 to launch not only a war on terror but also a massive military buildup under the cover of the politics created by that crisis and the wars. The resulting presidential power and congressional compliance produced eight years of ever-increasing military spending and martial commitments that would present the next president with bills and burdens exceeding the worst years of the Cold War.

Frequently public (and academic) discussions of national security policy feature a sharp contrast between arguments about ideas and those about interests. Foreign policy and national security can be seen as the product of a battle of ideas competing over the nature of threats and how to respond to them. Alternatively, arguments about interests invoke material incentives and forces that supposedly lie behind particular ideas, depicting military policy as the more or less direct product of material interests, whether in service of an executive branch strategy to advance economic interests, the influence of the military-industrial complex, or pork barrel logrolling in Congress. The Iraq War engendered a particularly acute version of this argument, with apologists for the war invoking in its defense reasons of security from terror, freedom, democracy, and other high-minded concepts, while others saw base material interests at work in the form of oil- and war-related contracts. This tussle between supporters and opponents of the war became acute, in part because the very sanctimony of the defense of a war of choice seemed at odds, to some, with the facts of the war. There were no weapons of mass destruction and no links to 9/11, and there was also a brazen disregard for the consequences. The only explanation, it seemed, for such a mismatch could be material concerns. Iraq thus became the latest in a long history of attempts to understand the United States' (or any other nation's) national security policy through ideational or material lenses.

Alas, this book will not attempt to cut the Gordian knot of this debate (either with particular reference to Iraq or the general question of ideas versus interests) —a debate that changes sides politically depending on who is winning or losing in the grand battle for control of American politics. But that inability to easily resolve this conflict is, in some ways, my point and what this book will discuss. Political arguments are usually both sincere and strategic. Everyone, from citizens to kings, is affected by these conflicting pressures. Some invoke lofty arguments in support of their material interests, while others change interests in service of principles; still others specialize in forming coalitions through the manipulation of both ideas and interests. Politicians must deal with this in a very real and unavoidable way since in the performance of their duties (even in most nondemocratic systems) they are adjusting and compromising to promote and win on issues of public policy. Politicians may mediate and shape the worlds of ideas and interests, but neither ideas nor interests reign supreme. Instead, both depend on the political process, and politics shapes or determines what emerges from their convergence and conflict.

The politics of national security are no more immune to this process than any other area of public policy. If anything, the arena of national security is more fraught with politics precisely because of the perceived stakes — more vulnerable to politics because the principles invoked are lofty, and the material interests involved are equally colossal. In no other arena is there such a caldron of wealth, prestige, power, and national identity. Once upon a time scholars of American politics argued that "politics stops at the water's edge." In other words, the ordinary pulling and hauling of partisan or parochial politics did not apply to foreign or national security policy. This was always more of an exhortation than an empirical claim, though it was given some historical credibility during the pre-Vietnam years of the Cold War when the two parties often cooperated on foreign and military policy (though there was no shortage of exceptions to this rule). For the most part, however, this adage was a bit of rhetoric used by politicians, and the very deployment of it by political actors belied its supposed message. When most commentators or public officials would make such a littoral reference, it was usually for the most partisan of purposes. Politics should stop at the water's edge so that my side can win. (The phrase "national interest" has a similar connotation.) The more it is said or implied the more political its intent.

My argument is a bit more specific than that, however. It is not simply that politics prevails even where national security is at stake. There is a political tilt in the world of military policy that tends to favor certain kinds of arguments and interests, which in turn tend to be more successful, especially over the long run. The combination of various factors, such as party competition, the nature of the issues involved, and the structure of the separation of powers, biases the system in favor of more hawkish or militaristic policies and therefore in favor of the arguments and interests that support such policies. On the one hand, because military policy is indeed deeply political it is more like other arenas of public policy than some theories and conceptions would have us believe. On the other, certain characteristics of its particular politics also distinguish it in important ways from other types of policymaking, as we shall see.

The Cold War was a study in how the limits of two-party competition influenced national security. Until the end of the Vietnam War, Republicans and Democrats cooperated or battled it out on almost exclusively hawkish terms. The Democrats lost China. The Eisenhower administration's moderation was attacked as weakness in the form of putative missile gaps and other indicators of decline, while the Johnson administration had to get tough in Vietnam for largely domestic reasons. After Vietnam the relatively dovish forces of Democratic liberalism lasted about four years until the second half of the Carter administration produced a desperate series of militaristic policies. Then came Ronald Reagan and the largest peacetime military buildup in the nation's history. Although nearly every phase of militarism (even Reagan's) produced its own partial backlash, there were severe limits to how far either party could go down the path of peace or restraint without getting penalized. The end of the Cold War did not eliminate this dynamic. Though the terms of debate were altered, much of the politics remained the same.

Why is this the case? One factor is the array of interests on each side. At the core of Jack Snyder's powerful explanation for military overexpansion is an argument about the power of interests. The multitude of forces at work pushing for, or receptive to, militarism, whether in a mild or more pernicious form, is ubiquitous, powerful, and often organized. This might not be an iron triangle — that is, an unbreakable set of interests linking military contractors, Pentagon bureaucrats, and members of Congress — but it is constituted by powerful, interconnected social and political actors and institutions. The potential interests that could be arrayed against militarism are relatively weak and unorganized; most do not even see militarism (at least publicly) as the enemy or competition. The logrolls that connect the forces in favor of militarism are relatively easy to get going and self-perpetuating. There is, by contrast, nothing like an iron triangle for peace.[7]

This does not mean and is not meant to imply that there is some military-industrial complex with overweening influence on outcomes in this policy arena. The material interests that comprise what might be called a military-industrial complex are often depicted as a causal force: they make things happen that otherwise would not. In some cases, undoubtedly that is true. Overall, however, I see a different pattern of cause and effect at work. The "unwarranted influence" to which President Dwight Eisenhower alerted us is more contingent. The military-industrial complex, such as it is, does not produce the propensity or predisposition for war or even hawkish policies short of conflict, as much as war or hawkish policies (driven primarily by political decisions) produce an opening for the military-industrial coalition to take advantage of the biases built into the system that favor, over the long run, hawkish policies. The complex could not stop the end of the Cold War or the drawdown that followed. Nor could the complex ignite an equivalent of a new cold war so soon after the end of the old one; that required the coincidence of 9/11 and an ideologically driven administration.

A second, seemingly more ideological factor reinforces the bias in the array of social forces. Historically, even minor international crises or events that at least superficially went against U.S. interests or plans were often interpreted by those out of power as a sign of weakness, or evidence of failure on the part of the president or party in power. Or if possible they were seized on by the president as a threat requiring a strong response that empowered the president and his party. But whatever the political outcome, the fight has been played out on this terrain. By contrast even powerful winds of peace dissipate rather quickly. It is easy to find examples where the two parties have tried to "out-hawk" one another. One finds it difficult to imagine the event or situation that would set in motion a comparable rivalry in a peace race. The end of the Cold War, as we shall see, was no exception. There are reasons this is not just an accident of history (and, again, not simply the work of the military-industrial complex).

National security features two characteristics that differentiate it from nearly any other issue: the perception of the costs and benefits at stake and the location of the problem or threat. The perceptions of the costs and benefits in the realm of national security are often quite dramatic. What is at stake? Whether an illusion or not, the stake is often blood and treasure, the homeland, or the free world. The potential costs of even perceived failure are high. The nature of two-party competition in the United States produces the classic competition over the median voter, who is usually in a relatively conservative or cautious position because of what is at stake, and because the external nature of the problem means many voters have less knowledge about how to assess threats to security.

The parties have to be extra cautious here because of the potential costs of missteps, more than gains from successful policies. You usually have less to lose by acting on the basis of "peace through strength" and tough talk than you do by, however symbolically, turning the other cheek or retrenching.[8] This kind of political deduction about the potential "security" costs and benefits intersects, of course, with the more directly material costs and benefits of military policy. That is, the distribution of the costs and benefits of military and national security policy is typically thought of as quite general or universal. The costs are distributed across all taxpayers. The benefits are often portrayed as similarly general — we are all made equally secure or insecure by national military policy. That way of looking at the costs and benefits of national defense is often politically relevant and powerful — we are all in this together! — but not entirely true. Aggressive national security and hawkish military policy produces rather particularized group and geographic benefits. As mentioned above, it is these group and geographic beneficiaries who form the hawkish logroll lobby.

The location of the problem — the threat, the enemy — is displaced; it is elsewhere. This relates to the relative lack of public knowledge on these issues, but it affects the politics of national security in another way as well. The issue is unlike most other issues in the United States, where the creation or identification of enemies and problems and the formulation of policies typically means setting one sector of America or Americans against another. The invocation of communism, the Soviet Union, rogue states, or international terrorism does not pit — typically — region against region, race against race, city against country, business against labor.[9] National security, viewed in this way, is not the Super Bowl but the World Cup. In another way national security is like both those sporting events. It's not just that military issues and national security often invoke some level of xenophobia and nationalism that displaces the conflict. In the American case the identity has a particular character. This nationalist identity has been organized historically around powerful and enduring conceptions of America's exceptional character and universalist mission in the world.[10] Based on a mix of historical fact and cultural mythology, American nationalism is periodically aroused in the form of a crusading spirit to remake the world. Related to, but also transcending the nationalist impulse, is the tendency for national security issues and policy to evoke jingoistic rhetoric, simplistic binaries (strength versus weakness), and empty tropes (the national interest, for example). It is not that such things always work, especially over the long run, but they constitute, along with some of the other factors discussed, a contrast to the political possibilities and propensities in other policy arenas.[11]

Separation of powers interacts with party competition in two ways that reinforce its less than salubrious effects on national security policy. When united in party and spirit, the president and Congress can act in a parliamentary fashion, but the temptations for the president to go it alone are powerful, especially in the realm of foreign and national security policy. Congress will often cheer the president on in such unilateral endeavors (Korea, Tonkin Gulf, Gulf War, Afghanistan, Iraq). Whether united or divided, Congress often follows the president's lead. This is not simply because of constitutional powers, including those of the commander in chief, or due to precedent. As U.S. Supreme Court Justice Robert H. Jackson recognized in 1952, the constitutional "zone of twilight" into which many areas of national security and foreign policy fall is one in which "congressional inertia, indifference or quiescence may sometimes, at least, as a practical matter, enable, if not invite, measures on independent presidential responsibility."[12] It also allows Congress to do what it does best—deal with and benefit from the particulars, rather than try to direct the show. The somewhat uncertain constitutional status of foreign and national security powers, and the tilt to the president, has often been characterized as "an invitation to struggle."[13] Congress, however, rarely RSVPs and if it accepts the invitation it is usually after the party is over and inebriation has been replaced by a hangover. So the invitation to struggle is rather more a presidential temptation toward unilateralism and a congressional tendency toward risk-avoiding parochialism: let out the leash on the dogs of war, concentrate on maximizing particular benefits, and await the results of the conflict you have facilitated.

This combination of issue structure, the array of interests, partisan competition, and the tendencies of the separation of powers becomes, at least as far as national security, a powerful mechanism for dysfunctional politics and irrational policies. In this way dysfunction and irrationality are not accidents; they are nearly the default setting of the system. The end of the Cold War offered a test of the system and of theories of policy formation. One could argue, as is implied in the conventional narrative, that the United States did react rationally to the end of the Cold War and then rationally again when attacked after 9/11. Indeed, the initial changes and reductions made as the Cold War ended were sensible and responsible, but it did not take long for the familiar arguments to be recast and for the biases I've described along with other circumstances to distort political possibilities and decisions. The American political system has been largely incapable of dealing with national security in a mature and rational manner—at least in a sustained fashion—and this book will show this process at work from the end of the Cold War through the aftermath of 9/11 and the end of the Bush presidency.

The transition from the end of the Cold War to the global war on terror occurred in roughly three phases. The drawdown, the period from about 1989 to 1994, saw a combination of rapid and substantial cuts in some aspects of the military and the initial attempts to redefine U.S. strategy under Presidents George H. W. Bush and Bill Clinton. Chapter 2 concentrates on the changes in force structure and their relationship to the generation of a new grand strategy based, ultimately, on regional conflicts and possible threats from major regional powers, such as Iraq. Culminating in the Clinton administration's Bottom-Up

Review, this process embodied the tensions of the era. The need to reduce was in part driven from without by altered geopolitical realities and from within by record deficits and the mounting burdens of the national debt. The end of the Cold War in many ways inflated American pretensions about dominating the world as the sole superpower even as it took away the grand cause and some of the military tools of the trade. American policymakers celebrated the "peace dividend" even as they sought to fill the "threat blank" left by the collapse of communism. Partly as a result of all these tensions, the Clinton administration produced a demanding two-war strategy and global role that in many ways was not supported by the kind of budgets and force structure they seemed to require.

The second phase, roughly from 1995 to the election of 2000, is the focus of chapter 3. This phase was characterized by a political stalemate between the parties and between the president and Congress, while moving unsteadily toward a politically powerful but not intellectually coherent consensus that the drawdown was over and that military spending, if nothing else, must increase in service of a strategy and purpose that had not been defined or agreed upon. This turnaround began early in Clinton's first term with a conservative counterattack on his military policies and performance as commander in chief. Clinton's political opponents derided his actions, including his attempt to permit homosexuals in the military, the debacle in Somalia, and involvement in Bosnia, but they had no international bugbear around which to mobilize. Instead the attacks were directed inward. Before Clinton's first full year was over, Republicans and conservative Democrats launched an attack on what they characterized as the nascent "hollow" armed forces. The threat was not from abroad but from the turmoil within the downsized and underfunded military, which was "going hollow" in a direct reference to the description of the post-Vietnam military in the mid-1970s. This was a largely elite effort whose arguments were repeated and echoed in the halls of the Capitol, but it was not a significant factor in the public disaffection and anger that produced a new Republican majority in Congress in the historic elections of 1994. Even with control of Congress, the Republicans' stance remained peevish and reactive. Much of this was symbolized by the fight over ballistic missile defense (BMD). No longer Reagan's massive umbrella, limited BMD became one of the most significant programs on which Clinton evaded a major decision for the entire eight years of his presidency. He kept up a relatively inexpensive research program that would ward off criticism from hawks but not bust the budget or produce a foreign policy problem. The GOP pushed for deployment in such a manner that it seemed the goal was deployment for its own symbolic sake, no matter whether the system worked or if it was directed at the relevant threat.

If conservatives and Republicans were struggling to find traction on security issues, the Democrats did little to institutionalize an alternative vision. Instead, Democrats and liberals sought more to exploit the putative disappearance of the problem for domestic purposes than to redefine what national security was now or could be. In the 1990s liberals seemed to assume that the end of the Cold War would entail ineluctable change in the powerfully entrenched politics of national security, that new national security politics and policies would naturally flow from the changed environment and replace the old. Although efforts were made to find a path in the new world order, they failed to realize that a new national security identity would have to be actively and aggressively constructed *domestically*. For example, a new norm or regime of collective security, involving allies in collective burden-sharing, would have to be packaged and sold, which it was not. No new paradigm was created and marketed at home or abroad.

Instead, a bipartisan consensus gradually took shape, epitomized by President Clinton's 1999 pronouncement that "it is time to reverse the decline in defense spending that began in 1985."[14] One of the ironies of the post–Cold War restructuring is how doubly irrational it was. Just as the drawdown was driven in part by the deficit and the need to save money, once that initial panic was over and the economy had turned around by the mid-1990s, then pressure came off the defense budget, and further cuts or adjustments were essentially taken off the table. This produced a kind of laxity about the military budget as many expensive cans (major procurement programs, further base closings) were kicked down the road during the economic boom and into the short-lived era of budget surpluses. In the adjustment, then, military contraction was minimized by the same forces and mechanisms that produce military overexpansion. By the late 1990s, it could be argued that a "new post–Cold War political coalition . . . [was] increasing the defense budget . . . much like the beginning of a new Cold War–era budget cycle, but this time without the Soviet threat."[15] In Jack Snyder's theory (and who would dispute this?) military overexpansion requires sociopolitical support, a coalition, however implicit, that provides support (however direct or indirect) for militaristic or expansionist policies. There was elite support for a more aggressive and militarized U.S. foreign policy. What was missing in the 1990s was the narrative framework to match elite interests to mass constituencies and broad public support.

This gap between mass and elite persisted through the election of 2000, which dealt little with foreign and military policy. As we will see in chapter 4, President George W. Bush entered office with hopes for a massive increase in military spending, but no geopolitical rationale. A conservative Congress was ready to grant his initial budget request, but it was not clear whether support existed for a sustained buildup. The attacks of September 11, 2001, changed this, nearly instantly. And so the final phase, reconstitution, began with the confluence of the militaristic designs of the Bush administration and the attacks of 9/11. The functional equivalent of a new Cold War was created nearly overnight. September 11 brought the longstanding arguments (though they had to be retooled a bit) of so-called neoconservatives to political life as they seized the opening it provided. But part of the reaction was fundamentally one of political interest, in a purely domestic sense. Whether conscious or not, the global war on terror as a national crusade was the psychologically motivated choice for an administration already in the doldrums, adrift, nearly bereft of purpose. It effected a rather seamless union of material, political, and moral interests across a wide range of social actors and forces. The economic odd couple of elite and mass was now linked by another bridge (beyond big government and taxes). The United States now had a mission based on a terse narrative: "We were attacked" in the Pearl Harbor of the twenty-first century. One of the first consequences of 9/11 was the unspoken ratification of Bush's preexisting plans for a major military buildup and a resurrection of presidential power. Chapter 4 concentrates on the new military doctrines—preemption, dissuasion, a new role for nuclear weapons—that the crisis of 9/11 made politically viable. The substance and politics of the vast military buildup that proceeded along with but separately from the wars is the subject of chapter 5. This buildup, which would eventually eclipse any rival since World War II, was accomplished under the political cover of the wars in Afghanistan and Iraq. Whereas the nation had a vigorous debate about the costs and consequences of the Reagan buildup, the politics of war hid the Bush buildup in plain sight.

In just a few years the war on terror recapitulated much of the Cold War, and chapter 6 examines some of the consequences of this for national politics through the elections of 2008. The considerable period of uncertainty and experimentation from 1945 to 1950 at the start of the Cold War was a longer span of time than the period after 9/11, when the U.S. military budget reached peak Cold War levels, launched two wars, got involved in other conflicts, and made a bold declaration of indefinite war (something the United States did not explicitly do during the Cold War). If anything, the war on terror was from the start even more open-ended and expansive in its objective than the Cold War. The consequences—for American politics and policy—have been as abrupt and may prove to be as profound. As the nation sailed, all canvas flying, into perpetual war on a vast sea of red ink, the war on terror reconfigured the political fortunes of parties and ideologies, produced a stark guns-versus-butter conflict, imposed severe constraints on other areas of U.S. policymaking, and facilitated a significant extension of domestic governmental surveillance and control over its citizenry. Whether this will endure and persist, as did the Cold War, remains to be seen, but one irony is that some of the roots of the war on terror and its dysfunctions are to be found in the earlier failure of the United States to disrupt and recast the institutional and political legacies of the Cold War. Instead the Bush presidency was able to implement policies that blended those of Lyndon Johnson and Ronald Reagan. Bush's policies combined a Vietnam War and a Reagan military buildup. His version of Vietnam, the Iraq War, became as contentious as its East Asian precursor. The military buildup, unlike that of his Californian predecessor and role model, was uncontroversial because the politics of war made any such examination politically unpalatable. The United States was stuck in a quagmire, building the arsenal of empire, racking up debt, ignoring or neglecting other urgent priorities, while doing nothing as far as energy policy, for example, to build a broader and more enduring national security. While the historic election of Barack Obama promised swift and significant change in the policies of his predecessor, the new president would inherit not only the wars in Iraq and Afghanistan but also the burdens—past, present, and future—of the buildup and problems it posed, amid an ocean of debt and economic chaos, for turning the ship of state in a new direction.

CHAPTER TWO

After the Cold War
From Buildup to Bottom-Up

> By the grace of God, America won the Cold War. . . . But even in the midst
> of celebration we must keep caution as a friend. For the world is still a dan-
> gerous place. Only the dead have seen the end of conflict. And though yes-
> terday's challenges are behind us, tomorrow's are being born.
>
> PRESIDENT GEORGE H. W. BUSH,
>
> STATE OF THE UNION ADDRESS, 1992

After the apparent collapse of the Soviet empire in 1989, there was a general
perception that peace had broken out all over and anticipation of a "peace dividend." How did the U.S. political system respond? What would be the new
grand strategy and military policy to direct national security policy through the
1990s and even beyond into the twenty-first century? And further, what changes
would be applied to the vast military apparatus and enormous defense budgets
amassed to "fight" the Cold War?

The end of the Cold War presented an unavoidable challenge to the basic
structure of U.S. foreign and military policy. The rather sudden finish to the
Cold War meant a traumatic adjustment for the national security establishment.
For forty-five years, everything about that massive operation—from nuclear
weapons to the CIA—had been determined by conflict with the Soviet Union
and the possibility of World War III. This transformation in U.S. and world
politics came just after the largest peacetime buildup in American history, a
buildup that had heightened the contrast between the old and new eras and both
eased and exacerbated the adjustment to the latter.

Although skeptics clung to pessimistic scenarios until the very end, after the
fall of the Berlin Wall nearly everyone—liberals and conservatives alike—agreed
that things had changed in two ways: first, the threat was reduced, and second,
the military budget would face cuts as forces and personnel were reduced. Beyond that, however, policy, programs, and priorities all seemed up for grabs as the

events of 1989 seemed to signal permanent change. What would emerge from this shift was unclear at the time. Resolution of this uncertainty would fall to the presidencies of George H. W. Bush and Bill Clinton, who each sought to put a stamp on national security policy in the emerging post–Cold War era.[1]

The Reagan Buildup

The Reagan military buildup, the largest in American history during peace, was already changing as the Cold War neared an end. The real dollar value of defense appropriations had been falling slowly since 1986.[2] Outlays, or the actual money spent each year, continued to rise through 1989, and these expenses dropped more slowly than appropriations thereafter. Billions of dollars in commitments made earlier in long-term contracts were coming due as budgetary outlays. This "stern wave" of expenditures meant that any decrease in actual spending would lag behind cuts in appropriations. Given that budget deficits are measured in outlays, not appropriations, this difference had political and fiscal implications.

Conservatives claimed that overall defense spending was already declining and that the buildup ended in 1985, but this argument was somewhat fatuous in light of the facts. From 1981 through 1985, national defense outlays were $1,610 billion in 2000 dollars; over the next five years, from 1986 through 1990, the total was $1,943 billion — nearly 21 percent greater. Budget reductions notwithstanding, during George H. W. Bush's first year in office, defense spending would still be more than 40 percent higher than during Ronald Reagan's first year as president. Thus, the buildup continued.

The 40 percent increase from 1981 to 1989 formed a new and rather lofty peak of military spending. Although by 1987 and 1988 many believed larger cuts were coming, the level of defense funding from the Reagan buildup altered political perceptions of what the right amount should be in subsequent years. From the vantage point of this peak in military spending, anything lower could be seen as an adjustment to the end of the Cold War rather than the effect of the previous buildup. In other words, the apex of the buildup could be used as the baseline, even if unconsciously, against which to measure restructuring after the Cold War. Another side of this same perception, and perhaps the more important part, was how it could be used politically. If policymakers made cuts in military spending, even if those levels of spending were inflated, they could be portrayed as being irresponsible or soft on defense. Thus, the huge military budgets of the late 1980s formed a standard that served as a political constraint, yet the deficit and domestic problems were realities that required attention. The Reagan legacy of a 40-plus percent real increase in defense spending and a 20 percent decrease in discretionary domestic programs, coupled with tax cuts and a large deficit, had taken a substantial toll on politics and policy. To many decision makers, greater cuts in defense spending seemed inevitable.

Nevertheless, reductions in defense spending remained controversial and could be made even more so when politics demanded. In August 1988, Reagan dramatically and for the first time vetoed a defense authorization bill passed by Congress. The president objected to several provisions on strategic programs, including cuts in the budget for the Strategic Defense Initiative, or SDI (Reagan's "Star Wars" ballistic missile defense program), a delay in the MX ICBM program, and other arms control restrictions. Reagan argued that the bill tied his hands in arms control negotiations, but he also made a much more sweeping condemnation: "This bill would signal a basic change in the direction of our national defense, a change away from strength and proven success and back toward the weakness and accommodation of the 1970s."[3] None of these congressional measures was new; Congress had added many similar stipulations and restrictions to past defense budgets, and large cuts in SDI had been made since 1985. But 1988 was an election year, and both sides of the political aisle understood the political motivations behind the presidential veto. Democrats accused the president of deliberately manufacturing the controversy to create and exploit perceptions of Democratic infirmity on defense, while Republicans charged that the Democrats, due to their politically motivated restrictions, had only themselves to blame for the veto. According to Republican Senator Pete Wilson, the veto was "one of those happy times when good government and good politics coincide."[4]

Whether politically inspired or not, Reagan's bit of lame duck bravado seemed a fleeting reminder of days gone by. But even if Reagan and his rhetoric would soon be gone, other peculiarities of the Reagan buildup remained, including Star Wars. The Strategic Defense Initiative stood apart as the major qualitative military innovation of the Reagan era and, for that matter, of the past two decades. To the end, President Reagan remained committed to his vision of a comprehensive defense. In 1988, in commemoration of the fifth anniversary of his Star Wars speech, Reagan promised that scientists were "not working late into the night to construct a bargaining chip" and that "we will continue to research SDI, to develop it and test it, and as it becomes ready, we will deploy it."[5] Despite the annual struggle over the program between the administration and congressional opponents, Reagan was able to transform SDI into an ongoing program costing $3 to $4 billion per year. No final decision to begin deployment of even a partial system was ever made, however, and SDI remained an extended and expensive array of research and development programs. In the days and years to follow, someone else would have to deal with Star Wars as well as the broader consequences of Reaganism and the military buildup.

That someone turned out to be Reagan's loyal vice president, George H. W. Bush. While the immediate successors to regime-builders often suffer politically, Bush was hamstrung by the legacy of his predecessor even more than earlier "faithful son" presidents.[6] As a Bush aide later put it, "It was awkward to follow Reagan and claim success. We couldn't say we'd be cleaning up the Reagan mess. We would just have to do it without talking about it."[7] Cleanup or not, Bush had to at least obscure or minimize the "Reagan mess." Though it included such things as the savings and loan industry bailout, the core of the Reagan mess was the budgetary crisis of deficits and debt. Bush was between a rock and a hard place. The country was weary of the Reagan revolution and its consequences and seemed to be swinging back toward expectations of governmental action in certain areas, including the environment and education. But the deficit overwhelmed nearly everything else. Imposing more tax cuts did not seem possible, due to several factors. The discretionary budget had been squeezed under Reagan. Entitlements, a politically intractable issue, were chewing up an ever-increasing portion of the budget. Bush complicated his leadership dilemma before his term had officially begun when, in his nomination acceptance speech, he asked Congress and America to "read his lips" as he vowed "no new taxes." Not only that, Bush also promised no cuts in core entitlement programs. The "read my lips" vow was the subject of heated debate among his advisors because they knew he probably could not hold to such a commitment. The election might demand this sort of grandstanding, but after the election the budgetary and political realities would require some sort of tax increase. It was, many felt, only a matter of how long the inevitable could be postponed.[8] As a result, Bush had precious little room to maneuver, even if he had been able to master the "vision thing." The defense budget was decreasing slowly but steadily, and Bush needed every penny he could get from the Reagan buildup. His presidency began with increasing evidence that the Cold War was ending if not over. The term "peace dividend" cropped up as a way to describe the substantial budgetary savings to be accrued and redistributed away from national security. Both fiscal and world politics were putting pressure on the administration to substantially revise U.S. military policy.

The Last Battle: How the Cold War Was Won

As Bush was confronting the reality of deficit government at home and the downfall of communism abroad, people around the world were contemplating the rapid demise of the fundamental conflict of the second half of the twentieth century. If the Cold War was ending, then had the United States won it, just like a traditional war such as World War II? And if so, how had it won? Interpretations of the past often influence the future. The adjustment to the end of the Cold War might have depended in part on the interpretation of how that epoch was brought to a close. Changes in military policy could or should have been influenced by perceptions of whether the vast resources and effort pumped into the Cold War had been worth it. In most ways this debate over "how the Cold War was won" was either the stuff of academic journals or partisan carping. Very little of it seemed to directly affect the discussion of what direction post–Cold War policy should take.

The debate, such as it was, tended to focus on either the success or failure of U.S. Cold War policy as a whole, or more specifically (and more politically and contentiously) on the immediate impact of the Reagan presidency and military buildup. And both involved questions that were difficult to answer, even in retrospect. Did U.S. policies (or those of the USSR) promote peace or conflict? In particular, did Reagan's policies precipitate the collapse of the Soviet Union? Many commentators drew sanguine conclusions from the fact that there had been no superpower war, no matter how many other wars occurred or how many millions died while the superpowers avoided Armageddon. For many commentators, the absence of a superpower war confirmed that deterrence and containment worked. It was not something that could be proven, but there was merit to the argument that nuclear weapons had made war so potentially devastating that neither side was willing to risk it. But there was also merit in the argument that the United States (and the Soviet Union) embraced many policies that exacerbated and protracted conflict, from Berlin and Cuba to Vietnam and Central America. The point is not so much whether either of these arguments was analytically superior but which prevailed politically. Those arguments that tended to accept or embrace the efficacy of past policies dominated the debate. The successful conclusion of the Cold War tended to trump criticism or second-guessing. Academic nuances aside, the arguments that prevailed in political discourse reinforced support for continued military superiority in the form of policies and programs that would maintain or enhance the United States' incipient status as the world's only superpower.

Scholarly debates ensued, but early on the impact on the press, public, and policymaking was minimal.[9] While the academic literature explored with great subtlety the relative influence of ideas, material forces, domestic politics, and changes in the global political economy — and was often critical at least implicitly of explanations that unambiguously gave credit to Reagan or contemporaneous U.S. policy — in the political world there was little questioning of the effect of the Reagan buildup or of the magnitude and costs of the Cold War effort as a whole. Instead, what tended to dominate was a form of elite vindication of peace through strength. This became known as "triumphalism." Triumphalist arguments were not all of a piece, but there was a common grounding in the idea that, details aside, the general policies of peace through strength (containment, nuclear deterrence) had worked. The United States had won the Cold War without fighting World War III. Even if one could not specifically link causes to effects or policies to outcomes in a scientifically satisfactory manner, the end or result justified the means. Triumphalism, by lending general support to the idea of peace through strength, bolstered the intellectual stock of hawks, even if it did little to alter the consensus about the desirability and rationality of a fairly substantial decline in military spending. If there was no comparable threat, then past success did not have obvious implications for the future of military budgets. Some Democratic or liberal commentators, including the father of containment, George Kennan, tended to laud the entire bipartisan Cold War effort from Truman to Reagan.[10] Fewer were willing to echo Strobe Talbott's assessment that the rapidly proceeding self-destruction of communism demonstrated that "the doves in the Great Debate of the past ten years were right all along."[11] Others at the time, in a more Republican spirit, emphasized Reagan's administration and policies and the seemingly direct link to the demise of the Soviet empire.[12]

The most sweeping and general verdict, and the most quoted, was rendered by Margaret Thatcher at a 1991 Heritage Foundation dinner: "He [Reagan] won the Cold War without firing a shot."[13] The firing of direct shots at the Soviets, one might argue, would have made it something other than an end to the Cold War, and victory in that case would have been Pyrrhic indeed. Indirect shots were

fired, if typically by proxies, and thousands died under Reagan's watch and policies, especially in Central America. Leaving aside the logical elisions and gaps in
this summation, how did the fortieth president accomplish this remarkable feat?

There are several layers to this contention. Besides the general temporal
association between Reagan's presidency and the collapse of communism, four
arguments tended to circulate.[14] The first, what might be called the "resolve"
argument, said that Reagan's rhetorical rejection of the Cold War status quo
(that is, detente) and challenges to communism ("Mr. Gorbachev, tear down this
wall") unhinged the Soviet leadership and fostered hope and dissent in Eastern
Europe. As Edwin Meese argued, "Reagan's strategic goal was to force the Soviets to choose: either stand down from their continuing confrontation with the
West, or face increasingly devastating pressures on the home front. He rejected
accommodation with the Soviets, on the grounds that it would postpone their
day of reckoning between their inherent domestic weaknesses and their globalist
ambitions."[15] Resolve was complemented by the second argument, resistance, or
what in earlier Cold War days was referred to as "rollback." The administration's
sometimes covert and sometimes quite public operations in Central America and
Afghanistan, for example, showed that the United States would use its power to
reverse real or perceived Soviet advances. The third argument, rearmament, or
peace through strength, was manifested in the military buildup and demonstrated to the Soviets that the United States would not be outdone in military
power. The fourth argument focused on Reagan's massive military buildup, even
if the price was a significant contribution to deficit spending and the national
debt, which forced the Soviets into a fiscal competition they could not sustain.
Summing it all up, Charles Krauthammer reminded Americans upon Reagan's
death in 2004 that the president's "policies of unrelenting toughness won the
Cold War and brought a new peace. . . . Reagan put relentless pressure on
the possessors of that power, the Soviet commissars, through his nuclear hard-
line, military buildup, Strategic Defense Initiative and the Reagan Doctrine of
supporting anti-communist guerrillas everywhere (and especially Nicaragua).
Ultimately, that pressure brought about the collapse of the overextended Soviet
Empire."[16]

As Krauthammer's verdict indicates, these arguments would become a cornerstone in the rapid elevation of Reagan to iconic status in the Republican Party.
Especially after what would turn out to be a lackluster performance by George
Bush Sr., and after memories of the less attractive aspects of the Reagan presidency had faded, the invocation by conservatives and Republicans of "Reagan"

and "Reaganite" became almost obligatory, particularly in reference to foreign and defense policy, as in a "Reaganite policy of peace through strength."

Over time one argument in particular about Reagan's victory in the Cold War—the one that gave direct credit to the financial scale of the buildup for putting the Soviets in an unsustainable position—was elevated into a central element in Reagan's strategic vision. What had been more general arguments about the economic burden the buildup would put on the Soviets and how that pressure might make them more eager for arms control agreements became a premeditated linchpin of the Reagan strategy and, in some accounts, the cause of Soviet capitulation. This mostly retroactive transformation of the fiscal impact of the buildup into a grand strategy required some distortion of history and amnesia regarding Reagan's public rhetoric and policies. President Reagan and his aides did not represent military spending and the buildup in this manner.[17] This way of looking at the buildup was largely an explanation after the fact. The manner of the collapse of the Soviet Union suggested that it was not able to sustain the competition. It was almost as if the Cold Warriors could not believe it had actually happened and so they forged a stronger link to Reagan's expensive belligerence. The country had gone several trillion dollars in debt due to the combination of military spending increases and tax cuts (a policy pairing that the forty-third president would replicate). An argument that tied the end of the Cold War to the expense of the buildup would surely help justify the less than sanguine fiscal situation at the end of the Reagan presidency. And as the Cold War receded into history, what could be dubbed "Operation Red Ink" (its proponents never gave it a name) was increasingly depicted as the main purpose of the buildup and the principal impetus for the Soviet collapse.

My point is not that the expense of the buildup is not plausibly related to developments that ended the Cold War, although I think the evidence in this regard is rather weak and conflicts with more credible arguments.[18] My argument, instead, is more about how this interpretation of Reagan's legacy developed. If Operation Red Ink was a conscious strategy, it was one based on deceiving the American public. Americans were not told that the United States would break the Soviet Union; instead, they were scared into thinking the Soviets were poised to crush them. Reagan attained office based in part on claims that our military was "second to one." We faced a nuclear "window of vulnerability," which if left unclosed might allow the Soviet Union to "take us out with a phone call," that is, "without firing a shot." The Republican platform of 1980 waxed hysterical about the country facing its darkest hour since World War II, saying it was "the most serious challenge to its survival in the two centuries of its existence." In fact, it posited, "if we let the drift go on," history might record "that the American experiment, so marvelously successful for 200 years, came strangely, needlessly, tragically to a dismal end early in our third century." In particular, achievement of Soviet superiority in nuclear weapons meant that the Soviet Union "for the first time is acquiring the means to obliterate or cripple our land-based missile system and blackmail us into submission."[19]

Through such hyperbole Reagan sold the military buildup almost exclusively on fear. Once in office the administration expended considerable energy justifying dozens of major weapon systems as vital to national security if not survival. As one example, the government twisted itself into knots trying to figure out how to deploy the MX missile system, which was seen as the essential element in reversing a perilous Soviet nuclear advantage.[20] As another, Reagan's pursuit of a comprehensive ballistic missile defense, or Star Wars, may have been quixotic but it was in earnest; it was not pursued because we could afford to throw money down the toilet and the Soviets could not. It is doubtful that a military power of such immensity and prowess (the Reagan and Republican vision of the Soviet Union) would capitulate because of several years of increases in U.S. military spending. In 1980 the Soviets were about to win the Cold War without firing a shot based on nuclear superiority, while a few years later they would concede the struggle and Reagan would win without firing a shot. As Robert Parry argued, "If the Soviet Union had been what the American conservatives claimed — a nation marching toward world supremacy in the early 1980s — how would one explain its rapid collapse only a few years later? After all, the Soviet Union wasn't invaded or conquered. Its troops did suffer losses in Afghanistan, but that would no more have brought down a true superpower than the Vietnam defeat could have caused the United States to collapse."[21]

Even if it was not so much the money as the demonstration of determination (denoted partly in dollars) that forced the Soviets to relent and transform, there is much left unexplained. Surely the wily Soviets could have placated the Reagan administration and waited for the next election without collapsing entirely just because the United States was going massively into debt. Positive Soviet change actually followed the mellowing of the Reagan presidency, after it was clear that the United States was reducing the military buildup. The Soviet Union's significant moves toward easing the arms race and general tensions came only when the buildup had peaked (in terms of congressional support and budgetary authorizations), the Senate had gone back to the Democrats, and Reagan had begun serious arms control negotiations and made widely disparaged offers to disarm and share Star Wars with the Soviets.[22]

The tension between the Reagan administration's public rhetoric, which sold the buildup on the basis of weakness and fear, and the ex post facto justification for the amount of money spent on the buildup was diminished as the latter was promoted after the Cold War and the former was overlooked or forgotten. Years later, Ronald Reagan's death, which came during George W. Bush's campaign for reelection, was used by some as leverage for current events, as a way to talk positively about military power and standing tall against national enemies, thereby reflecting positively on the wisdom of George Bush's policies in the war on terror. The arguments supporting Operation Red Ink reemerged with considerable force, and were readily parroted as fact by journalists, when Reagan died in June 2004. As one remembrance put it: "Against waves of 'expert opinion,' [Reagan] pursued his belief that the Soviet Union would crack under the pressure of an accelerated arms race."[23] Similarly, "Reagan had seen what few others recognized — that building up our defense would put the Soviets in an unanswerable bind. They could not afford to match us."[24] Reagan "boosted Cold War military spending in an attempt to bankrupt the Soviet Union."[25] The effects of these remembrances on public opinion about contemporary events were probably evanescent, but they showed that over time public arguments about the Cold War and the role of U.S. strategy and power in ending it had become, if anything, less subtle and more politicized, evincing a strong bias toward hawkish conclusions. Be that as it may, during the first Bush presidency the early attempts to draw political lessons from the Cold War for future U.S. policy were being outrun by subsequent events and political considerations.

Filling in the "Threat Blank": The Base Force and New Military Strategy under Bush

In some circles the reaction to the ending of the Cold War was less one of triumphalism or celebration than consternation. As if there had to be a new menace to replace the old one, the key question became, "What is the threat?" Among others, Democratic Senator Sam Nunn voiced this assumption in March 1990 when he criticized the Pentagon's plans, which under Secretary of Defense Dick Cheney were still Soviet-oriented. If the Pentagon were to expect congressional support, Nunn warned, military planners would have to "fill in the 'threat blank.' "[26] The national security elite had to have a vision and plan whether the motivation was to justify large-scale cuts or to protect as much of the Cold War force as possible.

For some, talk of a threat blank was premature, even after the fall of the Berlin Wall. Various hawks, in uniform, public office, and think tanks, argued that the Soviet Union could emerge from the turmoil just as powerful and dangerous as before. Some important actors in the national security establishment, however, saw the writing on the wall well before Nunn had raised his concern. As early as 1987 and 1988 the Pentagon's Joint Staff was debating a shift from the standard threat of global war with the Soviets to "indigenously caused conventional conflicts with little likelihood of direct Soviet intervention." And into 1989 military planners moved toward a strategy of "regional planning" based on aggression by a nation such as Iraq. Some, including Under Secretary of Defense for Policy Paul Wolfowitz, remained focused on Europe and resisted a significant shift away from the Soviet threat.[27] As noted earlier, adding to all this was intense pressure to make sensible cuts in the defense budget to help with the deficit and to adjust from the Reagan buildup to a sustainable level of military spending. The initial efforts of Bush and Defense Secretary Cheney reflected the global and domestic politics that complicated this project. On the one hand, Cheney sought to make some reductions to weapons programs that were potential long-term problems or no longer needed. As part of his first Pentagon budget Cheney retired one elderly aircraft carrier, ended production of the venerable F-14, and terminated the Osprey aircraft program, which was still being researched and developed. Congress, generally resistant to such things, fought back, saved the Osprey, and gave the F-14 a so-called soft landing by including funding for a final eighteen planes. Meanwhile, as if still in full-scale conflict with the Soviet Union, the administration — with congressional support — was pressing ahead with development of not one but two new land-based intercontinental ballistic nuclear missiles — the ten-warhead, train-transported MX and the single-warhead, truck-borne Midgetman.[28]

As Cheney and Congress were wrestling with these material adjustments, key figures were pushing forward revisions to grand strategy along the lines of the ideas percolating in the military bureaucracy. One of the most important of these individuals was Colin Powell, who was President Reagan's national security advisor as the Cold War thaw began to look like a long, warm spring. By 1988 Powell was convinced that change underway in the Soviet Union was essentially irreversible and that defense budgets would continue to decline. The armed services could either anticipate the implications of these changes and adjust with a new strategy and force structure or have unstructured reductions forced upon them by the political process, especially in Congress.[29] With massive deficits and global change pushing in the same direction, substantially lower defense budgets appeared inevitable. Powell (who served as commander in chief of the United States Army Forces Command, or FORSCOM, early in the Bush presidency) was highly motivated to avoid the creation of another "hollow force" army, which he had witnessed in the wake of Vietnam. In fact, much of Powell's thinking and efforts in this direction predated his appointment as chair of the Joint Chiefs of Staff (JCS) in October 1989, a month before the fall of the Berlin Wall. As FORSCOM commander, Powell gave a speech in May 1989 to a conference of army brass and defense contractors in which he warned his audience that "the future just ain't what it used to be." The Cold War was ending and defense budgets were going down; thus, he said, there was a need to plan accordingly. And plan he did. In late 1989 Powell began to formulate what would become the Base Force, and he expressed some of his thinking about this in the Senate hearings leading to his confirmation as chairman of the JCS.[30] Powell proposed a reorientation of U.S. national security strategy from the Soviet Union and Europe to regional conflicts. With the removal of the Soviet Union as a serious threat, the United States could make substantial reductions in its military forces and yet maintain and fulfill its obligations as the world's superpower. Though varied across services and weapons systems, the reduction in forces was in the range of 25 percent. For example, Powell envisioned a reduction in uniformed personnel from 2.1 million to 1.6 million.

Once he took the chair, Powell pushed forward aggressively with his ideas. This effort was resisted by, among others, Secretary Cheney and the recently appointed Under Secretary of Defense for Policy Wolfowitz, who, as mentioned earlier, believed the Soviet Union remained the principal threat.[31] Powell recounts that after his May 1989 speech to an important army seminar, during which he informed the audience that changes in the Soviet Union were profound and the army must adjust to that global reality and to leaner budgets, he learned of a conference held by the conservative Heritage Foundation that had reached nearly the opposite conclusion, saying that in the 1990s the Soviet Union would emerge from its restructuring stronger militarily.[32]

Powell chose the term "Base Force" to "convey that his proposed force structure represented a floor below which the United States could not go and carry out its responsibilities as a superpower, rather than a ceiling from which it could further reduce forces."[33] Determined to overcome resistance by the Office of the

Secretary of Defense and the services, and to begin to counter the criticism by Nunn and others, Powell went public with the Base Force concept in a series of speeches in the spring of 1990. By early summer Cheney and Wolfowitz were essentially on board. On June 26, 1990, he presented these arguments to the president, who endorsed the new strategy and force structure.[34] What President Bush approved was essentially Powell's Base Force joined to a still-evolving new national security strategy. The fundamental strategic change was a shift from more than forty years of focusing on World War III with the Soviet Union to indigenous regional conflicts without Soviet involvement (even if such conflicts were closer to the reality of the Cold War). As the president would later put it in announcing the changes, "In a world less driven by an immediate threat to Europe and the danger of global war, in a world where the size of our forces will increasingly be shaped by the needs of regional contingencies and peacetime presence, we know that our forces can be smaller. Secretary Cheney and General Powell are hard at work determining the precise combination of forces that we need. But I can tell you now, we calculate that by 1995 our security needs can be met by an active force 25 percent smaller than today's."[35]

As reported and later presented in the summer and fall of 1990, and then finally codified in the National Security Strategy of 1991, the changes represented by the Base Force and new strategy were important but floated seemingly between two eras, as perhaps was appropriate. The Bush administration took a fundamental but cautious step into the nascent post–Cold War world. One indication of the new strategy's ambiguous and tentative status is that it was nameless; it had no snappy moniker. Instead, in Washington the strategy was "known as the 'new strategy,' the 'new Defense Strategy,' the 'President's strategy,' and 'the U.S. military's new regional contingencies strategy.'"[36] Given the uncertainty of the post-Cold War period, the lack of a grand strategy with a memorable title was sensible enough. Things could change, and perhaps the new role for the United States was flexible and fluid enough that a master concept on the order of "containment" was neither necessary nor prudent.

The new strategy shifted away from war in Europe with the Soviet Union but kept a fairly keen eye on the old foe. The strategy's description of what would drive force planning and deployment began with the idea of "reconstitution," signifying that the United States would have a much longer period of warning — perhaps two years — in advance of Soviet aggression in or around Europe. This concept allowed the United States to reconstitute some of its forces in preparation for such a crisis or conflict. Nuclear weapons and strategic deterrence were next in the key considerations. Just as conventional conflict with the Russians was much less likely, the threat of nuclear war was greatly diminished, but strategic deterrence remained a vital component of national security. The final element of this revised view revolved around the need to respond to regional crises and conflicts. As we have seen, this shift toward regional conflicts had been in the works for many months, but the notable thing is its placement in and impact on the new strategy — it is a shift, but hardly a revolution. Aside from some language about the growing threat of regional conflict, there is no real attempt to fill the threat blank with what would later be called "rogue states," including Iraq, Iran, Syria, Libya, and North Korea. In fact, prior to the invasion of Kuwait, Operation Just Cause in Panama was probably as much or more a model for future contingencies as hypothetical aggression by Iraq.[37]

Powell, and no doubt others, worried that the Base Force, intended as it was to be a floor, would be thought of as a ceiling in light of other promising changes in the international environment and the formidable pressures of the budget deficit. The Base Force and the threat around which it was defined could be dead on arrival. The Pentagon and White House would have to sell the plan.[38] Bush was prepared to go public with the new strategy at the fortieth anniversary celebration of the Aspen Institute, an influential forum on national security issues. The date for the speech was August 2, 1990, the same day that, in a somewhat unsettling coincidence, Saddam Hussein invaded Kuwait.

The close relationship between the proposed new strategy and the crisis that would justify it brought to mind a similar situation forty years earlier at the beginning of the Cold War. As the nation was adjusting to uncertain conditions following World War II, NSC 68, the declaration of the Cold War, was put before President Truman in April 1950.[39] Unlike the Base Force and new strategy, NSC 68 was secret, but its invocation of imminent years of maximum danger and call for vastly increased defense budgets went against Truman's plans and the direction of public opinion. But on June 25, 1950 North Korea invaded South Korea, which turned NSC 68 into policy practically overnight, and there was no turning back. Despite the fact that the Base Force and emerging strategy were part of a plan to reduce force structure and spending, unlike NSC 68's call to arms, Bush and Powell's plans were nevertheless in a tentative and uncertain position, intellectually and politically. As noted earlier, they wanted to make the Base Force a floor and use the new strategy to draw a line against further cuts. The invasion of Kuwait, not unlike the invasion of South Korea, was a timely crisis that simultaneously clarified and justified their plans. It clarified the shift away from Europe to regional contingencies and gave life to what had been a percolating discussion of "rogue states" — without Soviet involvement — as the new threat to world order and U.S. national interests. It likewise tempered any talk of cuts beyond those planned by the administration.

As had Truman forty years earlier, President Bush took a decisive step immediately after Iraq's invasion with his declaration that "this will not stand." Following that, the historical parallels begin to diverge in important respects. Truman was compelled to commence military action to save South Korea. Tiny and defenseless Kuwait was already overrun. President Bush was in the Operation Desert Shield phase — the combination of economic sanctions and military buildup in the Gulf region which consumed over five months — for as long as it took U.S. troops in Korea to break out of the Pusan perimeter, advance into North Korea, and provoke a Chinese invasion of the peninsula. In Korea, the United States was on its way toward deadlock near the 38th parallel in the amount of time it took to initiate hostilities in the Gulf with the commencement of Operation Desert Storm. Then again, the Gulf War was over in less than six weeks while Korea dragged on into the Eisenhower presidency.

Brief as the actual war was, the eight months of Operations Desert Shield and Desert Storm were profoundly formative for postwar U.S. security policy. In what would become a common refrain of the post–Cold War adjustment, especially during and after the Gulf crisis and war, major regional conflicts were portrayed as a new and growing threat. Defense Secretary Cheney, for example, put it this way in the middle of Operation Desert Shield: "At the same time that the global Soviet threat is declining, the potential for major regional threats to U.S. interests is growing."[40] Just after the war, Army Chief of Staff General Carl Vuono echoed a now familiar refrain: "While the risk of a major conflict with the Soviet Union has certainly ebbed to a forty-five-year low, Iraq's aggression against Kuwait clearly demonstrates that the international environment remains dangerous and is in many respects growing more complex."[41] The logic of these statements, echoed in other documents, was left implicit and unspecified. Why did the end of the Soviet threat coincide with growing threats elsewhere? Was it that the end of the bipolar rivalry made independent action by lesser powers more likely? Was some other force such as globalization generating conflict? Or was it simply a matter of attention and expectation — that is, without the Soviet Union on which to focus, other areas of the world loomed larger, even if nothing had really gotten better or worse? The military's job was to plan for the worst, and in this case, the worst without the Soviet Union around.

Regardless, the threat to fill in the blank would be "rogue states" or regional powers, Third World nations with substantial militaries armed as a byproduct of the Cold War by either the United States or the Soviet Union (or both, such as in the case of Iraq). Instead of the decades-long plans and orientation around global war, military force structure and strategy would concentrate on potential "regional contingencies," which were most likely to be caused or precipitated by potentially expansionist and heavily militarized regional powers, rendered more dangerous by their actual or potential possession of weapons of mass destruction (nuclear, chemical, or biological matched to delivery systems). One problem was that several regional powers were "allies" or not a threat, including South Korea and Pakistan. This put the focus on a limited and in many ways unimpressive list: Syria, Iraq, North Korea, Iran, and Libya. Whether or not elite planners were losing sleep over the dangers of these regional "rogues," they were not, in and of themselves, enough to rally public opinion. Even so, the Pentagon and other interested actors were doing their best to substitute these states for the Soviet Union. Every aspect of this planning process began with the assumption that the United States must and would remain the world's military superpower and guarantor of stability. The deliberations that resulted in the regional defense concept and the Base Force show no evidence of calling into question what it meant for the United States to be the globe's paramount power. Likewise, the architects of the post–Cold War policy did not give significant consideration to rich and well-armed allies and a strategy of burden-sharing.

The Korean War had allowed policymakers to effectively enact NSC 68 without public debate. In a similar fashion, the Iraq invasion of Kuwait distracted attention from the new national security policy and Base Force concept. Bush's speech and its implications were covered by the press, but the ongoing crisis in the Gulf occupied the media and the public, as well as most policymakers.[42] Nevertheless, the Gulf War, at least initially, was a stark confirmation of the emerging doctrine just as NSC 68's vision of the Cold War as a real war was confirmed by the North Korean invasion. The Korean War certainly had a more profound impact. The increase in the military budget, much of which was devoted to a massive commitment to the defense of Europe, rather than the war in Asia, has no Desert Storm analogy. Desert Storm made the abstract quite real, even if that required some amnesia about how the United States failed to deter Iraq. Yet, owing to the awesome rapidity and nature of the U.S. victory, the most dangerous and well-armed regional power had been decisively dispatched in six weeks, with stunningly low American casualties, in the most one-sided victory in modern warfare. In some ways the Gulf War was in danger of backfiring as far as its larger impact on the political construction of a new U.S. national security policy. At the same time that the Iraq war validated the regional contingency scenario or rogue state concept, it significantly diminished a category that was to fill in the threat blank; the principal demon had been so easily crushed.

What the Gulf War Won

The Gulf War's destruction of the so-called Vietnam syndrome was one of the most immediate and explicit political consequences of the war for American military policy. As President Bush enthused, "By God, we've kicked the Vietnam Syndrome once and for all."[43] But four other political lessons emerged from the first Gulf War.[44] The first, as has been noted, was the substantiation and confirmation of regional conflicts as a focus of military power and rogue states as the principal threat; the second lesson was that the Reagan buildup paid off; third was the creation of what can be called the "Gulf War Standard" for the use of force in future wars; and fourth, all but inescapably, was the lesson that a massive military force was essential in a post–Cold War world to guarantee the kind of over-whelming victory represented by the Gulf War.

The two major wars fought by the United States during the Cold War — Korea and Vietnam — involved heavy casualties. They were also marked by cata-clysmic possibilities of a head-to-head confrontation with the Soviet Union, even if nuclear confrontation could be avoided. The Gulf War offered a new model, however potentially misleading, for the future of warfare. In a world devoid of highly trained and well-equipped enemies, swift and relatively costless victory was welcomed as an explicit military policy and viewed as a political necessity. In a way, the Gulf War resurrected one piece of the Vietnam syndrome even as it buried another part. We could fight, but it had to be quick and totally successful. This was the Gulf War Standard for future conflicts: a de facto policy that the United States could and should pursue a policy of total dominance, to the point where American casualties would become a nearly negligible factor. In fact, after Desert Storm, Powell wanted to add the term "overwhelming force" to be used as a new standard in the evolving national military strategy; Wolfowitz persuaded him to use "decisive force" instead.[45] The Gulf War Standard was possible in large measure because the demise of the Soviet Union (and the coincidental revelation that it was in part a paper tiger) in parallel with the full effects of the

Reagan buildup put the United States in an unprecedented position of military power, especially in terms of qualitative superiority.

The U.S. military on the eve of the Gulf War was more than a generation ahead of any rivals in the sophistication of its weaponry and the training of its personnel. The results of the war launched a debate about the near-revolution in military affairs supposedly represented by the conflict.[46] In the opinion of many, this conflict justified the Reagan buildup, which was being questioned by many for its effectiveness and flaws, including waste, fraud, and abuse; expensive and problematic programs, such as the B-1 bomber; and other programs that did not seem to work at all, such as the DIVAD anti-aircraft system. Iraq was a relatively easy showcase for the consequences of the largest buildup in peacetime history. Add the lessons of the danger of rogue states, the new standard, and the Reagan buildup, and the final lesson is evident. The Gulf War showed that a massively superior military force was still necessary to cope with conditions following the Cold War at minimum cost in American lives. Economic sanctions were not adequate. Though our allies might help (at least with the bills), unilateral U.S. force was necessary to enforce a new world order after the Cold War.

This quartet of lessons tended to brush aside concerns that the Gulf War was an "ideal war" (that is, waged against a relatively weak opponent without allies and in a completely exposed geographic setting). The performance of U.S. forces, while quite notable, was at least in some instances inflated. The Patriot missile system's effectiveness was distorted, and some of the high-tech weapons were not matched against comparable opposition (for example, the F-117 versus the Iraqi air defense system). Much of the grunt work was done by old fashioned carpet bombing by B-52s on totally exposed Iraqi desert positions.[47]

Conveniently there was no fifth lesson of the war, no lesson about the relationship between prewar U.S. national security policy toward Iraq and the obvious failure of deterrence. Why, with all its military might and vast intelligence apparatus, was the United States unable to predict Saddam Hussein's actions against Kuwait and/or unable (unwilling?) to deter an invasion of Kuwait?[48] One of the lessons of the Cold War was that deterrence had worked. With the Gulf War, the fact that deterrence had failed was never discussed seriously. In the Gulf, the failure or absence of deterrence was conveniently overlooked and, instead, the success of war proved the need for an expensive high-tech force. Lessons were drawn (and others ignored) to harmonize with the attempts to minimize the adjustments to American victories, whether in cold or hot wars.

Unlike NSC 68 and Korea, the regional contingency doctrine and Gulf War did not produce the equivalent of a new cold war. The Gulf War, however, put a psychological brake on the decline in defense spending, by justifying a new role for the United States as the world's SWAT team able to act with or without United Nations (UN) sanctions and with or without the help of allies. The Gulf conflict lent some credibility to the idea that a force nearly the size it was during the Cold War could be justified in a world without a threat comparable to the Soviet Union. Nevertheless, the Bush administration ended with what remained a broad, flexible strategic vision that did not emphasize major regional conflicts or future Iraqs. The National Security Strategy of 1991, written in the wake of the Gulf War, was remarkably measured in its references to the demands of regional conflict, and it did not focus on a single major threat to U.S. security. Apparently Pentagon planners and the Joint Chiefs of Staff specifically were recommending maintaining forces sufficient to fight two regional conflicts at the same time, but this did not appear in the new national security strategy. The document made no reference to simultaneous wars as a justification for the Base Force.[49] In early 1992 Joint Chiefs of Staff (JCS) chair Powell wrote that "the real threat we now face is the threat of the unknown, the uncertain."[50] A draft of the Defense Planning Guidance for fiscal years 1994–1999, leaked in March 1992 to considerable controversy (controversy that would be reignited in 2002, as we shall see in chapter 4), noted that regional conflicts "will be of primary concern" but concluded that U.S. "strategy must now refocus on precluding the emergence of any potential global competitor." In other words, the United States must remain a Cold War–sized superpower to reassure allies and convince potential foes "that they need not aspire to a greater role or pursue a more aggressive posture to protect their legitimate interests."[51]

Even on the eve of Clinton's inauguration, Secretary Cheney's "Defense Strategy for the 1990s: The Regional Defense Strategy" adhered to the premises and formulations of the Base Force. This "new military strategy" outlined a broad transition from containment to a multifaceted engagement with the major regions of the world, including Europe and Latin America. The document emphasized a preference for collective responses to threats and did not dwell on major regional conflicts as the primary scenario and specific justification for U.S. military power. This is significant inasmuch as the Clinton administration, ironically, would quickly adopt what was in important respects a more pointed, alarmist, and even hawkish military strategy.

Just as the impact of the Gulf War on the relationship between military strategy and budgets was real but limited, the political benefits of victory that accrued to the White House and Bush presidency were significant but unsustainable. In a remarkable reversal of presidential fortunes, the impact of Bush's Gulf War triumph dissipated over the next several months. Starting with the upturn in his popularity during Desert Shield in the late fall of 1990, and peaking at 89 percent as Desert Storm ended, the crisis and war gained Bush nearly a year's worth of support until fall 1991 when his approval rating returned to prewar levels and continued to fall through 1992, scraping as low as 39 percent.[52] The public did not care that much about the rest of the world, and the Gulf War had shown that Americans need not be overly concerned about military power. With the failure of the 1991 attempted Soviet coup and the subsequent end of the Soviet Union, this tendency was reinforced. What the public cared about was the economy because it was faring poorly. Even in early March 1991, barely a week after the war's conclusion, 24 percent of those polled listed the economy as the most important problem facing the country compared to 3 percent who cited international problems and tensions. A year later, in March 1992 amid the presidential primaries, 42 percent listed the economy as the most important problem (with 25 percent also listing unemployment and jobs).[53] That is in large part how Americans ended up electing Bill Clinton in 1992, despite Bush's Gulf War triumph, in a campaign and election that expended little in rhetoric or resources on the issues of foreign policy or national security.

Bill Clinton: The New Democrat, the Deficit, and the Peace Dividend

As a presidential candidate Bill Clinton did nothing to distract the American public from their lack of interest in national security policy. The campaign had all the appropriate press releases on such matters and Clinton did not avoid the subject, but his path to the presidency was paved with domestic politics, and this was to his liking and benefit. The 1992 Democratic Party platform focused on domestic issues, not on national security. To Democrats, the end of the Cold War was a reminder to turn homeward to ensure the stability and strength of what made the United States a beacon to the world.[54] The National Security section of the platform emphasized the need to implement new security policies for a changing world following the Cold War. "What the United States needs,"

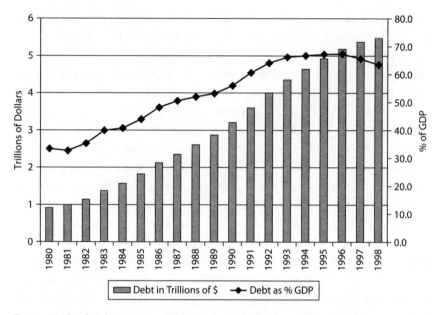

Fig. 2.1. Federal Debt, 1980–1998. *Source:* Office of Management and Budget.

argued the Democrats, "is not the Bush Administration's Cold War thinking on a smaller scale, but a comprehensive restructuring of the American military enterprise to meet the threats that remain," which included nuclear proliferation as well as "renegade dictators, terrorists, international drug traffickers, and the local armed conflicts that can threaten the peace of entire regions."[55] Clinton and Gore were not running on foreign policy, even less on military policy. The title of their campaign book, *Putting People First*, and the less elegant internal mantra of the campaign — "It's the economy, stupid" — symbolized the emphasis on domestic concerns, including health care, education, and the environment. If anything, the end of the Cold War was supposed to produce the so-called "peace dividend" that was to be cashed in for domestic priorities. However, anyone with even a modest awareness of the national budget knew there was a problem, a very big problem, and it was the same problem that had plagued Clinton's predecessor. The government was drowning in red ink (figs. 2.1 and 2.2).

President Bush lived the consequences of deficit government; President-elect Clinton was about to. On the eve of Clinton's inauguration, the character of American government had been altered significantly. The politics of deficit government had become the unspoken law of the land. The fiscal vise had been

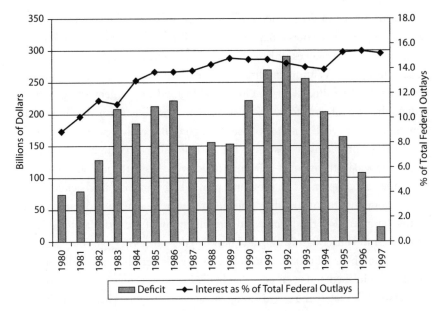

Fig. 2.2. Federal Deficit and Interest Outlays, 1980–1997. *Source:* Office of Management and Budget.

turned so tightly for such a long period that the discomfort and pain were taken for granted. The political and budgetary problems entailed by the burden of debt, deficit, and interest were so prominent and persistent that they were changing characteristics of government and politics in several areas, from institutions and procedures to public opinion and trust. What had been in part caused by underlying socioeconomic trends and political choices was now a cause, shaping politics and producing significant consequences for American government.[56] Despite or because of this, public expectations were high following the 1992 elections. Though based perhaps more on hope than hard facts, optimism about the prospects for fruitful united government was widely shared. Twelve years of divided government, the level of partisan hostility, and the lack of a clear mandate in the election were factors that tempered expectations among informed observers. Clinton and the Democratic majority in Congress presaged, if nothing else, a respite from the last several years of political acrimony and frustrations.

The optimism was rewarded by a productive first session of the 103rd Congress. Several bills that Bush had vetoed, including the Family Leave Act and the Brady Gun Control Bill, were easily enacted. Despite difficulties, Clinton pushed through the bulk of his economic plan. He then won a difficult fight to approve the North American Free Trade Agreement or NAFTA. Clinton's 1993 success rate on congressional votes (86.4 percent) nearly matched the very best first-year presidential performances of Eisenhower (89 percent in 1953) and Johnson (88 percent in 1964).[57] Within the administration, the process of reinventing government, led by Vice President Al Gore, was focused on implementing plans to reduce the federal workforce by over 250,000 positions (with the lion's share coming from the civilian sector of the Pentagon). But each victory seemed to be bracketed by problems or mistakes. The early legislative triumphs were at times overshadowed by the months-long imbroglio over gays in the military as we shall see in the next chapter.[58] The economic plan, which had combined deficit reduction (a combination of spending cuts and tax increases) with economic investments, became all of the former and virtually none of the latter as a result of a protracted and bitter fight within and between the parties in Congress. Later, the initial triumph of Clinton's campaign and agenda-setting on health care was quickly diminished and then completely dissipated as Congress struggled with the details. Ultimately the 103rd Congress failed to produce a health care bill and was brought to a lackluster finish when several other bills failed to pass for various reasons, including several Republican filibusters in the Senate.

Though media attention often focused on "mistakes" or "misjudgments" by Clinton or on the intrusions by the culture wars, the first two years of legislative work was dominated by the politics of the debt and deficit. And this was not just the case with the economic plan. The vast majority of Clinton's legislative triumphs did not involve any direct governmental spending, including family leave, the Brady Bill, and NAFTA. Only the Crime Bill cost real money. Clinton's small stimulus package could not survive cost-cutting politics. Even his health care plan, which was vulnerable on so many points, was doomed, in part because it would cost billions in the short run. Savings would come only later, if at all. The problem was that the deficit was such a tight political vise that politicians could not afford short-term costs, no matter what the eventual gains. The ugliness of deficit politics was soon evident to the young president, who griped, "Nobody knows we have any spending cuts. . . . We've got the worst of all worlds. We've gotten all this deficit reduction. We've made all the hard painful choices, and nobody even noticed."[59] In this kind of environment, the president and his party were relying on every penny they could squeeze out of the "peace dividend" to ease the fiscal pain. Clinton and his national security team needed a plan for military spending and a policy to deal with the fiscal realities and strategic concerns of the post–Cold War era.

The Bottom-Up Review

The Base Force was intended, as the name implies, to be an interim stopping-point or "transitional concept."[60] Military spending could go up or down depending on developments in global politics, even if Bush, Cheney, and Powell had sold the Base Force as a floor that must not be lowered. Every modern president seeks to put his stamp on national security policy, so it would be expected that Clinton would take some initiative. However, the uncertainty of the situation surrounding the Base Force and the subsequent changes in world politics (including the official demise of the Soviet Union and the results of the Gulf War) all pointed toward a thorough reassessment, as did the dire fiscal situation facing the new administration. In March 1993 Clinton's Secretary of Defense, Les Aspin, formerly chair of the House Armed Services Committee and known for years as a "defense intellectual," sought a post–Cold War foundation through a process he called the Bottom-Up Review (BUR), a department-wide and comprehensive evaluation "to reassess all of our defense concepts, plans, and programs from the ground up."[61] This fundamental reassessment was necessary, as Aspin argued in the resulting report, because "the Cold War is behind us." "The Soviet Union is no longer," and that was the threat "that drove our defense decision-making for four and a half decades." "In the aftermath of such epochal events" — including the Iraq war

> it has become clear that the framework that guided our security policy during the Cold War is inadequate for the future. We must determine the characteristics of this new era, develop a new strategy, and restructure our armed forces and defense programs accordingly. We cannot, as we did for the past several decades, premise this year's forces, programs, and budgets on incremental shifts from last year's efforts. We must rebuild our defense strategy, forces, and defense programs and budgets from the bottom up.[62]

Given this clarion call to action, the rest of the document was both reminiscent of the Bush administration and surprisingly hawkish by comparison. In what was fast becoming a familiar post–Cold War discursive sleight of hand, the BUR made a distinction between "old" and "new" dangers to U.S. interests. The danger of a global conflict, whether conventional, nuclear, or both, with the Soviet Union was "old." New dangers included the spread of nuclear, biological, and chemical weapons; aggression by major regional powers or ethnic and religious conflict; potential failure to build a strong and growing U.S. economy; and potential failure of democratic reform in the former Soviet Union and elsewhere.[63] With the exception of the last, none of these was "new," particularly the need to keep the United States economically strong. Proliferation of weapons of mass destruction had been a global security issue for decades and the subject of numerous negotiations and treaties. And while the argument was frequently made that the end of the bipolar power structure reduced the checks and balances that might have kept some countries from going to war or pursuing interests aggressively in their geographic neighborhoods, nothing was particularly new about regional or ethnic conflict. The United States fought a full-scale war in Vietnam, as had the Soviets in Afghanistan. For forty years the United States had maintained military forces in South Korea to deter the "major regional power" to the north. This exaggeration or distortion of the distinction between old and new threats was as revealing as it was analytically suspect. It made plain the effort to find substantial and compelling dangers, and it was all the better if they were "new."

In truth, it was not that most of these threats were new in any meaningful way as much as it was that their importance in any definition of national security had grown, not because of any systematic inflation of the danger they posed but due to the absence of the threat that had crowded them out in years past. In any case, the core of the BUR was a modest downward adjustment of the Base Force and a strategy that accepted the core Bush-Cheney-Powell assumptions about the trajectory of global affairs. Given Clinton's lack of emphasis on national security, his credentials as a "new Democrat" (that is, more conservative on matters of national security), and Powell's continued presence as chairman of the Joint Chiefs of Staff, the degree of continuity was not surprising. As Powell put it when introducing the BUR with Aspin, "The strategy underpinning is quite similar [to the Base Force] . . . because the world looks quite similar to us whether you're wearing base force eyes or bottom-up review eyes."[64]

And yet, unlike the Bush administration's official pronouncements (even after the Gulf War), the BUR made regional conflicts — aggression by Major Regional Powers (MRPs), the so-called rogue states — the near alpha and omega of U.S. strategy and forces structure. Major Regional Conflicts (MRCs, or elsewhere sometimes referred to as Gulf War Equivalents) became the primary class of military operations used to "evaluate the adequacy of future force structure" options.[65] Using the Persian Gulf region and Korean peninsula as analytic scenarios, the BUR put together what it called the "MRC Building Block," a roughly

Desert Storm–sized force necessary to check and reverse enemy aggression and then stabilize the region.[66] Some criticized this core conclusion of the BUR as falling into the old trap of fighting the last war by using the Gulf War as a "canonical scenario" for future planning, when future conflicts might not follow that pattern.[67] Even so, the MRC building block represented a measure of what it would take to defeat a foe of similar power and capabilities, a kind of worst case scenario for regional conflict. The BUR, however, took one giant step beyond this.

The principal conclusion was that the United States needed to maintain the ability to fight and win, nearly simultaneously, two "major regional conflicts" (each comparable to the Gulf War). The BUR — Bill Clinton's most significant effort to reshape military policy — contained the first explicit articulation of such a requirement in U.S. planning for the new era. This two-war standard, "decided early in the Bottom-Up Review" process, was "prudent for two reasons": first, it made a second war unlikely by having sufficient force to deter aggression elsewhere while engaged in conflict; second, having a military large enough to fight two MRC-sized wars "provides a hedge against the possibility that a future adversary — or coalition of adversaries — might one day confront us with a larger-than-expected threat."[68] Here was the post–Cold War worst case scenario, the combination of two wars at the same time and the potential adversary of the future. The Gulf War was used as the model of future conflicts, but deemed irrelevant was the fact that another "rogue" (North Korea) did not take advantage of the opportunity when the bulk of the U.S. military was surrounding Iraq for several months. The explicit two-war MRC scenario, in effect, compensated for the final demise of the Soviet Union in justifying what remained even in the BUR a very large post–Cold War military. The extent to which the BUR assumed that the United States would serve as the global SWAT team is reinforced by the fact that one of the other scenarios considered by the BUR was the ability to win two nearly simultaneous MRCs *and* conduct smaller military operations like those in Haiti or Panama.[69]

Not only would the United States be prepared to fight and win two wars at once, it would not demand or expect allied assistance. Despite a mention of possible allied contribution of "some support and combat forces," the bottom line was that "our forces must be sized and structured to preserve the flexibility and capability to act unilaterally."[70] Insofar as the BUR discusses allies and alliances, it does so mostly in the language of what would soon be known as "Engagement and Enlargement."[71] As the BUR was being unveiled in September, the Clinton administration began to articulate this other facet of its foreign and national security policy. On September 21, 1993, National Security Advisor Anthony Lake gave a speech entitled "From Containment to Enlargement." After half a century during which U.S. "engagement in the world revolved around containment of a hostile Soviet Union," the time had come to "think anew" as to America's role in the world. Unlike during the Cold War, "America's challenge today is to lead on the basis of opportunity more than fear." That opportunity flowed from the collapse of the Soviet Empire, the spread of democracy and markets, and the U.S. position amid all this change as the unchallenged superpower. With "no near-term threat to America's existence," the United States should not just engage with the world but make its central goal the "enlargement of the world's free community of market democracies."[72] But not, it would seem, the communal arsenal of democracy. The community of free market democracies could continue to free ride as the United States took it upon itself to bear the post–Cold War burden of policing the globe.

Despite the explicit two-war scenario and failure to include allied support, Aspin and Clinton planned for somewhat deeper cuts in personnel and force structure than the Base Force. The BUR determined that a force of 1.4 million active-duty personnel (compared to the Base Force floor of about 1.6 million) would meet the new strategic requirements. The army would be reduced from the 12 active divisions planned under the Base Force to 10; the air force, from 15 fighter wings to 13; and the navy, from 448 ships to 346, with 11 instead of 12 aircraft carriers. National guard and reserve forces would also be trimmed. As a result, the Pentagon foresaw further reductions in all the armed services until these levels were reached by 1999. This is in fact very much what would come to pass as the cuts were implemented over the course of the Clinton presidency (Table 2.1).

Whatever the strategic justifications and considerations that went into these reductions, much of the "peace dividend" or savings in the military budget would stem from the fact that Clinton would be the ironic beneficiary of the Reagan buildup. The Reagan era produced the most complete and comprehensive peacetime rebuilding of the armed services in the nation's history. In the first years after the Cold War, much of the emphasis in the news was put on the number of troops and civilian Pentagon officials that would be cut. Another less prominent or obvious factor was that virtually no new major weapons procurement programs were necessary. The core of the Reagan buildup had been the recapitalization of the military. Major weapons systems were finished for every service, and they

Table 2.1. Post–Cold War Cuts in Personnel and Force Structure

	1990	1995	2000
Total Active Uniformed	2,070,000	1,518,000	1,384,400
Total Reserve	1,128,000	945,800	864,600
DoD Civilian	1,070,000	865,200	698,300
Army Divisions	18	12	10
Navy Ships	546	372	318
Air Force Tactical Squadrons	76	53	47

Source: Secretary of Defense, *Annual Report to the President and the Congress*, 1995, 1999, 2001.

comprised a lengthy and expensive list, including the M-1 tank, the Bradley fighting vehicle, the B-1 bomber, several new aircraft carrier groups, the Trident program, the MX, cruise missiles for three services, and so on. With the considerable reduction in the size of the armed forces, there were too many weapons, and in the next chapter we will deal more directly with the problems produced by this surfeit. For now, however, the point is that Clinton faced no pressing decisions on weapons programs (aside for some pressure on ballistic missile defense), and he would derive some savings simply by living off the martial fruits of the Reagan buildup.

The BUR got some press, but it was also overshadowed by other events, some quite germane to national security policy. As always, Clinton's focus was on other things, including NAFTA, which he was working hard to get passed in Congress, along with his budgetary package. The BUR was previewed in early September to a rather muted and mixed reception in Congress and the media. This unveiling was unfortunately coincidental with two other significant and symbolic events. As part of the annual defense authorization bill, Congress codified a rebuke to President Clinton's campaign promise to lift the ban on homosexuals in the U.S. military (discussed in more detail in chapter 3). Legislating a strict version of what had become known as the "don't ask, don't tell" compromise, the actions of the Democratic Congress brought a vexing issue for the president back into the news.[73] At the same time, U.S. military forces were involved in a small conflict in an obscure country and for obscure reasons. In December 1992 President Bush, in one of the last significant actions of his presidency, sent over 28,000 U.S. troops to strife-ridden Somalia, ostensibly to protect a UN humanitarian mission to provide food to starving Somalis. This was just the sort of post–Cold War nation-building mission that would later become fodder for a Republican counterattack against Clinton's foreign and national security policy (centered on overextending U.S. forces in such missions, putting them under UN command, failure to pursue BMD aggressively, and generally underfunding the military). On October 3 and 4, 1993, in the firefight that became infamous as the "Blackhawk Down" episode and often referred to as the Battle of Mogadishu, 18 U.S. soldiers were killed and 73 wounded. If not already concerned, many Americans now wondered why U.S. soldiers were fighting and dying in a "humanitarian" operation. News stories about each of these events bracketed and sometimes overshadowed coverage of the BUR and its implications. The symbolism, perhaps in retrospect, was pretty thick. Clinton's major effort to reorient U.S. military policy, in part to acquire leeway for domestic initiatives was at times overwhelmed by events that symbolized the past and future problems he would face as commander in chief—the opening debacle over gays in the military (and the culture wars that involved) and the alleged misuse of American military power in peacekeeping and nation-building. Meanwhile, the BUR would get little respect either from liberals or conservatives.

For some the Bottom-Up Review raised as many questions as it answered about the probable threats to our security and how to address them. From a more liberal perspective, most controversial was the conclusion that the United States must maintain a force capable of fighting and winning two nearly simultaneous regional wars without allied assistance. Both assumptions—two simultaneous wars and no allied support—were all too questionable and sounded more like something from the dire days of the Cold War. Critics argued that the planned force was excessive given the limited capabilities of potential enemies and the formidable capabilities of our allies. The United States and its allies accounted for over 70 percent of world military expenditures and possessed the vast majority of the world's advanced military equipment and well-trained forces. Several experts including Lawrence Korb, a former under secretary of defense in the Reagan administration, argued that the United States could cut deeper and still maintain a superpower force relative to other nations. Trenchant as these critiques were, they were hardly audible compared to the more conservative criticism of the BUR.[74]

The bulk of the criticism, typically from more conservative and hawkish quarters, focused principally on the apparent gap between mission and resources. The force structure was too small given the BUR's own requirements and the projected budgets would not even maintain that force structure, especially after the first few years. These critics saw the BUR as a sham exercise in which budgetary concerns were driving defense planning—Clinton needed a bigger "peace dividend" for his own budgetary priorities and the BUR was intended to find the extra savings. The fiscal cart was leading the strategic horse. It was no secret that the Clinton administration's fiscal plans called for a $104 billion reduction in projected military spending from 1995 to 1999, and Aspin claimed that the BUR as written would result in $91 billion in savings over that period. Later, during a November 1993 press conference, Secretary Aspin would essentially confirm the accusations that budgetary concerns shaped the process as much or more than strategic decisions. Aspin said that the BUR was designed "to meet the targets of the original budget resolution, the deficit reduction, the economic package that the President proposed in February."[75] The administration argued that it had fully budgeted for its planned force structure; only changes in inflation rates could change funding needs. Indeed, some of this debate was rather technical, involving disagreements about projected inflation and other future unknowns.

The 1995 budget and five-year defense plan implemented the Bottom-Up Review. The president planned to spend nearly $264 billion on defense in 1995 and $1.3 trillion over the next five years. The 1995 budget made a small nominal increase over 1994, but this was a one percent drop when adjusted for inflation. The decline would continue in 1996 and 1997 but level off or increase slightly in 1998 and 1999, especially as new procurement programs began. Some experts, however, disputed whether the armed forces would be fully budgeted in the last years of the five-year plan. The most pessimistic estimates predicted a funding gap as high as $20 billion a year by the end of the five years as new procurement programs were projected to swell funding requirements.[76] The BUR apparently asked for too much and too little — for some, too much in the way of military responsibilities and force structure; for others, too small a force and budget. It was a rocky start for the new president's attempt to define the course of military policy and spending for a new era.

Star Wars: From SDI to GPALS

The end of the Cold War, as we have seen, was a combination of opportunities and dangers for the various actors and interests involved in and affected by U.S. military policy. Most welcomed the termination of the overarching threat even as some of the same folks and others searched for the closest thing to a substitute. Many welcomed the relief a peace dividend would bring to the budgetary process even as others sought ways to justify the largest possible military budget. This same dualism carried over to specific military programs. Now that the Cold War was over, what programs, particularly major weapons platforms in development, might be cancelled or significantly reduced? Of course, even as this question was being asked, others were seeking ways to justify their Cold War weapon in the New World Order. Most prominent and controversial among these was one of the singular legacies of the Reagan presidency, Star Wars or the Strategic Defense Initiative (SDI). President Reagan remained committed, as we have seen, to his vision of a comprehensive defense. In October 1988, less than a month before the elections, the Defense Acquisition Board approved plans for development of a Phase I Strategic Defense System (SDS). This partial defense would have been composed of kinetic weapons based in satellites and terminal defenses on the ground, with a projected cost, according to the Pentagon, of $74 billion. Presidential candidate George Bush and his party also remained committed to SDI. The 1988 party platform stated that the Republican Party was "committed to rapid and certain deployment of SDI," which was the "most significant investment we can make in our nation's future security."[77] Bush proclaimed during the 1988 presidential debate that "I will research it fully, go forward as fast as we can. . . . And when it's deployable, I will deploy it."[78]

As president, George Bush inherited an SDI that was deeply rooted, if not quite flourishing. In the first budget he prepared as president, Bush requested, unsuccessfully, a 21 percent real increase in funding for Star Wars. Over the next five years the administration planned to spend an additional $31 billion for SDI research and development. In spite of congressional cuts and global change, the administration defended the proposed increases for fiscal 1991 and beyond. Even Budget Director Richard Darman justified the funding by saying that "there are third parties now, non-superpowers, who have ballistic missile capability."[79] Soon thereafter, President Bush gave a speech in which he argued that "strategic defense makes more sense than ever before."[80] These statements show how at this uncertain moment in history Star Wars was poised between two worlds, still justified by the uncertain future of the Soviet Union along with the emerging fallback of rogue states that were seeking ballistic missile capability and nuclear weapons. But the implications of these two threats were rather different. The reason Reagan's comprehensive Star Wars was so implausible to many was that to be effective against the Soviet Union it needed to be able to defend against thousands of warheads. Rogue states, however, none of whom at this point possessed nuclear weapons, had at best missiles of limited range. They could not threaten the continental United States. Moreover, the number of missiles and warheads involved would be very small.

With peace breaking out all over, many thought Star Wars was dead. As we have seen, some credited it specifically with helping to end the Cold War. Star Wars and Reagan's nearly religious commitment to it demonstrated to the Soviet leadership just how far the United States would go financially and technologically to overwhelm the Soviets militarily. In any event, as the Iron Curtain collapsed so did much of the justification and support for BMD. Either Star Wars had served its purpose, or its status had just changed from dangerous to ridiculous. And yet, ironically, Star Wars was saved by the demise of the very thing that had been its sole justification. If the idea of a comprehensive defense against hundreds or thousands of intercontinental ballistic missiles had always been risible, defense against a handful of technologically unsophisticated theater-range or even intercontinental missiles was not. Consequently, Star Wars needed a post–Cold War transformation and got one via the rogue state doctrine. In fact, in the same speech of August 2, 1990 that Bush used to announce the Base Force/regional conflict strategy, he emphasized again that he was "convinced that a defensive — and I reemphasize that word — a defensive strategic deterrent makes more sense in the nineties than ever before."[81] And just as the rogue state doctrine would get a timely demonstration in the Gulf War, ballistic missile defense would get its first post–Cold War test in the same conflict. With Patriot missiles flying in the Gulf as the Soviet Union disintegrated, the idea of a more pedestrian form of missile defense seemed plausible. In yet another dichotomy, the use of Patriots in the Gulf War helped and hurt the cause of missile defense. Proponents viewed the Patriot system's limited success as a testament to the ability to pull off the trick of hitting a bullet with a bullet; opponents saw in the Patriot's performance further evidence of an expensive and quixotic program.

With the end of the Soviet Union and the putative lessons of the Gulf War in mind, the Bush administration substantially repackaged and refocused Star Wars. In short order, the Strategic Defense Initiative or SDI became Global Protection against Limited Strikes or GPALS. Instead of a massive Soviet first strike, the post–Cold War threat could come in three basic forms: an accidental or unauthorized launch from the former Soviet Union or China; a deliberate attack by Russia or China; or use of shorter-range missiles against U.S. forces or allies within a region of conflict, such as the Persian Gulf. As Secretary of Defense Dick Cheney explained in early 1992, the "DoD has embarked on an aggressive program of strategic defense — centered on the Global Protection Against Limited Strikes (GPALS) system — to protect U.S. troops in the field and our allies from tactical ballistic missile attack, and to protect the United States itself from a ballistic missile attack."[82] This was codified in the Missile Defense Act of 1991, which "established the goals of deploying a highly effective defense of the United States against limited attacks while maintaining strategic stability, and providing highly effective theater missile defense to forward-deployed U.S. forces, and to our friends and allies." The act called for deployment at the earliest possible date or by 1996 of "operationally cost-effective" ABM capability at a single site for defense against a limited attack.[83] Star Wars — a comprehensive defense against a large-scale attack — was dead. While the Bush administration had dramatically reduced the technological demands and economic costs of national missile defense and made deployment of the resulting GPALS an important national goal, the fate of GPALS would pass to his successor.

The Clinton administration was predictably more circumspect about the importance and feasibility of even the less demanding GPALS. In his first budget plans, Clinton reduced BMD funding from $6.3 billion planned by Bush to $3.8 billion, and later the BUR explained that "this reduction reflected this Administration's skepticism about the need for early deployment of a national missile defense system and a desire both to reorient the program toward theater missile defense and to fund overall missile defense research and development at a sustainable level." The administration would seek "options that could meet future threats at an affordable cost."[84] This was a sensible approach but one that also fit Clinton's need to save money where possible. Ballistic missile defense would receive about $18 billion in funding over five years compared to the $39 billion planned by Bush and Cheney. The $21 billion in savings was not insignificant and provided an interesting contrast to some of the aforementioned conservative and partisan criticisms directed at the BUR. Critics accused the administration of underfunding readiness and procurement, but many of these same critics would have spent at least as much and probably more than the Bush administration planned on BMD. Perhaps they could have found the money to do everything they wanted as far as military programs, but more likely their emphasis on BMD would have conflicted with more prosaic but vital elements of military power and preparedness.

Be that as it may, the Clinton administration would emphasize development of theater defenses, including improvements to the Patriot system, that would be used to defend "forward-deployed U.S. forces," while pursuing a "more limited NMD technology program."[85] In other words, Clinton had no desire to move toward deployment of even a limited system designed to protect the continental United States. The administration would kick this can, along with other difficult military policy decisions if possible, down the road. But even as some the earliest experiences of the administration had indicated (as we shall see in the next chapter), Clinton might have expected that he would have trouble exercising his role as commander in chief. Little could he or most Americans imagine how much the 1994 midterm election, less than two years into his first term, would exacerbate his problems, producing a bitter partisan division between the White House and Congress that would distort and delay the process of adjusting military policy and thereby contribute mightily to the politics of irrational security.

CHAPTER THREE

WHAT COMES DOWN MUST GO UP
Clinton and the Politics of Military Spending

> With the dwindling Soviet threat, we can cut defense spending over a
> third by 1997. BILL CLINTON, NOVEMBER 1991

> It is time to reverse the decline in defense spending that began in 1985.
> BILL CLINTON, JANUARY 1999

Military policy during the Clinton presidency was dominated by a confluence of fiscal politics and the culture wars. The deficit and debt led Clinton to look for every penny that could be saved from the "peace dividend" while he lived off the Reagan buildup, hoping the Bottom-Up Review would settle the structure and purpose of the post–Cold War military. He would also try to square the circle by managing the downturn in military spending with an effort to revive the economy. This effort involved a public but lackluster attempt at conversion of military industries into commercial ones, an emphasis on preserving the industrial base, and a much less publicized or noticed explosion of arm sales abroad. Meanwhile Republicans struggled to repackage their national security platform. Lacking a notable or credible external enemy, they would create enemies within, based on cultural and fiscal politics. As Clinton found himself increasingly enmeshed in international crises that seemed to require the use of U.S. military power, the Republican critique about a new decade of neglect and a hollow force was reinforced by arguments that the United States was squandering its military power in hazardous adventures in nation-building. During his second term, when Clinton was faced with a rapidly expanding economy and a disappearing deficit, he was able to mitigate some of his difficulties with military policy by allowing military spending to rise again. The fiscal situation that only a few years earlier had put tremendous pressure on the president to maximize the peace dividend now allowed him to relax a bit and cooperate with the Republican Congress to begin real increases in military spending, while delaying any significant decisions about the major weapons systems that would empower the American armed forces of the twenty-first century. In the end, despite the significant reductions in military forces at the beginning of the decade, defense policy during the 1990s would end up in a kind of holding pattern, awaiting the next president and a new century.

Harbinger: Clinton and the Postmodern Military

In the 1992 presidential contest, following the end of the Cold War, the campaign focused on the economy, jobs, and such things as health care and other domestic concerns. What little discussion there was of military spending and policy often had a pronounced domestic cant. Clinton pledged, as we will see, to build one more Seawolf submarine to preserve the military-industrial base and win the Connecticut primary. Whether this was good national security policy or not, it was standard campaign fare. While Clinton's campaign focused on the economy and jobs, it included as well some items in step with a liberal social agenda. One of Clinton's promises was that he would issue an executive order ending the ban on homosexuals in the military. This promise provoked little controversy during the campaign even though it was included in the national party platform, which pledged to "provide civil rights protection for gay men and lesbians and an end to Defense Department discrimination."[1]

Once Clinton was elected, however, that commitment was among the first and most important controversies that got his presidency off to a somewhat rocky start. The issue of gays in the military commenced a long line of episodes in the culture wars of the Clinton presidency, which provided rallying points for social conservatives and the Republican Party. This conflict began not long after the election, while the president-elect was still in Little Rock, when a reporter asked him if he would follow through on his campaign pledge. The president's reply, "I am going to move forward on that," set the stage for the fight that would soon follow as religious conservatives, Republicans in Congress, and the military commanders who would soon be serving under him were alerted to the first issue that would unite them against the incoming administration.[2]

"The first week of the administration [was] chaos, with all the media attention focused on the controversy over allowing gays in the military and on [attorney general nominee] Zoe Baird's nanny problems," despite the fact that Clinton had already backed away from an immediate executive order to fulfill his promise on ending discrimination in the military based on sexual orientation.[3] His plan was to delay formal implementation to defuse the issue. Meanwhile Secretary of Defense Les Aspin proposed having the military stop asking recruits about their sexual orientation and end discharge proceedings. But that approach did not hold. In fact, during his first week in office, Clinton held separate meetings with the Joint Chiefs and leading members of Congress and both groups told Clinton they opposed the change; in addition, the members of Congress threatened to pass a law codifying existing policy. Many Southern Democrats found the issue politically dangerous and Republicans were happy to be given this early angle of attack on the new president. With influential Democratic Senator Sam Nunn of Georgia, chairman of the Armed Services Committee, leading the opposition (and also leading the media on a tour of a submarine to show how little privacy could be found on board), there was little hope for Clinton's pledge. On January 29, 1993, the new president announced a compromise. A decision would be delayed six months to await a Department of Defense study of the issue. In the interim, the military would stop asking recruits about their sexual orientation but would continue to discharge members of the armed services identified as gay. Six months later the president announced the implementation of what many called the "don't ask, don't tell" policy, a compromise the president acknowledged "will not please everyone, perhaps not anyone."[4]

The reaction to Clinton's proposed executive order was not surprising, given the conservatism of the military and the strength of the religious right. Clinton was not the president to take the nation and the military on this journey. The liberal Democrat Clinton had not served in the military and lacked rapport with military leaders, so this was the wrong issue with which to commence his presidency. It seems, however, that there was more to it than that. With the end of the Cold War and the decline in military spending, one suspects that deeper psychological forces were at work as well in the intensity of the opposition. Our national purpose was gone; budgets were down; weapons were being taken away. In this climate we had a draft-dodger as president, and he wanted to allow gays in the military. This change would never have been easy, but the timing during Clinton's presidency was particularly inauspicious. The issue of gays in the military forged a powerful symbolic link between foreign and domestic politics. Clinton's social liberalism seemed to affect or undermine American national security policy. This impression was augmented by other aspects of Clinton's early national security agenda, including, as we shall see, his emphasis on conversion of defense industries and his use of reinventing government to cut civilian Pentagon bureaucrats. And as we saw in the last chapter, the Bottom-Up Review was not very successful in allowing Clinton to define his military policy and set an agenda for national security strategy.

Cleaning Up: The Cold War Legacies of Bombs and Bases

The issue of gays in the military demonstrated the unexpected pitfalls for the commander in chief in what would otherwise seem to be the promising circumstances of a post–Cold War world and became the new president's initial and unsuccessful foray into shaping the armed forces of the new era. Other national security issues took Clinton and his administration into the past, as they were forced to confront some of the domestic consequences of the Cold War. For example, Secretary of Energy Hazel O'Leary spearheaded an investigation into nuclear radiation experiments conducted on U.S. soldiers and citizens during the Cold War. The Democratic Congress held some hearings on the matter, and in January 1994 President Clinton formed the Advisory Committee on Human Radiation Experiments, which issued a report about a year and a half later. The committee documented thousands of experiments conducted between 1944 and 1974, including hundreds of deliberate releases of radiation. Not much came of this study, but it was, however briefly, a powerful reminder of what had been allowed under the supposed exigencies of national security.[5]

As awful as the radiation experiments were, they seemed quite small and of largely historical interest when compared to a present danger — the monumental problem of waste from nuclear weapons production and the astronomical costs of cleaning up plants and facilities across the country. Essentially the whole Cold War was spent paying as little attention as possible to the vast problems being created by the production of nuclear weapons. During those years 99 percent of all high-level nuclear waste came from this weapons-making activity, not the production of nuclear energy, as well as about 70 percent of all low-level waste and virtually all transuranic waste. Nuclear weapons production took place in a vast complex controlled first by the Atomic Energy Commission and later by the Department of Energy (DOE), at one point covering 2.3 million acres with 120 million square feet of buildings at fifteen major production facilities in thirteen states, with additional smaller facilities throughout the country. At the end of the Cold War there were estimated to be 4,500 contaminated sites. High-level nuclear waste, for example, was held in temporary surface storage facilities located at 131 sites in thirty-nine states. An estimated 300,000 barrels of transuranic waste were stored in various locations. The waste included the hulls of decommissioned nuclear submarines and some of the by-products of deconstructed nuclear warheads.[6]

Three very expensive and complicated problems confronted the Clinton administration in its efforts to deal with this legacy: emergency remediation (short-term containment of high-risk sites); long-term safe storage; and environmental restoration or cleanup. There was, however, no agreed on, guaranteed solution for long-term secure storage of either low- or high-level nuclear waste, and the cleanup would involve working on the far frontiers of environmental technologies. Billions would be spent just to figure out how to restore sites. Ground zero for these challenges was the Hanford Nuclear Reservation in Washington, where plutonium was manufactured for the first nuclear weapons. One of many problems at Hanford was that thousands of gallons of radioactive sludge in basins had leaked into the ground and moved toward the Columbia River a few hundred yards away. The cleanup at Hanford began with over $1 billion a year spent for research and development (R&D) on how to proceed and with an estimated thirty years and $50 billion to accomplish the actual restoration. In 1993 the DOE's budget for cleanup of nuclear facilities was about $9 billion; the entire budget of the Environmental Protection Agency (EPA) was only $7 billion. Most of the DOE's budget in the 1990s and into the new century was for cleaning up from the Cold War. Initial estimates for the entire cleanup projected the expenditure of hundreds of billions of dollars across several decades.[7]

Nuclear production facilities were not the only form of Cold War real estate requiring attention and action. Even in the middle of the Cold War the Pentagon decided that it had too many military installations or bases in the United States and asked Congress for permission to close or reduce a number of them. Many were badly outdated and remained open largely for political reasons — Congress members could not bear closing bases in their districts and a relatively easy logroll had members often supporting one another even if their district or state was not on the line that year. Nevertheless, Congress did allow many smaller installations to be closed. Major installations were a different story, and between 1977 and 1987 Congress prevented the closure of any large bases.[8] As the end of the Cold War came into view, however, Congress passed a law that evaded the politics that kept bases from being closed by delegating the most difficult decisions to an independent commission and limiting congressional participation in the decision. The legislation passed in 1988 created the Base Realignment and Closure Commission (BRAC) process. Following this law, the secretary of defense produced a list of bases for closure or realignment; the BRAC, appointed for that one round of closures, met and refined the list; the list was approved by the president and then sent to Congress. The crucial restriction on legislative action was that Congress had forty-five days during which a vote of disapproval could be taken, but no changes or amendments were allowed to the list. If Congress did not vote, the list went into effect automatically. This was a painful but highly successful process. Four rounds of BRAC—in 1988, 1991, 1993, and 1995—resulted in 97 closures and 55 realignments of major installations as well as over 200 minor closures and realignments.[9]

The elimination of excess base capacity was another vital adjustment to the end of the Cold War, but the financial benefits of this were not forthcoming. The costs of closing, including the direct expenditures to shut or realign facilities, dominated the fiscal equation of base reductions for several years. As with everything else, the Pentagon was prone to exaggerate the savings, but one principal reason for the imbalance between costs and savings was that almost every base was a toxic waste site, and sometimes an explosive toxic waste site. In a nonnuclear version of the weapons complex cleanup, thousands of sites—whether closed or not—required some form of environmental restoration. And as with almost any major Pentagon program, the estimated costs grew as time passed. According to the Congressional Budget Office, "In 1988, DoD estimated that the [base environmental cleanup] program would cost between $14 billion and $18 billion in 1994 dollars. In 1992, the department estimated that it would cost $26.6 billion in 1994 dollars. According to the most recent DoD estimates, the program could cost as much as $30 billion."[10] At one point in the 1990s tens of thousands of acres still in government hands after the closures contained unexploded bombs, including 7,200 acres at Fort Ord, which bordered the Pacific Ocean in a resort-like setting. In a large chunk of the 55,000 acres at the Jefferson Proving Ground in Indiana, an area about four times the size of Manhattan Island, some 25 million rounds of artillery and tank ammunition had been fired over several decades with an estimated 1.5 million rounds remaining unexploded, some buried up to twenty feet deep, including depleted uranium munitions. Here and elsewhere there were also more mundane problems, including poorly stored used motor oil leaking into the ground. The Pentagon was never held to the same environmental standards as other entities. One result of this environmental nightmare was that the Pentagon's projected $1.2 billion in real estate sales from closed or reduced bases shrank to only $92 million in actual income through the early 1990s. In the short run, at least for the first five years, the cleanup costs exceeded the savings and sales.[11] With hundreds of billions of taxpayer dollars in hock to the environmental legacies of the Cold War, the peace dividend proved to be an elusive prospect.

Falling Down: The Political Economy of Post–Cold War Military Spending

The effort to adapt to the end of the Cold War was a complex blend of good faith attempts to shift to a changed world and lingering addictions to Cold War spending and politics. Part of this effort, as we have seen, came with the attempt to recast the "threat" and design an appropriate new strategy, an exercise that featured both rational changes and familiar adherence to unlikely worst case scenarios. Another facet of the issue was a sometimes desperate attempt to ameliorate the economic impact of the drop in military spending. Chapter 2 showed how Clinton's revision of military policy and spending was motivated in part by the formidable problem of deficit politics, especially amid a weak economy. Insofar as he could manufacture a peace dividend by downsizing the Pentagon, all of it could be consumed by the need to lower the deficit; at best, this dividend might provide a little wiggle room for small domestic initiatives. Demobilization after a war has often produced political concerns about the economy. Nothing compares to the scale of demobilization after World War II, when the United States went from twelve million to three million in uniform in one year, and from $83 billion in military spending in 1945 to just $9 billion in 1948. The prospect of this transformation alarmed policymakers well before the war's end, and resulted in, among other things, the GI Bill. After World War II, mass-production industrial manufacturing absorbed much of the fallout from the transition to peacetime in the late 1940s and flourished with the economy's transition to consumer products. The end of the Cold War entailed a far smaller "demobilization" in a much larger economy and population. Nevertheless, American leaders worried about the potential economic and social dislocations that would be produced by the substantial downturn in military spending.[12] Over 500,000 uniformed personnel would leave the military in five years, and 216,000 civilian Pentagon positions disappeared between 1989 and 1994. Perhaps most importantly, billions of dollars in military spending would no longer be going to the private economy either directly or indirectly. Procurement of weapons and other goods was dropping off rapidly from the Reagan buildup. It was not clear what kind of employment weapons makers or their employees could find in the increasingly service-based economy. The result at the end of the Cold War was not a coherent policy initiative, such as the GI Bill. Instead, a hodgepodge and scramble ensued, which combined an overt willingness to justify military spending purely in economic terms and a backdoor industrial policy of liberal arms sales to protect defense spending and ease the economic impact of the post–Cold War drawdown.

The Economic Threat of Peace and the New Justification for Defense Spending

By the end of the Reagan administration, military contractors who were not in a state of denial could see bad times ahead. They knew that the outlays that were keeping defense spending at record levels would soon dwindle even without the promise of a peace dividend. The contractors knew that procurement dollars would disappear faster than other parts of the military budget. Early in the Bush presidency, the Base Force provided a blueprint for a much smaller force only a few years away.

The Gulf War, once again, cut both ways. It vindicated the buildup and provided an unprecedented display of American weaponry, but the very speed and success of the war in eradicating one of the only dangers in a new era underscored how the world had changed and demonstrated how advanced the United States was in military power. Americans quickly evinced their concern for the economy and the deficit over martial elements of national security. The election of Bill Clinton provided no comfort or prospect of relief for military contractors. In fact, during the first year of the administration, Defense Secretary Aspin hosted a dinner with executives from over a dozen major military contractors during which Deputy Secretary of Defense William Perry informed them that "there were twice as many military suppliers as he wanted to see in five years and that the Government was prepared to watch some go out of business."[13] Perry, a former business executive in the industry, was no dove; this was a message of tough love — the decline in defense spending would not sustain the number of major contractors that flourished in the Cold War and under Reagan.

Contractors were faced with three options: get out, get it just right, or get even bigger. A few sizeable corporations such as General Electric (GE), Unisys, and Westinghouse — all of which had substantial commercial operations — got out of the military sector altogether. Others chose to downsize and specialize, including General Dynamics, which decided to focus on ships and tanks but not diversify to commercial products. Hughes Electronics reduced its military division by laying off some 14,000 workers and developing new commercial products. Hughes's dependency on military production declined from 75 percent in 1990 to 40 percent in 1995. Finally, gambling on a strategy of getting even bigger, some of the largest defense contactors decided to merge and dominate. Martin Marietta, which had absorbed GE's defense unit, joined with Lockheed and later bought the much smaller Loral. Boeing, which had already taken on Rockwell International, took over McDonnell Douglas. Northrop and Grumman merged to form Northrop Grumman and acquired Newport News shipyards. These mega-mergers, along with numerous adjustments and closures by smaller firms, produced mega-layoffs. Approximately 1.6 million jobs were lost in private sector defense firms between 1987 and 1999, a decline of 45 percent, with the vast bulk disappearing by 1995 and California accounting for nearly one-third of the losses.[14]

In addition to the difficulties faced by the millions of Americans who lost jobs, the consolidation produced the danger of near monopolies in certain sectors of military production. The risk was that the government might suffer accordingly in a situation with little or no competition for contracts to produce weapons for the Pentagon.[15] There was tension between the reality of too many large firms to support on a post–Cold War diet and the Pentagon's desire for competitive benefits from future contracts. With the Pentagon's support, the Department of Justice blocked the merger of Lockheed Martin and Northrop Grumman but none of the other corporate marriages. While most laid-off workers received nothing in the way of help from the government, the CEOs and shareholders of many companies were rewarded handsomely. The government provided financial assistance to encourage and facilitate the mergers, greasing the palm of the market's invisible hand. Starting in 1993, for the first time in postwar history, the Pentagon allowed companies to bill the government for expenses related to mergers of firms, often referred to as "post-merger restructuring costs." By September 1996 the Pentagon had paid nearly $180 million in such costs to merged firms, and it anticipated a responsibility for a total of over $750 million. Only about 10 percent of these costs benefited laid-off workers. A disproportionate sum went to CEOs. Martin Marietta, for example, submitted a bill to the Pentagon that included $31 million to be distributed among executives (though they did not get all they asked for). This practice came to be known around Congress and elsewhere as "payoffs for layoffs" and led to changes in the law to limit such payouts.[16]

Defense Conversion and the Industrial Base

Beyond the reimbursement or subsidization of restructuring costs, the desire to mitigate the dire straits for arms manufacturers took other forms. One policy was a rather feeble effort to promote conversion from defense to civilian production. "Conversion" is a general term covering nearly any and all initiatives to convert military industries to commercial production. One avenue touted in the 1990s was dual-use technology. The objective was "to 'spin-off' defense technologies into commercial fields, 'spin-on' commercial technologies to lower costs for new defense technologies, and invest in new technologies with both military and commercial use." Clinton and Gore gave speeches promoting conversion and dual-use technologies but very little seemed to go into the effort or come out of it, at least compared to the scope of the changes to the industry. Clinton promised to invest about $20 billion over five years, but much of what was spent ended up going toward easing the local economic pain caused by closures of military bases, not to transform industries or help their dislocated workers.[17]

The other effort to assist the transition elevated parts of the defense industry into a national security program and an asset to be protected. New phrases entered the public discourse, euphemisms such as the need to "preserve the defense industrial base." To some, the only slightly facetious translation of this was, "We will build weapons we don't need to keep military contractors in business and save jobs." This program had, however, a rational military justification. At the end of the twentieth century the weapons of warfare were too complicated to let the technological base lapse. The Ford Motor Company could go into the bomber business in World War II and go back to making cars at the war's end, but that kind of flexibility was less feasible nearly five decades later. The United States did not need more technologically superior attack submarines in 1993, but it might in the near future, and the manufacturing skills involved in that kind of specialized production might not be easy to regenerate in a timely fashion. In fact, the poster child for the industrial base argument was a submarine known as the Seawolf. Designed in the 1980s to be the next generation of attack submarines in the Cold War cat-and-mouse game with the Soviet Navy, the Seawolf reached production stage just as that struggle was coming to a close. With the navy planning to build about thirty of the boats in all, the first Seawolf was under construction when President George H. W. Bush and Defense Secretary Richard B. Cheney decided in early 1992 to rescind funding for the second and third subs (Bush even made it part of his State of the Union address). In an election year dominated by a slack economy, the Seawolf became a political football. Candidate Bill Clinton promised to build a second Seawolf, and the Democratic Congress balked at President Bush's request, retained funding for the second submarine, and provided money that could be used to start a third boat. Meanwhile, the former Soviet Navy was all but mothballed, and the United States still had a full fleet of the best attack submarines in the world. Once president, Clinton made the strategic preservation of the defense infrastructure or industrial base part of official national security policy in the Bottom-Up Review, which used the industrial base argument as justification for the third Seawolf submarine as a transition to a "more cost-effective follow-on" attack submarine, with construction slated to begin at the end of the 1990s.[18] Consequently, to "protect the industrial base" and to hedge against an uncertain future, the United States would end up spending at least $7.5 billion to produce three Seawolf submarines. This very limited Seawolf production would end up bridging the gap until production of the Virginia-class attack submarine could begin.[19]

With the economy in the doldrums, it was not difficult for military programs to be justified unabashedly in purely economic terms. The Pentagon, contractors, and members of Congress had never been shy about using the economic benefits of particular programs to help them along, but in the early 1990s this became at times the sole argument for certain programs, sometimes with specific reference to the states that would benefit from the weapon's production. Advertisements in publications focused on Congress (*Congressional Quarterly Weekly Report*, for example) featured ads for helicopters, tanks, and other weapons that said little or nothing about the threat the weapon countered. Instead, the ads touted the distribution of jobs around the country that would be made possible by continued weapons production, made a link to the defense industrial base if plausible, or emphasized the weapons' cost-effectiveness in an era of tighter budgets. A 1994 advertisement for the V-22 Osprey — a weapon Defense Secretary Cheney tried to kill without success in the late 1980s and that would not be ready for combat even by the time Cheney ended his eight years as vice president in 2009 — promoted the "21st century infrastructure," spawned by V-22 development, "that means jobs in virtually every state in the country."[20]

Speeches on the floor of Congress sometimes had the same character. In 1994 one representative, for example, gave an impassioned plea to save a weapons program by invoking the workers, the jobs, and the fact that his great state needed the program. He was turning from the podium to return to his seat when he remembered to add, "And it's vital for national security."[21]

No one reflected this schizophrenia of conflicting goals and priorities more than Bill Clinton as both candidate and president. Clinton needed the military cuts for deficit reduction and to provide a little fiscal wiggle-room for his domestic priorities. At the same time, he had to engage in a form of damage limitation by keeping some military programs going, especially in key states. Even so, the U.S. government would not be buying enough to keep many contractors in business. The military-industrial complex needed another source of demand. This led to one of the most perverse policies of the early period following the Cold period. It was one of the least discussed aspects of the Bush and Clinton presidencies and one of the most dubious and contradictory policies of U.S. foreign and national security policy during these years. While cutting military spending, Bush and especially Clinton opened the floodgates to arms exports. In so doing they sustained a governmental welfare program (because the government also contributed taxpayer dollars to this process) to help save defense contractors and the economy. Arms sales became a backdoor, seemingly costless way to cushion the blow from the defense downturn and its potentially devastating impact on American arms manufacturers and the economy more generally. This was the quiet policy pursued by the Bush and Clinton administrations. If the United States had no reason to buy more weapons and could not afford to anyway, that did not mean the rest of the world did not and could not. They could, and they did.

The New World Order of American Arms Sales

The demise of the Soviet Union meant not only the end of bipolarity in military power, it entailed as well the near disappearance of the United States' main competitor in arms exports. Part of this competition stemmed from the Cold War itself as each side armed its allies and wooed those not committed to either camp. Consequently, it was not surprising that in the years directly following the Cold War, worldwide arms sales dropped by over 30 percent.[22] Soviet/Russian sales plummeted by over 80 percent, accounting for most of the decline from 1989 to 1994. All else staying equal, the United States would have been thrust by default into the position of top dealer in the arms trade, and in fact the United States increased its market share dramatically, from just over 30 percent to nearly 60 percent between 1989 and 1993 (fig. 3.1). Yet it was hardly the case that the

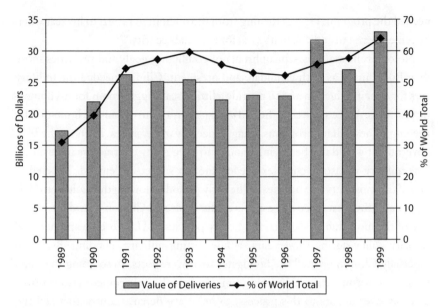

Fig. 3.1. U.S. Arms Sales, 1989–1999. *Source:* U.S. State Department.

United States found itself in this position by accident. The U.S. government was aware of the economic benefits from arms sales following the Cold War, and the Bush and Clinton administrations aggressively pursued the biggest possible piece of the global arms pie. The U.S. State Department's data show that the United States actually increased the value of its arms exports by about 8 percent (in nominal dollars), comparing the periods from 1986 to 1989 and from 1991 to 1994. In fact, the efforts of the two administrations were so successful that in 1994 sales dropped somewhat in response to what some experts saw as a saturation of the market from 1990 to 1993.

While probably exaggerating the contrast between the Cold War and after, David Mussington, writing in the early 1990s, argued that:

> During the Cold War, international politics determined the character of global arms transfers. In the post–Cold War period, however, domestic economic imperatives have become the dominant factor. Defense exporters faced with declining orders look to foreign markets to maintain production levels, and as a means of financing continuing R&D in weapons and dual-use technologies. Western governments have encouraged this, as it coincides with their diminishing willingness (or ability) to subsidize weapons research and production.[23]

Or in the words of another contemporaneous assessment, "The pure economics of weapons production is only expressing itself now that the Cold War is over. Previously, inefficient industries were kept alive around the world for allegedly strategic reasons, although most of the time that was just a euphemism for protectionism."[24] Whether strategic concerns were paramount or not during the Cold War, economic considerations dominated in its immediate aftermath. In the United States the Reagan buildup entailed a massive overhang of productive capacity in the weapons industry at the same time as a recession was threatening post–Cold War prosperity. The government was highly motivated to seek a soft landing for the engorged defense industry and mitigate the effect on the economy.

The contrasts and contradictions in this situation were extraordinary, though largely unnoticed amid the historic transition to the brave new world. The global arms trade was decreasing, but the U.S. share was increasing. Even as U.S. involvement in the arms trade continued to rise by default and then by design during Bush Senior's time in office, some policymakers sought to reduce the number of weapons being sold by the United States because such sales were unnecessary, often unseemly, and potentially counterproductive in a more peaceful era. The Democratic Congress was evincing concern about the rampant proliferation of arms around the globe, which seemed to be propelled in good part by the arms trade in the United States.[25] In a time of relative peace it hardly seemed necessary to continue the trend of dramatically high arms sales that were all too common during the final stages of the Cold War in the late 1980s. At times, ironically, the Bush administration sounded the same theme. Near the beginning of his speech to Congress at the conclusion of the Gulf War, President Bush noted that "it would be tragic if the nations of the Middle East and the Persian Gulf were now, in the wake of war to embark on a new arms race." Bush followed this up with a short-lived program, the so-called Middle East Arms Control Initiative, which sought to restrict the flow of arms to the Mideast. Nevertheless, "the plan to control arms exports to the Middle East would not diminish the heavy flow of U.S. arms to that region."[26] Much like Cold War policy, and despite the arms control initiative, the Bush administration was seeking to solidify alliances with states in the Persian Gulf, including Saudi Arabia, Kuwait, and the United Arab Emirates, and arm them to deter aggression by other nations in the region.[27] Instead of arms control, the reality was that the United States sold about $21.4 billion in weapons to the Middle East from the start of the Gulf crisis in August 1990 through spring 1992. The United States was sending about $1 billion in arms a month to the region while spending only about $580 million a month on procurement for the army.

What drove the contradiction between the supposed arms control initiative and actual policy? The reason becomes evident in an extraordinary letter to Bush from the leaders of six major defense contractors urging Bush's approval of the proposed sale of seventy-five F-15s to Saudi Arabia. The sale, they argued, "would rapidly inject $5 billion into the economy, reduce the U.S. trade deficit, and sustain 40,000 U.S. aerospace jobs and a corresponding number of jobs in the non-aerospace sector of the economy—all at no cost to the US taxpayer." As the election of 1992 neared, Bush responded to this request. He reversed a long-standing U.S. policy prohibiting sales of the most advanced weapons to Middle Eastern nations other than Israel. Then in a speech to McDonnell Douglas employees in St. Louis in September 1992 announcing his approval of the F-15 sale, the president addressed the economic motive directly and somewhat iron-ically: "I'm . . . aware that the past few years have been difficult for this company, for a lot of Americans, as Americans have had to adjust to the reality of a new and more peaceful world. And I know that many of you have been anxious about what the future will bring especially about the status of the Eagle, about the F-15. And I have been sensitive to the impact of this contract on your production line, your jobs."[28] Bush ended his term with "a flurry of arms sales, quietly announcing major weapon shipments to China and Kuwait," and in the two months before the election the administration "rushed through the equivalent of a year's worth of weapons exports."[29] The sale to China lifted an arms ban that had been im-posed following the events in Tiananmen Square in 1989 and had been strictly enforced up to the point of this deal.[30] These types of mass arms sales from the United States were all too common during early part of the 1990s. By the time that Bush left office, his "policies of using State Department, Pentagon, and active duty military personnel as virtual sales representatives for the arms indus-try helped contribute to a surge in U.S. sales in 1992."[31]

In 1992 presidential candidate Bill Clinton ran on a platform that called for change, and change included a reduction of arms sales coming out of the United States. In mid-1993 Clinton gave a speech to the United Nations in which he "outlined his administration's arms control policies, urging tighter restraints on international export control policies and measures to enhance nuclear non-proliferation."[32] In practice, however, "during Bill Clinton's tenure, the United States . . . emerged as the world's premier arms-trading nation, racking up sales numbers that equal the busiest years of the Nixon/Kissinger weapons export boom of the mid-1970s. In 1993, Clinton's first full year in office, the Pentagon and State department helped U.S. firms close a record $36 billion in new arms deals, and American firms controlled 72 percent of all new arms sales agreements with the Third World."[33]

Given the prominent role of the United States in the world, it was always possible for the Clinton administration to argue that such sales were subsidiary to geopolitical policy. According to Pentagon spokesman Ken Bacon, "The basic reason for selling weapons overseas has been to advance our foreign policy goals. . . . It's not to create jobs in the U.S." At the same time, however, there were plenty of indications that the economy and jobs were a primary motivation, and the administration was not particularly concerned about hiding the evidence. In 1993, Commerce Secretary Ron Brown told military contractors that "we will work with you to help you find buyers for your products in the world marketplace, and then we will work to help you close the deal," and Clinton's State Department informed embassies to push weapons sales.[34] The United States spent an estimated $3.8 billion between 1991 and 1994 to send personnel and weapons to arms bazaars around the world, and about 6,500 people were employed by the government to promote and service arms sales.

In the meantime, Clinton did a review of U.S. arms sales policy that culminated in a February 1995 revision. In the latter part of his first term as president, Clinton signed Presidential Decision Directive 34, which was a "new conventional arms transfer policy . . . formalizing his administration's support for continued high levels of U.S. arms sales and its commitment to help the U.S. defense industry maintain its predominance in international markets."[35] In addition to other rather liberal criteria, for the first time U.S. policy included the following as one of the five explicit criteria to be consider for any sale or transfer: "To enhance the ability of the U.S. defense industrial base to meet U.S. defense requirements and maintain long-term military technological superiority at lower costs." One arms lobbyist called this "the most positive statement on defense trade that has been enumerated by any administration."[36] The administration went out of its way to show that it meant business. In 1997 the administration decided to allow F-16s to be sold to Chile, which had no need for them. Clinton overturned a policy in place since 1977 to ban the introduction of advanced tactical aircraft in Latin America.

Congress did not require much encouragement to use this backdoor industrial policy. In addition to the usual arguments about jobs, a trump card was often thrown down: If we don't sell, someone else will. The United States might as well enjoy the benefits. Also, we can be trusted to use greater oversight and restraint than other nations. Just as contractors' magazine ads aimed at Congress often touted the economic benefits of their wares, they often emphasized foreign sales as unambiguously in the national interest. For example, General Dynamics, maker of the M1 Main Battle Tank (of which the U.S. Army had too many after reductions following the Cold War) called its product "One of America's Most Potent Economic Weapons." "The Development of the M1A2 Main Battle Tank by the U.S. Army," the ad continued, "is a defense program that offers the potential for over $10 billion in Defense Trade Sales. These sales to our allies will generate billions of dollars in federal, state, and local taxes. Keeps tens of thousands of highly skilled Americans at work. Retains a unique industrial/technology base. Contributes to a favorable balance of trade. Funding the M1A2 program assures American and Allied forces have the weapon system they need to win on future battlefields and creates a potent economic weapon."[37]

Arms transfers from the United States to other nations take two primary forms. Foreign Military Sales (FMS) are government-to-government sales managed by the Department of Defense (DoD). The weapons may come directly from Pentagon stocks or involve new production, which the DoD contracts from the manufacturer. The second type of arms transaction is through industry-negotiated sales licensed by the State Department and referred to as Direct Commercial Sales. Military contractors can negotiate with foreign governments for sales, but the sales have to be licensed. In the 1990s, both types of sales were used extensively by the United States, but the industry-negotiated sales flourished in the more open and economically motivated environment after the Cold War.

The decade, however, would see a third form of sales become famous (or infamous). In the Excess Defense Articles (EDA) program, used weapons and equipment were given away for free to foreign governments. With plenty of weapons left over from the drawdown, the United States dramatically increased its use of the program. In 1990, the United States gave Egypt 700 M-60 tanks for free. Egypt paid only the transportation cost of about $1 million. Other states that received M-60 surplus tanks included Bahrain, Greece, Morocco, Oman, Portugal, Spain, Taiwan, and Turkey (notice the Turkey-Greece pairing). Overall, from 1990 through 1995 the United States transferred $7 billion in military equipment, primarily to developing countries, including 3,900 heavy tanks and 500 ground attack jets as well as large quantities of surplus small arms and light weapons. Giving these items away was often cheaper than destroying or storing them, and such transfers were seen as an easy way to curry diplomatic favor. Some EDA deals were used at least putatively in furtherance of U.S. goals, such as for narcotics control.

Another form of excess, surplus military parts, caused a brief uproar and scandal at the end of Clinton's first term. The Pentagon was unloading all sorts of surplus equipment, including parts from sophisticated weapons such as helicopters and rocket launchers — even virtually intact and complete weapons — and selling them to the American public. *Newsweek* and *60 Minutes* teamed up for an expose that revealed a slipshod system awash with technologically advanced parts and potentially dangerous weapons available not only to ordinary Americans but also to arms traffickers and agents for foreign governments who might have obtained sophisticated parts to be reverse-engineered abroad.[38]

Arms sales became an easy way to mitigate the post–Cold War dilemma because of the harmonious set of political relationships involved. Arms sales provided economic benefits to the general economy and to geographically concentrated constituents. Unlike an arms buildup driven by U.S. spending, arms sales were either cost-free or involved relatively low costs invisible to the American taxpayer. Finally, in the relative worldwide calm following the end of the Cold War, arms sales were not a salient issue. Public consciousness was extremely low and there was no immediate or direct relation between arms sales and global events or outcomes. Some portion of the sales was no doubt justifiable, but most sales were made without any compelling strategic rationale or clear relation to larger security goals. They were instead an easy way for the interests of military contractors, the Pentagon, and politicians to coincide in an era of declining military spending.

Privatization

Another element of military downsizing during the Clinton administration, privatization, also sought to balance various interests amid this period of relative austerity for the Pentagon. Increasing reliance on private contractors, like other elements of the Clinton adjustment, would prove to have significant implications a decade later in the so-called war on terror. The Pentagon had always used private companies for weapons procurement and R&D — these were the corporate interests implied in the phrase "military-industrial complex." After the Cold War the U.S. military began to increase its use of private contractors for services in support of operations and personnel. This built on some precedents from the

Cold War. In the Vietnam War private companies provided tens of thousands of logistical support workers who constructed bases and provided food for U.S. soldiers. Particularly with the end of the draft in 1973, "the Pentagon began contracting mundane jobs like cleaning and cooking to private firms" to lure recruits.[39] In 1985 the army adopted the Logistics Civil Augmentation Program (LOGCAP), the regulation that, in its own words, "covers the planning process for the use of civilian contractors during wartime situations."[40] But it was not until the end of the Cold War that LOGCAP was first put to use and the role of logistical-support military contractors began to expand significantly. This expansion could be seen both in the amount of money dedicated to hiring contractors and in the breadth of the tasks they were hired to do. In addition to an increasingly important logistics role, private contractors began to provide skilled engineers for weapons technical support, language experts, security, and even training for foreign militaries.[41]

The major reason given for increasing military outsourcing was to save money in the face of post–Cold War budget constraints. Privatization holds the potential to create cost savings in a number of ways. First, it reduces the size of the standing army. Unlike soldiers who are always on the payroll, contractors can be called up when needed and are therefore only a cost to the government when the extra numbers and services are required. The second way contracting can lead to cost savings is through competition. In order to win government contracts, private companies will compete to offer the needed services at the lowest possible cost.[42] A 1995 report by the Defense Science Board, written at the request of the Pentagon acquisition chief, asserted that the DoD could save $12 billion a year by 2002 if it outsourced "all of its support functions to private vendors . . . except those that deal directly with warfighting or are not readily available commercially."[43] In addition to saving money, another reason for the increasing use of contractors after the Cold War was its compatibility with the general move toward an embrace of the free market and belief in the inherent efficiency of private business over government that began in the Reagan era. This " 'privatization revolution' . . . provided the logic, legitimacy, and models for the entrance of markets into formerly state domains."[44]

As far as privatization of the military, however, little change occurred under Reagan. Steps in that direction began during George H. W. Bush's presidency as the Cold War was ending. His secretary of defense, Dick Cheney, advanced this agenda. In 1992 Brown & Root Services (BRS) received a Pentagon contract to "produce a classified report on how private companies — *such as itself* — could help provide logistics for U.S. troops deployed into potential war zones around the world."[45] Subsequently the army awarded BRS the first LOGCAP contract, which would lead directly to the first major use of LOGCAP in the Balkans during the Clinton administration.[46] Halliburton, the parent company of BRS, later hired Cheney as its CEO in 1995.[47] In 1993, under Clinton, the Commission on Roles and Missions, established by Congress to determine how best to streamline the military, lent its support to privatization. The commission determined that "more than a quarter of a million DoD employees engage in commercial-type activities that could be performed by competitively selected private companies." According to one commission member, "There's a growing consensus that we need to move toward more privatization. The burden of proof in the future should be why something shouldn't be privatized rather than why it should be."[48] The pace of privatization began to pick up from 1995 when the Pentagon

> began to give outsourcing renewed attention, and momentum continued to build for what proved to be a significant expansion of the private military industry. By 1996, Congress directed DOD to begin privatizing support services considered commercial in nature. It instructed the Pentagon to submit a plan for increased use of the private sector for services not central to the military's warfighting mission, and it required the DOD to provide a justification when it recommended that a function not be outsourced.[49]

A major Defense Department study released in May 1997, the Quadrennial Defense Review, which will be discussed in more detail later in this chapter, was the first major Pentagon planning document to put considerable emphasis on privatization, primarily as a cost-saving measure. Later that year, "the Pentagon launched its Defense Reform Initiative, which targeted 237,000 additional civilian and military positions for public-private competition . . . with the prospect of shifting 15–30 percent more jobs into the private sector."[50]

Well before the Iraq War would showcase U.S. dependency on private military contractors, some warned against the potential problems posed by extensive privatization.[51] The savings might prove elusive, critics said; and using private contracts could offer a more politically palatable way for the United States to carry out unpopular or legally murky foreign policy goals. The Defense and State departments increasingly contracted with private companies "to go into danger zones that are too risky or unsavory to commit conventional U.S. forces" such as Haiti, Sierra Leone, and Liberia.[52] As noted above, private contracting firms also played a significant role in the war in Bosnia, both to provide important logistical support for U.S. troops and to train the Croatian military in the face of a United Nations arms embargo.[53] Such involvement could decrease public scrutiny or debate that would be required by a larger mobilization of U.S. troops. Public concern or outrage might be dampened if private contractors rather than soldiers were killed in such missions. Finally, privatization could leave the mission vulnerable because of dependence on contractors for essential operational support. What if contractors abandoned their contracts and the theater of operations? Overall, could privatization make going to war politically easier but then in turn endanger and complicate the mission? A few years after these warnings were first raised they would be given substantial credibility by the Iraq War. Meanwhile, as privatization quietly proceeded in the quest for greater savings, the Clinton administration faced increasingly hostile opposition to its plans for national security.

The Enemy Within: The Return of the "Hollow Force"

The initial battle over homosexuals in the military revealed how vulnerable Clinton was on issues of national security. While that shot across the bow was important, it could take hawks only so far, especially once the compromise removed the drama from the headlines. The issue of gays in the military was as much about the so-called culture wars over moral values as it was any sort of genuine debate over national security. Conservatives still lacked a notable threat to national security around which to rally. In the environment following the Cold War, if an external threat or enemy was not forthcoming, then something else would have to do. In a remarkable coincidence of political timing, just as a Democrat for the first time in twelve years was adjusting to the White House, opponents of further cuts in the military budget rallied around the issue of military "readiness." The charge was that the decline in military spending was reaching the point where readiness — the degree to which forces are actually prepared to fight — was endangered.

More directly related to military power and effectiveness than the controversy over homosexuals in military service, readiness nevertheless was similarly focused on an internal threat — something the United States was supposedly doing to itself, regardless of any external threats. Despite the fact that the defense budget had been declining for several years, hawks managed to settle on this issue only once Bill Clinton was president. By the summer of 1993, charges were increasingly common that readiness was threatened by the post–Cold War drawdown and overseas operations in Iraq, Somalia, Bosnia, and Haiti. Those who sounded this alarm had a name for the threat: the "hollow force."

The opening barrage of this campaign came in July 1993 with Senator John McCain's report, "Going Hollow: The Warnings of Our Chiefs of Staff."[54] This softened the ground for what would become several months of attacks based on this critique. Readiness is a measure of the gap, if any, between the military's numbers on paper of its troops, units, ships, aircraft, and other elements versus the number ready at any given moment to take part effectively in potential or actual conflict. A "hollow force" is one in which that gap is large, to the point where significant sectors of the military are not prepared to fight efficiently and effectively or at all. Readiness thus encompasses everything from procurement to pay, and McCain's report listed over a dozen vital elements of readiness that were compromised by underfunding. Critics argued that readiness had begun to deteriorate. All agreed that, as far as weapons procurement, we had the best-equipped armed forces in the world by a comfortable margin. Those concerned about readiness emphasized the other aspects, including training tempos, depot maintenance backlogs, and recruiting and retention trends. The critics, however, were charging the administration with threatening the very thing the White House and Department of Defense claimed was their highest priority in the military budget. The timing of McCain's report is suggestive of the politics involved. The report has a rushed quality and is comprised of a seven-page summary followed by transcripts of speeches given by McCain on the Senate floor, responses by members of the Joint Chiefs to questions posed to them by Senator McCain, and supporting documentation. Senator McCain wrote the chiefs in spring of 1993 just as consideration of the FY 1994 defense budget, Clinton's first, was starting. It is possible but doubtful that the difficulties alleged in the report did not appear until Bush lost the election and Clinton was sworn in as president.

This "going hollow" argument was not unprecedented. It paralleled the critique in the 1970s of the post-Vietnam American military, which many argued was not ready to fight quickly and effectively for lack of training, equipment, key personnel, and morale. In the wake of Vietnam, as the United States demobilized from that conflict and military spending headed toward a Cold War low, hawks raised similar concerns about budgets but also other aspects, including the quality of the troops in a relatively unpopular postdraft military. Some of the critiques from the 1970s were valid, considering the potential threat at the time. The United States was out of Vietnam but there was still the Soviet Union with which to contend. A notable part of the post-Vietnam critique was that we had neglected nuclear weapons in particular. While we fought in Vietnam and licked our wounds afterward, the Soviet Union was catching up in strategic nuclear capability.

Compared to the 1970s critique, even if it was exaggerated, the 1990s version of the hollow force argument lacked some punch. The Soviet Union was gone and no one was questioning the conclusion that we had too many nuclear weapons. So this hollow force was more narrowly framed and without reference to any particular threat. The hawks had to work with what the circumstances offered. Nevertheless, members of Congress harkened back to those dark days as a reminder of the dire circumstances that faced the United States both then and now. For example, Senator Daniel Inouye (at the time chair of the Defense Appropriation Subcommittee) reminded his fellow Senators that "many of us look back to that period [the 1970s] with some horror when we found this nation with hollow military forces. By hollow forces I will just give one example which I provided yesterday. Very few Americans recall that during that period, about one-third of our naval vessels were not ready for combat."[55] Or as Democratic Representative Norm Dicks put it: "In 1979, America, by its own military leadership's self-recognition had a hollow force. Today we are on the verge of having that hollow military back again. In fact, if Members talk to some of our military leaders, they say it is already there. We are starting to delay key maintenance projects. We are not maintaining our equipment as well. We are having a difficult time with retention. We are having a harder time recruiting people."[56]

The "hollow force" or readiness argument was the dominant controversy and trope surrounding military spending from late 1993 through much of 1994, especially in Congress.[57] Four Republican members of the House Armed Services Committee formed a Hollow Forces Update Commission.[58] The debate in both houses of Congress over an emergency supplemental spending bill — primarily meant as relief for the January 17, 1994 Northridge earthquake near Los Angeles, California — became a somewhat surprising showcase for the hollow force arguments and their proponents. Hollow force hawks used this opportunity to attach an amendment adding $1.2 billion to the supplemental so the Pentagon could pay for military operations in and around Somalia, Iraq, Haiti, and Bosnia. Liberals and some deficit hawks in the House sought to delete the military portion of the supplemental via an amendment offered by Barney Frank (D-MA).

The debate over the amendment to excise the military money from the emergency spending bill prompted another debate in which the hollow force argument featured prominently. John Murtha (D-PA), chair of the Defense Appropriations Subcommittee, rose in opposition to the amendment that sought to delete the $1.2 billion. He warned, "I believe that we are now seeing a reduction in readiness all over the country. I have come to the conclusion it would be very difficult for the U.S. forces to be projected forward in a one-front war on a timely basis, let alone a two-front war. . . . We are still on the edge of a hollow force. It is important to defeat this amendment because I am concerned we are on the verge of a hollow force." "We are, under the best of circumstances, heading for a train wreck in the Department of Defense," argued Joseph McDade (R-PA), the ranking minority member on Murtha's important subcommittee. "A vote for this amendment," continued McDade, "is a vote for a hollow Army, a hollow Navy, a hollow military." According to Randy Cunningham, the San Diego Republican who would in 2007 be convicted and imprisoned for taking bribes from a defense contractor during the Bush buildup, cuts to the military "are putting us below a hollow force." "If we do not replace this $1.2 billion," said Norm Dicks (D-WA), "we are going to cut further into readiness, training, all the things that we have to have to have a competent qualified military. All the money that we spent in the 1980s to build up our readiness and training will go for naught."

Frank responded in part by arguing that overseas operations should increase readiness as they involved real training that would decrease the need for other forms of military exercises, flying time, and so forth, especially as troops were rotated in and out of operations. Frank lost on a vote of 158–260, which featured odd bedfellows. The other key sponsor of the resolution was ultraconservative and hawk Dan Burton (R-IN), who argued that the emergency bill should not be the place to add defense money, even though he agreed that the military had been cut too much already. He was joined in the vote by others, including conservatives such as Dana Rohrabacher and Charles Stenholm, as well as liberals like Bernie Sanders and Neil Abercrombie.[59]

The United States was undergoing the largest demobilization of military forces since World War II. This side of the readiness or "going hollow" story was rarely if ever mentioned. Instead, according to most critics, the cuts had gone too far and we were not spending enough money. The main point of contention should have been whether the signs of diminished readiness were real and indicative of long-term problems or largely a product of the inevitable but temporary turbulence that accompanies rapid cuts and restructuring. It was true to some extent that the Pentagon was having trouble managing the pace of the builddown, just as they had trouble managing the pace of the buildup (for which they were rarely criticized by hawks). An argument can be made that some of the concern about the defense budget stemmed not only from the Pentagon's natural reactions to its reversal of fortune but also from its difficulties coping with the process. For example, the transfer of excess military equipment from deactivated units costs money, which contributes to work and expenditures because the equipment to be moved has to be run through depot maintenance before going to, say, a reserve unit. As a result, some of the reports of delays and backlogs were a result of the process of reductions rather than a long-term shortage of maintenance funds. The hawks in this debate might have been right about the short-term difficulties, but wrong about the long-term prognosis. Much of the drawdown, including base closings and realignments, would cause disruptions and cost money in the short run, but would produce long-run savings. When the dust settled from the declines and decreases, the "hollow force" hawks might have discovered a military that had adjusted easily to this relatively high level of peacetime spending for a greatly reduced force.[60]

In political terms, military "readiness" is very much a motherhood and apple pie position. Much like the catchphrase "support the troops," who could be against it? As such it had become, over the years, a "political shibboleth for left and right alike."[61] Some liberals used it against Reagan's extravagant spending on weapons programs; conservatives could trot it out against cuts in military spending. What made this episode of alleged dangers to readiness and the putative return of a hollow force different was that the end of the Cold War and recent defeat of Iraq put a political premium on such arguments, even if the objective need for high readiness had been greatly reduced. Without some attention-grabbing external threat, this was about all that was available to opponents of lower military spending.

The 1994 Elections, the Contract with America, and the Republican Counterattack on National Security

The lack of traction on the issue of national security was evident in the highly successful campaign the Republicans waged in anticipation of the 1994 midterm elections. Relying on the ability of the minority in the Senate to frustrate major Democratic initiatives, the Republicans in both chambers tied Clinton's government in knots during his second year in office, especially over the course of the summer of 1994. Several measures were defeated or blocked, including a comprehensive congressional reform measure that could have been popular with voters. The plug was pulled on the effort to legislate Clinton's health care plan.

Meanwhile the Whitewater investigation, a rather petty affair involving the actions of Clinton and his associates in Arkansas when he was governor in the early 1980s, was joined by other putative scandals, including Travelgate.

Republicans ran against Congress, the president, and the federal government as a whole, concentrating nearly exclusively on domestic issues and fomenting a general turn against Washington. As one high-level Republican Party official put it, "Washington has replaced communism as the glue for conservatives . . . people that love their country but hate their federal government. Where is the evil empire? The evil empire is Washington."[62] This politics of resentment and antipathy toward the federal government was facilitated and amplified by an important new phenomenon in American politics, talk radio and its most influential pioneer Rush Limbaugh. It also tied into the citizen militia groups blossoming around the country.[63] The militia movement was fueled by two incidents, the Ruby Ridge raid in the summer of 1992 during Bush Senior's presidency and the siege of the Branch Davidian compound near Waco, Texas, which took place February 28 to April 19, 1993. And it was around these two events that a link, however delusional, was forged to national security issues. A national security issue that had some play, at least with the likes of Rush Limbaugh and the militias, was U.S. involvement in United Nations (UN) peacekeeping operations. To some this issue was a legitimate concern over control of U.S. troops and foreign policy; to others it played into fears of a post–Cold War world government signaled by UN black helicopters allegedly crisscrossing the United States.[64] The hapless UN had, like Washington, D.C., morphed into the former Soviet Union. Even this shift symbolized the threat from within, and it was hardly the stuff to turn a national election. Potent as this apparition was to a narrow segment of Americans, the GOP concentrated almost exclusively on domestic matters.[65]

This domestic focus was expressed most clearly in the "Contract with America," the unprecedented midterm election platform on which many Republican candidates ran for Congress. The brainchild of Minority Whip Newt Gingrich and Representative Dick Armey, the Contract was a specific legislative agenda backed by a promise that the Republican House would vote on every item in the Contract within the first 100 days of the new Congress. The Contract went public in a September 27, 1994 Capitol ceremony and was eventually signed by over 350 House Republican incumbents and candidates. The core of the Contract with America consisted of items predicated on the existence of deficit politics, including passage of a balanced budget amendment, an end to unfunded federal mandates, and adoption of the line-item veto. Other planks in the contract promised tax cuts, term limits for Congress, welfare reform, and get-tough-on-crime measures, among other things.[66] It was a House-only affair, however, a promise made by the would-be Republican House majority.[67] Some Republican Senate candidates did sign on to a conservative Contract-like proposal called the "Agenda for a Republican Majority," an initiative led by Spencer Abraham and other Republican challengers. And the incumbent Senate Republicans produced an agenda called "Seven More in '94," an allusion to the number of seats they needed to gain to reach a majority. It contained seven measures: "a balanced budget constitutional amendment, an increase in the income tax exemption for children, a modest health care overhaul, a radical redesign of federal welfare, another crime bill with stiffer death penalty provisions, an expansion of Social Security benefits for the working elderly, and an end to further defense cuts."[68] All in all, it was a less ambitious or radical agenda than in the House, but as far as military policy, not very different. In fact, the remarkable thing about the Contract with America was its relative silence on issues of national security. The military, national security, and foreign policy were crammed into just one of the ten planks that composed the Contract, and even this plank lacked focus and passion. It called for the United States to shun UN peacekeeping missions and to build a strategic missile defense system; it also specified that any further cuts in defense spending had to be used to reduce the deficit, not to fund social programs. The Republicans had yet to find a national security mission.[69]

Whether or not the Contract played a significant role in the election, the Republicans were successful in a historic fashion.[70] The House and Senate were both given Republican majorities for the first time since 1952, and no president since Eisenhower had lost both houses in the midterm elections of his first term. The overturn in the House majority was particularly stunning; it had been controlled by Democrats since 1955. Clinton's losses, however, were much greater than Ike's, who had begun his presidency with very narrow margins in both houses and lost control in 1954 to equally small Democratic majorities. On the whole, one had to go back exactly a century, to the midterm elections of 1894, to find comparable losses in both houses.

The 1994 elections, stunning in and of themselves, were read as a decisive verdict that Clinton and the Democratic majority failed to produce significant change. In a year, the presidency and Democratic Congress had gone from a rousing success to a government in crisis. Following the elections, the Clinton presidency seemed a shambles. Indeed, in early January 1995, at the start of the 104th Congress, Clinton's presidency was characterized as a sideshow to the actions of the new Republican majority. Never in the era of the modern presidency had the locus of political initiative and action shifted so suddenly and decisively to Congress. Even so, it did not take long for the Republicans to experience the challenges of being the governing majority, and some of the antigovernment sentiments they drew from and incited proved difficult to control. One facet of the Republican politics of resentment came to a tragically ironic close on April 19, 1995 when 168 people were killed in the bombing of the federal building in Oklahoma City. Escaping any repercussions for their support, however tacit, of the militia movement and its delusional arguments, members of the new Republican majority in Congress would have to soldier on without pandering as much to antigovernment extremists.[71] Gingrich and company would find it increasingly difficult to advance their agenda. Despite passing several of the less significant items in the Contract, many of the major measures, such as a balanced budget amendment and term limits, failed.

More importantly, Clinton began his remarkable comeback by standing up to key elements of the Contract and portraying them as mean-spirited and the wrong direction for the country. His use of the veto and willingness to confront the Republicans with a budget crisis ultimately restored his presidency and put the GOP on the defensive. Clinton issued twelve vetoes between June 1995 and January 1996 and only one, on a relatively unimportant litigation reform, was overridden. Among his successful vetoes was the Defense Authorization Act, which contained Contract language calling for deployment of a missile defense system (discussed below). Provisions about preventing U.S. troops from serving under UN command did not make it past the Senate. The Republican national security agenda, modest and reactive to begin with, was all but dead in the water.[72] The president and Congress had fought to a standstill on the military and other issues, but that contest did not solve the difficult choices facing the country in the balancing act between national security strategy and resources. Instead, the growing economy would play the major role in allowing Clinton and Congress to take some pressure off defense planning and budgets. Defense spending would start to go up again, largely because it could.

Stalemate: The Quadrennial Defense Review of 1997

In 1993, as part of the 1994 Defense Authorization Act, Congress authorized a Commission on Roles and Missions of the Armed Forces (CORM) to evaluate the military's structure. Among its May 1995 recommendations, in addition to its

endorsement of privatization discussed earlier, the commission called for a review every four years of overall military policy and implementation. This produced what has become known as the quadrennial defense review (QDR) process. After the Republicans took control of Congress they wrote the Quadrennial
Defense Review into the National Defense Authorization Act of 1996 and made
direct reference to the central criticisms of the BUR, the last major review. This
first QDR was intended to revisit and modify the Bottom-Up Review and to
consider lingering questions raised by the CORM, working toward a new strategy for the armed forces of the twenty-first century. The Republican majority, no
doubt suspicious that the Clinton administration would not necessarily evaluate
matters as the Republicans would, took an additional step. The same legislation
created a National Defense Panel of private sector experts appointed by the
secretary of defense in consultation with the chairs and ranking members of the
Senate Armed Services and House National Security Committees. The National
Defense Panel was directed to review the QDR and make its own recommendations if necessary.

Clinton's secretary of defense was by this point William Cohen, a moderate
Republican and former Senator from Maine. Rehearsing the president's recent
National Security Strategy, the QDR's strategic theme was "shape, respond, and
prepare."[73] That is, shape the current strategic environment to advance U.S.
interests, respond to current threats, and prepare for future threats. Beyond that,
under Cohen's leadership, the first QDR, with a few minor embellishments,
replayed the familiar post–Cold War tune. The initial attempt to redefine military policy under Clinton, the 1993 Bottom-Up Review, justified its twenty-first
century force structure with the assumption that we must be prepared to fight
two wars on the scale of the Gulf War, simultaneously, without allied help. The
Quadrennial Review changed nothing about those core assumptions. Both major
reviews under Clinton in effect justified the largest possible military forces in a
world devoid of significant military threats and replete with well-armed and
wealthy allies.

Despite major concerns about the tension between missions and money —
that is, the gap between U.S. military commitments and needs and future budget
projections — the QDR made no tough decisions about either. In particular, the
document evaded decisions about future major weapons programs. Instead the
QDR concluded that all the systems were needed, just fewer of each. For example, the QDR reduced the number of F-22 fighters the air force would procure
from 438 to 339. But the air force would also get the vast bulk of the 2,852 Joint

Strike Fighters (JSF) built early in the next century. The navy was also to get several hundred JSFs, along with 548 F-18 fighters. This came at a time when many in Washington were feeling that the "procurement holiday" from the end of the Cold War should be over and when many new weapons programs were heading toward production. As the QDR noted, "That drawdown is now over, the dividend from procurement reductions has been spent, the procurement holiday must end, and investment in modernization needs to rebound" because "it has become clear that we are failing to acquire the modern technology and systems that will be essential for our forces to successfully protect our national security interests in the future."[74]

The difficulty was, as the QDR recognized, that this shift to the production of new systems was to take place in a budgetary environment in which, "absent a marked deterioration in world events, the nation is unlikely to support significantly greater resources dedicated to national defense than it does now—about $250 billion in constant 1997 dollars per year."[75] This begged the question of where the money would come from to pay for this expensive array of new weapons. The QDR and Secretary Cohen emphasized two equally dubious sources— base closings and management reforms—along with some modest further reductions in uniformed and civilian personnel. Just as the Pentagon, White House, and Congress have been prone over the decades to inflate the dangers posed by various threats, they have been equally liable to exaggerate the budgetary benefits of various reforms, and to underestimate the real final costs of major weapons systems. Even by 1997, as we saw earlier, the available data indicated that base closings had not produced net savings, largely because the environmental cleanup costs outstripped the gains from property sales and consolidation. The Pentagon has frequently trotted out management reforms as a way to economize, and the QDR had the audacity to label its version the "Revolution in Business Affairs." Even so, anyone familiar with the history of such things would have bet that the weapons of the future, such as the F-22s, would cost billions more than the current projections, and the various reforms and base closings would save billions less than projected. Not many seemed to notice, however. Not long after the release of the QDR, the big story involving the military was an imbroglio over adultery in the Pentagon, unfolding in considerable detail on the front pages of newspapers and at the start of news broadcasts. This scandal culminated in the withdrawal of Air Force General Joseph Ralston, vice chairman of the Joint Chiefs, as a candidate for chairman of the Joint Chiefs of Staff.

If the QDR of 1997 was a major if unsurprising reminder of the extent to which the Clinton administration refused to make difficult decisions about national security policy, an actual decision from 1997 was perhaps unexpected insofar as it revealed the distance which Clinton had retreated from any sort of liberal policies or even inclinations as far as national security policy. By 1997 negotiations for an international treaty to ban the use of land mines were reaching a positive conclusion and over a hundred nations were ready to sign the agreement. Despite his initial desire to support the treaty, Clinton bowed to pressure from the Pentagon and kowtowed to their rather lame arguments. The Pentagon argued that the United States needed to retain the right to use land mines in South Korea and that so-called smart land mines (more technologically sophisticated land mines that are built to self-destruct after a short time) should be allowed on the battlefield. One common refrain was that it was not U.S. landmines that were killing or maiming children around the world. That the world's only military superpower would make such arguments should have been a major embarrassment to be quashed by a confident president with the support of ample arguments to the contrary. Such was not to be the case. After some hemming and hawing, and a feeble and ludicrous attempt to have the treaty make exceptions for the United States, Clinton announced on September 17 that the United States would not become a signatory to the treaty, a position that would align it with such nations as Iran, Iraq, China, Russia, Somalia, and Libya. Instead, Clinton directed the Pentagon to find alternatives that would end the use of land mines by 2003 (except in Korea), well after the end of his presidency. One month later the Nobel Peace Prize was awarded to the International Campaign to Ban Landmines and its coordinator Jody Williams.[76]

The Economy, the Surplus, and the Turnaround in Military Spending

While never able to comfortably inhabit the role of commander in chief, and unable to make decisions about military policy that might have produced a smoother and more durable transition to a new era, President Clinton benefitted from the end of the Cold War primarily because of its impact on the budget. Defense spending was coming down regardless as the nation transitioned to the significantly smaller force structure called for by the Base Force and Bottom-Up Review. This helpful trend was augmented, however, by the legacy of the Reagan buildup. Capital spending, especially on military procurement, declined more rapidly than the rest of the Pentagon budget (fig. 3.2). As we have seen, this was

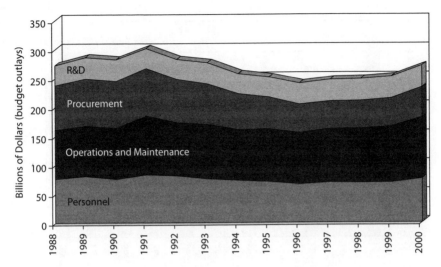

Fig. 3.2. Military Spending by Function, 1988–2000. *Source*: Office of Management and Budget.

rational insofar as the near-simultaneous combination of the Reagan buildup, with outlays peaking in 1989, and the end of the Cold War left the nation with too many relatively new weapons. Some notable forms of procurement were unlikely to be needed even in the long term. During the core years of the Reagan buildup, nuclear weapons programs composed from 25 to 30 percent of the total procurement budget. With the exception of Trident missiles and a few B-2 bombers, this line of procurement was finished in the early 1990s, with no need for further production in the foreseeable future. Unlike many conventional programs this constituted a large and "permanent" reduction in procurement requirements. As everyone recognized, the broader procurement holiday could not go on for ever, but for several years it kept pressure off the defense budget, which declined in real terms through 1998 even though small nominal budget increases started in 1995 (fig. 3.3).

The decline in military spending was, in some ways, greatly exaggerated and frequently not put into any larger historical context. Military spending had descended considerably from the mountaintop of the Reagan buildup, but even though the Cold War had ended and the armed forces were considerably smaller than during the 1980s, the budget by many measures was still high in relative terms. Historical comparisons of real (adjusted for inflation) military spending show that the defense budget was not gutted, especially given the reductions in

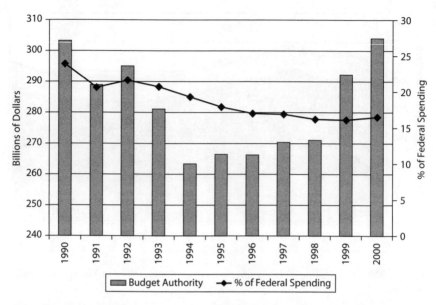

Fig. 3.3. Military Spending, 1990–2000. *Source*: Office of Management and Budget.

force structure. By 1993 Bush and Clinton had cut outlays by nearly 23 percent from the peak in 1989 but the nation was still spending 10 percent above the level in 1980, which was two years into real increases made by Carter and Congress. Even from the perspective of the entire Cold War, the military budgets of the 1990s were surprisingly high. The average annual outlay for national defense from 1950 to 1989 was $317 billion per year (in FY 2000 dollars). This includes, of course, the Korean and Vietnam wars and the Reagan buildup. In 1994 the United States was still just above the Cold War average by about 2 percent. The 1994 defense budget was spent, however, on a force that was approaching a 25 percent reduction in overall size from the levels of 1980. Even in 1998, the low point in post–Cold War military budgets, the nation was allocating only 11 percent less than the average from the Cold War.[77] Operations and maintenance budgets (per personnel) were at very high levels in real terms, despite the arguments about a "hollow force." In fact, the Pentagon budget as a whole was quite high when measured in terms of the amount of spending per active duty personnel, higher than it was at the peak of the Reagan buildup (fig. 3.4).[78] In 1995 the Pentagon spent about 49 percent more per capita than it did in 1980. Even if we concede the arguments about a hollow force in the 1970s, it was implausible that

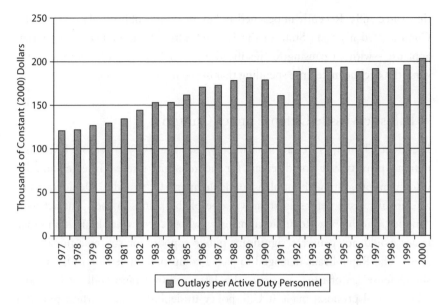

Fig. 3.4. Military Spending per Active Duty Personnel. *Source:* Office of Management and Budget and Department of Defense, Comptroller.

the U.S. military establishment could not maintain a quite solid and robust force with that level of funding in the 1990s.[79]

The pressure — political and otherwise — to increase defense spending stayed low long enough for the economy to rebound and loosen the vise grip of deficit politics. If neither the BUR in 1993 nor the QDR in 1997 were going to make substantial reductions in major weapons procurement programs, then the procurement holiday was going to end with rather large bills due as production increased. In the meantime, however, the economy had picked up and tax revenues were pouring into the federal treasury. The government was projecting, realistically for once, an end to the deficit, with a surplus by perhaps 2000. Revenues increased by 33 percent in real terms from 1994 through 1999 and the surplus made a shockingly early return at nearly $70 billion in 1998, to be followed by $126 billion in 1999 and $236 billion in 2000.[80] With this remarkable change in fiscal fortunes, Clinton could allow defense spending to increase, thereby appeasing his critics and providing cover for his fellow Democrats and potential successor without endangering other priorities. In 1999, budget authority for defense spending increased in real terms (by 5 percent) for the first time since 1985. Recently impeached and in the middle of his trial in the Senate, Clinton used his 1999 State of the Union address to announce to bipartisan applause — without pausing for justification or analysis — that "it is time to reverse the decline in defense spending that began in 1985."

Ballistic Missile Defense under Clinton

President Clinton, as we saw in chapter 3, used the BUR to demote BMD as a national priority.[81] It would remain for the indefinite future a research and development program without plans for deployment. Or would it? Deployment of a national missile defense system was one of the planks in the Contract with America, but the new Republican majority, whose success was limited on other issues, could not generate significant public support for strategic missile defense. The Republicans managed to pass a compromised version of their Missile Defense Act of 1995, as part of the defense authorization bill for FY 1996. The original proposal made it U.S. policy to deploy at the "earliest practical date" effective theater and national missile defense systems; whereas, among other modifications, the final legislation called for the deployment of "affordable and operationally effective" systems with no temporal reference. Unsatisfied with this outcome, Speaker Gingrich and Majority Leader Bob Dole, who was running for president against Clinton, introduced in the House and Senate in March 1996 the Defend America Act. The act would have required deployment by 2003 of a national missile defense system that "is capable of providing a highly-effective defense of the territory of the United States against limited, unauthorized, or accidental ballistic missile attacks; and will be augmented over time to provide a layered defense against larger and more sophisticated ballistic missile threats as they emerge."[82] Candidate Dole framed the issue this way: "If I ask most people what would you have the President do if there was an incoming missile, ballistic missile, you would say shoot it down. We can't because President Clinton opposes it. And we support it."[83] The legislation, however, never came to a vote in the House and fell short on a vote to cut off debate in the Senate. By this point Clinton had triangulated the controversy by once again putting off any decisions with the so-called 3+3 plan, which mandated three more years of research and development from 1997 through 1999, to be followed by a decision in 2000 about deployment of a system to protect against an attack by a small number of warheads, which if approved would be completed by 2003.[84] The decision would be contingent on the effectiveness of the technology, its affordability, and the threat at that time.

Still dissatisfied and frustrated, the Republican Congress passed legislation in 1996 to mandate an assessment by actors outside the government of the threat to the United States by ballistic missiles. This produced the Commission to Assess the Ballistic Missile Threat to the United States, which was composed of nine members, private citizens with expertise in this area, appointed by the CIA, but with six of the nine members essentially selected by the House and Senate majority leaders. This effort was motivated in part by the obstacle to the Republican majority's plans for BMD posed by the 1995 National Intelligence Estimate (NIE). In that estimate, the collective wisdom of the nation's intelligence agencies was that a long-range missile threat to the continental United States from regional powers was not likely for at least fifteen years.[85] This move, to create a competitive analysis of a disagreeable NIE, was reminiscent of the creation of Team B by CIA Director George H. W. Bush to produce an outside evaluation to challenge that era's NIE about the Soviet missile threat. Team B's report leaked after the 1976 elections painted an alarming picture of the Soviet threat, its level of military expenditures, and especially its ballistic missile capability. The report gave support, among other things, to the idea of a "window of vulnerability" in strategic nuclear capabilities, with the Soviets moving toward a first strike capability. Paul Wolfowitz was an advisor to Team B, along with Paul Nitze (who wrote NSC 68 back in 1950) and Donald Rumsfeld, who as secretary of defense under President Gerald Ford had pushed for this kind of competitive analysis.[86] Both Rumsfeld and Wolfowitz resurfaced twenty years later to be appointed members of this new Team B, on the threat of ballistic missiles, with Rumsfeld as chair. In July 1998 the Rumsfeld Commission issued its report, and like Team B, its assessment was that the threat was both larger and closer than imagined. In this case, the threat of attack by intercontinental missiles in the hands of regional powers, such as North Korea, Iran, and Iraq, was, regarding capabilities (as opposed to motivation), as close as five years. The report called into question the ability of the intelligence community to know if and when countries were undertaking such an effort and consequently the warning might be much less than five years.[87]

Amid the ongoing investigation and pending impeachment of President Clinton, the Rumsfeld Commission report failed to generate much in the way of headlines or national panic. It did, however, provide Republicans with enough ammunition to pass, after some compromises, the 1999 National Missile Defense Act. In yet another version of the familiar language, the act stated that "it is the policy of the United States to deploy as soon as is technologically possible an effective National Missile Defense system capable of defending the territory of the United States against limited ballistic missile attack (whether accidental, unauthorized, or deliberate)." In his signing statement for the bill, President Clinton emphasized that no decision had been made and that any "NMD system we deploy must be operationally effective, cost-effective, and enhance our security."[88] This was his way of clarifying the conditions that would govern a decision to deploy, including cost-effectiveness, which was not implied in the original language of the proposed legislation. Despite actions and pronouncements that made it seem that the administration would proceed with deployment, Clinton decided in September 2000 that the time was not ripe; he did not have "enough confidence in the technology, and the operational effectiveness of the entire NMD system, to move forward to deployment."[89]

Into the New Century

Clinton's decision on national missile defense exemplified the costly political stalemate and gamesmanship that characterized military policymaking in the 1990s. The serious if flawed efforts early in the decade to adjust to the most dramatic change in world politics in half a century were not pursued and augmented by other decisions that would have matched resources to commitments, preferably by scaling back commitments (such as the two-war scenario and the self-sustaining assumption of no allied support) and making tough decisions about the dozens of expensive weapons systems awaiting production. Instead Clinton, who never wanted to base his presidency on national security, and the Republican Congress, which had found little purchase on these issues, fought it out for six years mostly on other matters, culminating in the Monica Lewinsky scandal and impeachment. Despite largely symbolic fights over such things as national missile defense, national security and military policy suffered from a lack of commitment and attention. Politically, as we have seen, this neglect was made possible by the combination of the Reagan buildup's legacy of a procurement holiday and the turnaround in the economy that allowed Clinton to agree to increase military spending at the end of his presidency, but with no clear picture of where this was all heading.

If conservatives and Republicans struggled to find traction on security issues,

Clinton and the Democrats did little to institutionalize an alternative vision. In the 1990s Democrats and liberals either ignored national security whenever possible or seemed to assume that the historic change brought by the end of the Cold War would take care of military spending and policy. National security politics and policies would naturally flow from the changed environment. Although efforts were made to find a path in the new world order, they failed to realize that a new national security identity would have to be actively and aggressively constructed *domestically*. For example, a new norm or regime of collective security, involving allies in collective burden-sharing, would have to be packaged and sold, which it was not. No new paradigm was created and marketed at home.

President Clinton might have been kicking various military cans down the road for his political purposes, but the Republicans were no less irresponsible. They would have committed the country to a very expensive deployment of a missile defense system of dubious effectiveness against a remote and unlikely threat. The fervor with which they pursued this in disregard of cost, effectiveness, and purpose raised the suspicion that it was mostly for political reasons. It was something tangible to offer Americans — who had always expressed surprise that we could not stop such missiles and generally liked the idea of being able to do so — in an era devoid of significant demons. In the end, however, their belief in national security and the need for strong leadership in what they portrayed as a dangerous world took a back seat to impeaching the president over alleged misconduct in the Monica Lewinsky investigation. The extent to which the Republican Party, the party of Ronald Reagan and victory in the Cold War, was so adrift and aimless in the 1990s on issues of national security was remarkable. Its entire focus was inward. From the gays in the military, to the hollow force, to the Contract with America, to the politics of resentment represented by militias, to Clinton's impeachment, the GOP had become not so much isolationist as solipsistic. Having no vision for foreign or national security policy, it sought to frustrate actions taken by the president in those areas and elsewhere. The party of presidential power did its best to destroy just that. Into this morass stepped a man who embodied the time and tenor of the Republican Party at the turn of the century, George W. Bush, a one-term governor of Texas, with no foreign policy or national security experience or portfolio. As we shall see in the next chapter, the campaign of 2000 was hardly fought on issues of national security, but insofar as the issue was broached candidate Bush criticized Clinton's military policy in familiar fashion. "Eight years ago," Bush noted on the eve of the election, "the Clinton-Gore administration inherited a military ready for dangers and challenges facing our nation. The next president will inherit a military in decline. But if the next president is George W. Bush, the days of decline will be over." Bringing his running mate into this pledge, Bush added, "Dick Cheney and I have a message to all of our men and women in uniform and to their parents and to their families: Help is on the way."[90] Little could candidate Bush imagine how true his statement would in some ways prove and in other ways how tragically ironic.

CHAPTER FOUR

From AMBITION TO Empire

Bush and Military Policy before and after 9/11

"Our country, after an era of drift, must now set itself to important tasks and higher goals."[1] So opened the Republican Party Platform of 2000. "An era of drift" cagily evoked the panoply of conservative criticisms of President Bill Clinton and his administration from beginning to end, across nearly every arena of policy and action. In particular, however, the contrast of the terms "drift" and "higher goals" in this statement played upon widespread public disgust with the Monica Lewinsky scandal. In comparison to that episode, anything would seem more vital or lofty. But this disparagement of the Clinton years cut both ways. The Republicans took no responsibility, of course, for the sense of drift, despite years of sniping at and harping over what later (especially after 9/11) seemed to be rather petty matters, including the Whitewater scandal, Travelgate, and the myriad other alleged crimes committed by President Clinton and First Lady Hillary Rodham Clinton. The Republicans accepted no blame for their own Herculean efforts to run down public opinion about and to foster hostility toward the federal government and its policies. Little wonder, then, that the country might drift while tangled for nearly two years in the politics of sexual scandal and impeachment. Nearly anything might be a higher goal or a more important task than the Republicans' protracted and futile attempt to remove a president from office for lying about consensual sex.

The "era of drift" referred as well, as we saw in the last chapter, to what Republicans and conservatives saw as the squandered opportunity after the Cold

War to preserve and extend American power. During the election campaign of 2000 the Republican Party, along with candidate George W. Bush and conservative elites who would become key figures in the Bush administration, criticized Clinton's military policies and budgets. Though vague about budgetary implications, they argued for strategies, pay increases, and programs such as ballistic missile defense, which all implied a significant increase in spending. Overall, however, national security was a relatively minor issue during the campaign. Despite the invocation of Ronald Reagan's policy of "peace through strength," the Republicans could not replicate, amid the relatively placid and prosperous times, the kind of public concern about national security that helped them gain power two decades earlier.

Nevertheless, in its first year the Bush administration worked toward a more aggressive and expensive national security policy. This policy was based on doctrines and strategies that sought to extend American influence through military power and envisioned the budgets necessary to create the means to that end. The administration was off to a relatively slow start in this regard when the events of September 11, 2001 made possible the military policies and programs for which they had been planning — and even more. This chapter concentrates on the new military doctrines and strategies produced by the administration both before and after 9/11, while the next chapter examines the character and politics of the concomitant military buildup.

Bush, National Security, and the Election of 2000

George W. Bush campaigned for and entered the presidency espousing and echoing the familiar litany of Republican attacks on the national security policies of the Clinton administration. His campaign did not differ much from the 1994 "Contract with America," which first outlined the elements of the Republican alternative for foreign and military policy: provide more money for defense in general; deploy a ballistic missile defense; and limit, if not eliminate, U.S. involvement in peacekeeping or nation-building efforts, especially if tied to the United Nations. That was about all there was to the Bush campaign, however.[2] On occasion Bush articulated a more complete vision of what national security and military policy would look like under his leadership, including an emphasis on the transformation of U.S. forces through further qualitative advances in the application of technology. The United States could take advantage of the relative peace of the post–Cold War era and "use this window of opportunity to skip a generation of technology" in order to create the unrivaled force of the future.[3] And yet no commanding vision of a threat or grand design for national security framed what became, as the campaign developed, little more than a series of talking points. Candidate Bush, for example, was rarely more precise or detailed than this: "If we don't have a clear vision of the military, if we don't stop extending our troops all around the world and nation building missions, then we're going to have a serious problem coming down the road, and I'm going to prevent that. I'm going to rebuild our military power. It's one of the major priorities of my administration."[4] In another refrain from the campaign trail, Bush, as we've seen, would tell the "men and women in uniform" that "help is on the way."[5]

The campaign of 2000 dealt very little with national security or military policy. Neither candidate, Bush or Gore, had a distinct advantage on the issue. As a senator, Gore had been knowledgeable and influential in areas such as nuclear weapons, but as vice president he had emphasized domestic policies including the reinvention of government (which had involved shedding many civilian employees at the Pentagon). Bush was a governor with absolutely no foreign policy portfolio or experience with military policy (and an embarrassing service record from the Vietnam era). As world events and the country's mood did not demand a national dialogue on national security and the military, the candidates were probably happy to oblige. For example, when the opening question of the presidential debates allowed Gore to comment on Bush's lack of experience for the office, he did not mention national security and instead talked about Bush's domestic priorities. Less than 22 percent of the debates were devoted to issues of national security, the military, or foreign policy.

In the final debate, where audience members asked the questions, only two of the fifteen questions touched on these subjects.[6] The candidates said almost nothing specific about military spending or programs, not even mentioning ballistic missile defense. What little was said was devoted to mostly general discussions about when to use military force and commit American troops and the pros and cons of peacekeeping operations and nation-building. It was on these topics that Bush made some of his most ironic statements, including his assessment of how the conduct of U.S. foreign policy is perceived by the rest of the world: "It really depends upon how our nation conducts itself in foreign policy. If we're an arrogant nation, they'll resent us. If we're a humble nation, but strong, they'll welcome us. And it's — our nation stands alone right now in the world in terms of power, and that's why we have to be humble. . . . We're a freedom-loving nation and if we're an arrogant nation they'll view us that way, but if we're a humble nation they'll respect us."[7]

Humble or arrogant, the international manners of the United States were not much on the minds of the American voter. One is hard-pressed to find *any* mention of foreign policy, national security, or military spending in accounts of the presidential election in 2000.[8] In the Voter News Service exit poll, 12 percent of voters mentioned the generic category of "world affairs" as a factor in deciding their vote.[9] Such international issues are often swamped by domestic concerns and debates, but with the world at relative peace, the campaign seemed to hinge inevitably on perceptions of character, leadership, and issues such as social security, education, and the economy. If anything, Gore had a slight advantage as far as the impression voters had of his ability to handle a world crisis.[10] Bush's unprecedented victory in the U.S. Supreme Court provided the hairbreadth margin for a win via the electoral college in the face of Gore's constitutionally irrelevant popular vote majority. Given this vexed and vexing outcome of the election, no one could say the voters had sent a clear signal about what mattered in this election, let alone about who should be president.

The Bush Presidency before September 11

Nevertheless, the lack of voter interest or debate about national security issues did not mean that Bush and his supporters lacked important, far-reaching, expensive, and debatable plans for military spending and policy. The American public did not get to consider what would prove to be the most expensive part of the Bush agenda — even without counting the costs of the wars that would follow 9/11. Bush devoted only a few sentences in his inaugural address to national security and foreign policy, following his pledge to lower taxes with one to "build our defenses beyond challenge, lest weakness invite challenge."[11] Likewise, in his first address to Congress to announce the goals of his administration, Bush made education his "top priority." After spending most of his time on education, Medicare, Social Security, and tax cuts, he announced a modest increase in "military pay and benefits and health care and housing." Furthermore, as part of confronting the threats of the twenty-first century, including terrorists and "tyrants in rogue nations intent upon developing weapons of mass destruction," he said that the nation "must develop and we must deploy effective missile defenses." This rhetoric added little to the generalities of the campaign. Only later in the address did he devote a few more sentences to national security policy when he announced that he had "asked the Secretary of Defense to review America's Armed Forces and prepare to transform them to meet emerging threats. My budget makes a down payment on the research and development that will be required. Yet, in our broader transformation effort, we must put strategy first, then spending. Our defense vision will drive our defense budget, not the other way around."[12]

The words "transform" and "transformation" evoked the essence of the new administration's plans for the military and defense spending. It was no secret that Defense Secretary Donald Rumsfeld's review of national security and military policy would revolve around these concepts; for example, they were the basis of comments about skipping "a generation of technology" in weaponry. But what was the real nature of these plans? While having manifold implications, including the general adaptation of U.S. military power to changing security conditions and requirements, the core of transformation was more specific. In short, transformation was the implementation of the revolution in military affairs (RMA) and the reorganization of the U.S. armed services around that revolution. The RMA was a theory about the future of warfare that emerged in the early 1980s as advances in microelectronics implied significant advancements in military capabilities. As the implementation of the RMA, "transformation can mean fully *adopting new information technology* and *restructuring the armed forces* in order to produce an 'information age' military."[13]

This technological revolution had the potential to change nearly everything about warfare through two key elements: first, the accuracy and precision in weapons, and second, vastly improved intelligence and communications. Highly accurate weapons reduced the need for quantity, numbers of troops, or the use of potentially excessive force. Computer-age intelligence and communications would provide an initial and ongoing superiority that would not only help win wars but also perhaps even prevent them. Together, precision weapons and the information network to utilize them would supposedly dominate the battlefield — if conflict was even necessary. Transformation could make the United States so manifestly superior, argued some of its proponents, that others might not dare to fight.

Even back in 1999 Governor Bush was quite explicit about the link between transformation and the broader goals of national security and foreign policy. He argued that one of his national security goals was to take advantage of a tremendous opportunity—given few nations in history—to extend the current peace into the far realm of the future. A chance to project America's peaceful influence, not just across the world, but across the years. This opportunity is created by a revolution in the technology of war. Power is increasingly defined, not by mass or size, but by mobility and swiftness. Influence is measured in information, safety is gained in stealth, and force is projected on the long arc of precision-guided weapons. This revolution perfectly matches the strengths of our country—the skill of our people and the superiority of our technology. The best way to keep the peace is to redefine war on our terms.[14]

War on "our terms" required a major overhaul of existing U.S. forces, still oriented toward massive conflicts including the Gulf War, into forces that are

agile, lethal, readily deployable, and require a minimum of logistical support. We must be able to project our power over long distances, in days or weeks rather than months. Our military must be able to identify targets by a variety of means—from a Marine patrol to a satellite. Then be able to destroy those targets almost instantly, with an array of weapons, from a submarine-launched cruise missile, to mobile long-range artillery."[15]

The concept of transformation predated the Bush campaign and was even in some forms moving toward implementation in the Pentagon. For example, the army was already at work on what it called its Objective Force, a version of transformation from the end of the Clinton years. The Objective Force as articulated in late 1999 by Army Chief of Staff General Eric K. Shinseki involved selective recapitalization of so-called legacy forces while working toward new weapons (with an emphasis on the family of Future Combat Systems), communication-information networks, and reorganization of combat units. For the military services, transformation was the classic combination of a threat combined with opportunity. Transformation promised new programs and resources but at the same time entailed dramatic changes that might upset vested roles and interests within the services. The service facing the greatest risk and opportunity was the army. Although the army was at work on the Objective Force, talk by candidate Bush and later Secretary Rumsfeld of perhaps skipping a generation of weapons made the army anxious.[16] The army might have to leap into an unknown and untested future while sacrificing more traditional weapons programs intended to replace aging systems from the 1970s and 1980s. All this, however, would await Rumsfeld's review.

In the meantime, Bush tried to live up to his promises to be the president of tax cuts and educational reform. In a near replay of the Reagan agenda from 1980, Bush's budgetary priorities combined tax cuts, defense spending increases, and an attempt to hold the line on domestic programs. Unlike Reagan, as we have seen, Bush had no leverage and little support for a substantial increase in military spending prior to September 11, 2001. Although no manifest threat to national security could be found or conjured, a sizable budgetary surplus projected well into the future made tax cuts an attractive and easy political initiative. The Congressional Budget Office projected a $282 billion surplus for 2001 and a rather astounding accumulated $5.6 trillion surplus over the next decade.[17] During the 2000 presidential campaign, candidate George W. Bush began pushing tax cuts that he said would return money to the American taxpayer because "the surplus is not the government's money. The surplus is the people's money."[18] The implication was that once he became president, the tax cuts were sure to follow. If proposed and backed by a president, tax cuts become almost impossible for members of Congress to resist. And once Bush was in office, the tax cuts became his most vigorously pursued priority.

Bush detailed his large package of tax reductions not long after taking office, giving the subject the most coverage when he delivered his first address to a joint session of Congress on February 27, 2001.[19] Justifications for the massive cuts multiplied as the economy took a downward turn. With growing fears of recession, the president urged passage of his proposal as a way to "give the economy a timely second wind" or to keep it from crashing altogether.[20] The goal of returning the people's money morphed into stimulating the economy. Before Bush took office, economic experts expressed doubt that the cuts would provide short-term economic stimulation, arguing instead that recession was best avoided by adjustments in interest rates.[21] When questioned about the logic behind the revenue reductions, the White House also argued that the proposed tax cuts would benefit low-income earners and would also help people handle the climbing costs of energy.[22] The changes passed by Congress that spring were estimated to reduce the surplus by at least $1.35 trillion over eleven years.[23] The Economic Growth and Tax Relief Reconciliation Act (EGTRRA) reduced tax rates across all brackets, raised the child tax credit from $500 to $1,000, and phased out the estate or "death" tax, in addition to several other provisions, including rebates on 2001 taxes mailed to millions of Americans during the summer.[24]

A vigorous debate ensued over whether the tax package benefited the wealthy disproportionately. Whatever the merits of that debate, for our purposes the important point is that the somewhat hypothetical surplus was slashed by very real reductions in revenue. Amazingly, even after the events of 9/11 and a declaration of a war on terror, Bush proposed and Congress passed two more rounds of tax cuts, the Job Creation and Worker Assistance Act of 2002 and the Jobs and Growth Tax Relief and Reconciliation Act of 2003. Tax cuts passed during these three years added up to more than the Kennedy and Reagan cuts combined.[25] By 2002 the surplus was gone, replaced by deficits that were Reaganesque in size and circumstance insofar as they were likewise the product of the combination tax cuts and substantial increases in military spending. Tax cuts were, in fact, Bush's only significant legislative accomplishment before September 11, 2001. Although he had made education a top priority, the centerpiece of that agenda, the No Child Left Behind Act, would not reach his desk until January 2002. His much touted and criticized energy task force, led by the vice president, produced as it were great heat, little light, and certainly no legislation.

By the summer of his first year as president, Bush was squaring off against Congress and the Democrats on the budget. As the president noted only two weeks before 9/11, "If Congress goes off on a spending spree in other areas, it's going to create a competition for defense dollars" and that competition was "going to be a battle" if Congress did not come up with the money for the military. The president even welcomed news about the rapidly shrinking surplus as "incredibly positive news" because it would create "a fiscal straitjacket for Congress" that would check government spending and growth.[26] The president had noted more than once before September 11 that only three circumstances would justify the use of the Social Security "surplus": economic recession, an emergency, or war. The economic slowdown in 2001 provided a modest level of recession, which, as we have seen, was one of the justifications for the tax cuts. September 11 provided the other two. As Mitch Daniels, Bush's Office of Management and Budget (OMB) director, related it, soon after 9/11 Bush remarked that he had "hit the trifecta."[27] Whether Bush was being glib or lamenting his plight, the main effect of hitting the trifecta was not on the somewhat mythical Social Security surplus but rather on presidential power and military spending.

The initial emphasis on tax cuts along with less successful initiatives in education and energy show that the administration's ambitions for national security were not matched by a comparable degree of public support. In fact, the administration's initial budget (FY 2002) proposed an increase in military spending of $14.2 billion, or 4.8 percent over 2001, relatively modest growth in line with other increases since 1999.[28] This addition was characterized as a down payment toward transformation of the military, which had been, for the most part, in a strategic and structural holding pattern since the end of the Cold War. Because the new strategy would drive the budget, details about future programs and budgets were put on hold. But some things could not wait, and in late June 2001 Rumsfeld announced a rather significant increase in the 2002 military budget first proposed by the administration — another $18.4 billion to be added to the earlier increase for a total of $32.6 billion, or 11 percent over 2001 (over 7 percent adjusted for inflation). That growth was more in line with the rapid peacetime buildup under Ronald Reagan. Yet by September 2001 the Bush administration had not presented the promised review and justification for the increases in military spending that had been added to the budget.

Rally around the Flag: The Political Impact of September 11

Before Rumsfeld could deliver his report, four airliners were turned into instruments of terror and mass murder. The political impact of the 9/11 attacks was profound. One of the more predictable consequences was a "rally around the flag" effect for President Bush. His approval ratings had been modulating all year between 55 and 65 percent, a modest but acceptable level for a new president. The percentage who disapproved of his performance, however, had been climbing into the summer of 2001, rising from the 20 percent range to 40 percent or more as August turned to September. Immediately after 9/11, approval of the president vaulted to between 80 percent and 92 percent depending on the exact date and survey, by some measures the highest approval rating attained by any modern president.[29] The all-encompassing impact of the rally around the flag effect was evidenced by the fact that approval for the president's handling of the economy went up nearly as dramatically.[30] But all this of course had nothing to do with economics — the real impact was on the president's role in national security and military policy. The president had a sweeping warrant for the use of his powers as commander in chief. This mandate was confirmed by the authorization of use of force passed three days later by an all but unanimous Congress.[31]

The great unknown of the presidency of George W. Bush is what its general fate and place in history would have been absent 9/11. Those attacks were so momentous that they affected everything else about Bush's eight years in office. Bush and his colleagues came into office with grand and aggressive dreams (if not exact plans) for U.S. foreign and military policy, including regime change in Iraq.[32] Given world events and public opinion before September 11, however, it is not at all clear whether or to what extent these dreams or plans could have been implemented. Without the events of 9/11, would a war against Iraq have been politically feasible? Or, more to the purposes of this analysis, how far could Bush have increased military spending without a clear and present danger abroad and amid a rapidly ballooning deficit, created in part by the tax cuts that had been his top priority after taking office? We have, in effect, no test of this proposition. It certainly appeared as though Congress was more than ready prior to 9/11 to go along with the 4.8 percent increase originally planned for the 2002 budget. But the additional $18.4 billion tacked on that summer had yet to face a decisive test in Congress. The defense appropriations bill was taken up by the House Appropriations Committee the day of the attacks. Delays followed and Congress did not debate the bill until nearly the end of November. The bill did not pass the Senate until December 7. And by that point, politics of war had rendered opposition to vast increases in military spending not just impotent but nearly nonexistent.

Because 9/11 quickly overshadowed everything, we cannot know what would have happened to the Bush plans to rebuild and transform the military if the attacks had not occurred or if they had been foiled in a relatively undramatic fashion. Until 9/11 the only tangible indication of the kind of resources and efforts underlying the Bush administration's rhetoric about unrivaled military power came in the form of the $18.4 billion increase to the original FY 2002 budget request. What we have not examined, but need to, are the justifications for such increases that preceded the political leverage of 9/11 and what, if anything, changed or was added to those strategic rationales after 9/11. What were the strategic principles and doctrines that the Bush administration used to justify its military programs and budgets before and after 9/11? The short answer is that although the administration prior to 9/11 had explicit plans for a very assertive national security policy, some elements it would have liked to include were not politically feasible before the attacks. As we shall see in the next chapter, 9/11 meant there was no longer any need to justify the plans, and the Bush administration was able to spend more than it had hoped for on the military even though most of the spending was essentially unrelated to 9/11.

The 2001 Quadrennial Defense Review: Military Doctrine before 9/11

The major review of military strategy and priorities that Bush had asked Rumsfeld to do coincided with the congressionally mandated Quadrennial Defense

Review (QDR) that was due at the end of September. Although Rumsfeld had previewed elements of the "new strategy" over the summer, the QDR would be the vehicle for its full release and exposition.[33] Released on September 30, 2001, the QDR, according to Secretary Rumsfeld, was "largely completed before the September 11, 2001 terror attacks on the United States."[34] Besides a foreword to the document by the secretary of defense and some brief references to the attacks and their implications, the QDR is the justification for the kind of robust military budgets the Bush administration had looked forward to, whether politically feasible or not, prior to the attacks.

A Post–Cold War Military Strategy

The QDR purported to change U.S. military policy significantly, and the core of that change was determined before the attacks. As Rumsfeld noted, "Even before the attack of September 11, 2001, the senior leaders of the Defense Department set out to establish a new strategy for America's defense." That new strategy would be "built around four key goals that will guide the development of U.S. forces and capabilities, their deployment and use." Those four goals were "assuring allies and friends; dissuading future military competition; deterring threats and coercion against U.S. interests; and if deterrence fails, decisively defeating any adversary."[35] This formulation is quite similar to what Rumsfeld previewed before the Senate Armed Services Committee in late June.[36]

Rumsfeld emphasized that a "central objective of the review was to shift the basis of defense planning from a 'threat-based' model that has dominated thinking in the past to a 'capabilities-based' model for the future." A capabilities-based model "focuses more on how an adversary might fight rather than specifically whom the adversary might be or where a war might occur. It recognizes that it is not enough to plan for large conventional wars in distant theaters. Instead, the United States must identify the capabilities required to deter and defeat adversaries who will rely on surprise, deception, and asymmetric warfare to achieve their objectives."[37] In essence this meant that military planning would shift from defining existing specific threats to assessing present, future, and hypothetical capabilities.

As with any revision of military doctrine one immediately suspected that some old wine was being poured into a new bottle. There was fancy and somewhat obfuscatory language, with a dramatic turn of phrase, but did it mean anything new? Would any previous Pentagon planner have agreed with the claim that they focused exclusively on concrete, existing threats when planning U.S. force structures and deployments? Certainly Cold War planning was dominated by assessment, whether wholly realistic or not, of the Soviet threat, and as we have seen Clinton's Bottom-Up Review revolved around the Gulf War–like scenarios of major regional conflicts.[38] Nevertheless capabilities still had to be linked to states or entities that potentially threatened us — the Pentagon was not going to start planning based on the military capabilities of Great Britain. Some tended to dismiss this threats-capabilities shift as a distinction without much of a difference and emphasized the relatively modest nature of the material changes proposed.[39] As defense expert Michael O'Hanlon noted, "The 2001 QDR contained the fewest programmatic and force structure initiatives of any of the four major U.S. defense reviews since the end of the cold war (as it contained virtually none)."[40] The conservative nature of the review included both its lack of proposed new programs or initiatives (increases) and no cuts in weapons programs or reductions of overseas deployments (decreases), both of which might be part of the much-vaunted "transformation" process.

This line of analysis, however valid in some respects, understates the importance of the policy changes, especially when combined with the paradigm-shifting effect of 9/11. When joined with the events of 9/11, the doctrine of a capabilities-based analysis of threats along with other elements of the QDR added another element to the worst case scenario that was so important to the high military budgets of the Cold War and to the attempts we have examined to minimize the post–Cold War downturn. The QDR made clear

> that [capabilities-based] concept reflects the fact that the United States cannot know with confidence what nation, combination of nations, or non-state actor will pose threats to vital U.S. interests or those of U.S. allies and friends decades from now. It is possible, however, to anticipate the capabilities that an adversary *might* employ to coerce its neighbors, deter the United States from acting in defense of its allies and friends, or directly attack the United States or its deployed forces. A capabilities-based model — one that focuses more on how an adversary *might* fight than who the adversary might be and where *a war might occur — broadens the strategic perspective.*[41]

That would be an understatement. Given the formidable resources and talents of the United States and its allies and the rather paltry capabilities of the few potential foes, a focus on potential capabilities that might be used by unspecified foes in the indefinite future had the effect of taking what was then a historically unprecedented positive correlation of forces and rendering it irrelevant. In this worst case scenario, there was no obvious limit to what was plausible. The bitter irony is that the QDR was mostly written prior to 9/11 when the new administration, by many accounts, was not doing its best to "anticipate the capabilities that an adversary," such as Al Qaeda, "*might* employ to . . . directly attack the United States." By that measure, the advantages of capabilities-based planning were already in doubt.[42]

Moreover, capabilities-based planning is a reflexive concept; it is as much about U.S. capabilities as those of potential foes. Instead of threats from specific enemies, military planning would anticipate potential capabilities known and unknown enemies might use. But with all the hypotheticals involved (What enemy? Which capabilities?), capabilities-based planning really turns back on itself by allowing U.S. planners to imagine the capabilities the United States *might* need to combat threats that *might* exist now or in the future. As Rumsfeld noted above, "The United States must identify the capabilities required to deter and defeat adversaries," both known and unknown. A few months later one of Rumsfeld's assistant secretaries argued that a capabilities-based approach meant that "we're focusing on how we will fight, how we will have to fight, not who or when, and we don't really know. We expect to be surprised, and so we have to have capabilities that would deal with a broad range of the potential capabilities that adversaries may array against us."[43]

Because this concept predated 9/11 it can be interpreted as an attempt to reconfigure what was becoming a rather stale debate about the kind of military threats faced by the United States. In essence it was an attempt to bolster and expand the somewhat tired two-war standard based on the Major Regional Conflict concept from the 1990s, which had been the reigning worst case scenario. Capabilities-based planning shifted the burden of proof. Now hypothetical future possibilities would be privileged, especially when demonstrable threats were lacking. Given the events of 9/11 one might consider this sensible except for the fact that the job of intelligence services has always been to consider what might happen — and the possibility of terrorists using airliners as weapons was on their radar screen. The problem was not imagination, but prevention. Moreover, it was not clear how 9/11 and a capabilities-based approach applied to the military budget. If the enemy was going to attack with dramatically unconventional means then perhaps increased military spending on exotic capabilities was not the appropriate response. Such contrarian thoughts, of course, did not have a place in the QDR or in the administration more generally. Instead, the QDR's kind of thinking did not just broaden the strategic perspective, it lowered the threshold justification for military programs that could be funded on the basis of hypothetical capabilities possessed by potential enemies.

Dissuasion

The QDR added another concept that, when paired with capabilities-based planning, synergistically justified vastly increased military spending without having to demonstrate an increased threat to U.S. national security. While three of the "key goals" enunciated by the QDR — assurance, deterrence, and decisive victory — were hardly new strategic concepts, the fourth, dissuasion, was more innovative. It was not an entirely novel idea, but its inclusion as an explicit pillar of military policy was unprecedented and significant. In fact, it was potentially the most open-ended and demanding of the four. Not only must one prepare for uncertain threats, one must prepare and build capabilities so that others might be dissuaded from even the attempt to compete, regardless of intent. Or as the 2002 *National Security Strategy of the United States* characterized it, "Our forces will be strong enough to dissuade potential adversaries from pursuing a military build-up in the hopes of surpassing or equaling the power of the United States."[44] This policy is not about dissuading a nation or entity from *attacking* the United States or one of its interests; that is covered by deterrence. Dissuasion takes aim at an earlier step in the process — persuading others not to even spend the money, do the research, or build the weapons that would be necessary to undertake a military operation against the United States or its vital national interests.

Dissuasion made it official policy for the United States to be not just superior, but so strong that it could dissuade others from even trying to compete. This doctrine transcended what was always the general idea that the United States would try to maintain some degree of superiority. But even that was a relatively new concept insofar as the Cold War was nothing if not an ongoing (and often spurious) debate over whether the USSR had achieved a "margin of superiority" over the United States in one or another category of weaponry. In other words, only with the end of the Cold War was the United States able to conceive of something like dissuasion as a policy because it was already so far ahead of the rest of the world.

What would be part of a dissuasive policy? As described in the QDR, dissuasion was an ecumenical concept — very little if anything escaped its coverage, and this expansiveness is worth quoting at length:

Through its strategy and actions, the United States influences the nature of future military competitions, channels threats in certain directions, and complicates military planning for potential adversaries in the future. Well targeted strategy and policy can therefore dissuade other countries from initiating future military competitions. The United States can exert such influence through the conduct of its research, development, test, and demonstration programs. It can do so by maintaining or enhancing advantages in key areas of military capability. Given the availability of advanced technology and systems to potential adversaries, dissuasion will also require the United States to experiment with revolutionary operational concepts, capabilities, and organizational arrangements and to encourage the development of a culture within the military that embraces innovation and risk-taking. To have a dissuasive effect, this combination of technical, experimental, and operational activity has to have a clear strategic focus. New processes and organizations are needed within the defense establishment to provide this focus."[45]

Dissuasion was bold and far-reaching, but also a little at odds with post–Cold War patterns of international military expenditures; it was also irrelevant in the face of the events of 9/11. The statement about others "surpassing or equaling" the U.S. military budget was somewhat absurd given that the United States had maintained its massive lead over the rest of the world even after the post–Cold War drawdown in defense spending. The United States significantly decreased its military budget and force structure under Bush and Clinton, but as the United States cut expenses so did most other nations of any significance — most of which were close allies of the United States — and the military budget of the former Soviet Union nearly disappeared. Most did not cut as much as the United States because they did not have as large an adjustment to make to the end of the Cold War. They were already spending too little or about the right amount depending on one's political perspective on what the Cold War required. Dissuasion was hardly necessary. In fact, the evidence from the 1990s pointed to the effectiveness of what one might call "persuasion" or "leading by example." Cutting the U.S. defense budget seemed to be a signal to others that they could do the same. The only notable exceptions to this were China and perhaps not coincidentally Japan and India. These three Asian giants produced modest but real increases in military spending in the 1990s, but China and India were still spending under half of what Japan, Germany, and the United Kingdom were spending individually on their defense. The European Union, unlikely in any event to be able to coordinate such an effort, was the only economic entity in the post–Cold War world capable of trying to match the United States, and there was, of course, no reason for Europeans to undertake such a project.

Given the attacks of September 11, what exactly would dissuade terrorists from the use of violence in an attempt to accomplish their objectives? Surely not the size and scope of the U.S. military budget and establishment. Clearly dissuasion did not (and does not) apply to terrorist tactics and groups that don't care how large the U.S. military is. They are, if anything, provoked and valorized by the kind of imperial power expressed by a massive American military. Moreover, the supposed "rogue states" were utterly incapable of "surpassing or equaling" the United States, even if they were able to function as a true "axis of evil." In an era when supposedly everything had changed, dissuasion was a doctrine aimed exclusively at the relatively small number of nation-states with large GNPs, nearly all of whom were close allies of the United States.

Moreover, dissuasion probably had a perverse effect on those nations whose interests might be antithetical to the United States but whose resources were quite limited. The doctrine's logic did not explain in what way it would discourage nations (North Korea and Iran in particular) from seeking relatively cheap "asymmetrical" deterrents — nuclear weapons — that could offset unmatchable American superiority. If anything a policy of dissuasion (later reinforced by the policy of preemption, as we shall see) would seem to encourage countries to embrace and acquire nuclear weapons — the only thing capable of deterring the United States from using its awesome military power. Regardless of the absurd logic, dissuasion was, if taken at face value, one of the only concepts that could justify the administration's policy of outspending the rest of the world by post-9/11 margins. In other words, it became official U.S. policy to have an excessively large military budget — regardless of the actual threats. Finally, dissuasion was also another reason not to forego new programs because of budgetary constraints or due to the "lack of a current threat" because "the decision not to pursue a new technology . . . entails risk: introducing it early provides a military advantage for a time, and it may dissuade any potential adversary from pursuing similar capabilities."[46]

Moreover, the incredibly expansive range of research, development, and deployment justified by dissuasion would be so formidable that potential enemies would be paralyzed — not only could they not afford to compete, they would not know where to begin:

> By enabling the creation of a range of capabilities and warfighting options, field exercises and experimentation can compel future competitors into an unenviable

choice. They can seek to develop responses to most or all of the U.S. capabilities and options and consequently stretch their limited resources thin, or they can choose the high-risk option of focusing their efforts on offsetting only one or a few of the new warfighting options, leaving themselves vulnerable to the others. When confronted with this dilemma, potential adversaries may find themselves dissuaded from entering into a military competition in the first place.[47]

As this analysis has implied, dissuasion probably worked better on allies than enemies. Dissuasion was yet another reminder, whether intentional or not, to the United States' friends around the world that it would pay any price and bear any burden to facilitate free-riding by affluent allies. Why waste valuable resources on cutting-edge military research and development, and even procurement, when the Americans were determined to foot the bill? Even some of more prosaic elements of the QDR such as the assurance of allies — what could be read as mere boilerplate — ironically ended up being an affirmation of the principle that the United States military would not rely on allies or define its needs in conjunction with allied capabilities. In essence, assurance amounted to a more or less direct admission that the United States would do much more than its share. Assurance in the QDR meant continued American presence overseas and helping "allies and friends create favorable balances of military power in critical areas of the world to deter aggression or coercion."[48] The QDR devotes not a substantive word to burden-sharing or the wealth and formidable military capabilities of allies. The only explicit role for rich and well-armed friends is to help the United States conduct a limited number of "smaller-scale contingency operations in peacetime, preferably in concert with allies."[49]

With a commitment to bear the burden and build to dissuade, perhaps the Bush Pentagon would be compelled to trim the two-war guideline. Instead, the 2001 QDR added substantially to the commitment. "U.S. is not abandoning planning for two conflicts to plan for fewer than two," the QDR assured its readers. "On the contrary, DoD is changing the concept altogether by planning for victory across the spectrum of possible conflict."[50] The expansion is evident in one requirement. The U.S. military must have the ability to "swiftly defeat aggression in overlapping major conflicts *while preserving for the President the option to call for a decisive victory in one of those conflicts — including the possibility of regime change or occupation.*"[51] One can see in this not only an increase in the two-war requirement but also an explicit comment on the results of the Gulf War, a less than subtle allusion to neoconservative critiques of the elder Bush's failure to destroy the Hussein regime, if not an outright anticipation of the coming war on Iraq.

Even in the immediate wake of 9/11 it was difficult not to read the QDR without seeing a kind of global paranoia based on several premises and conclusions. The brave new world entailed movement from the "enduring . . . geopolitical blocs" of the Cold War to "fluid and unpredictable" geopolitical dynamics and the "increasing diversity in the sources and unpredictability of the locations of conflict."[52] The QDR viewed the Cold War as a period of stability and known threats, as if to say, alas, if only we had the Cold War back, we could relax. The QDR was not the first such pronouncement to look back on the Cold War through rose-colored glasses; it was a common sentiment in the 1990s as well. September 11 provided some substantive plausibility for that point of view, even if overall it remained historically quite questionable. This was bad revisionist history combined with a somewhat risible analysis of current events, especially given the number and power of America's allies. The language of uncertainty and unpredictability was less a comment on the objective geopolitical situation than a revelation of the state of mind of Pentagon planners and like-minded politicians and analysts. How else can one interpret such language in a world that featured more coherence and alignment of democratic and capitalist power than ever before?

Transformation

What capabilities would supposedly dissuade martial competition with the United States? It was not that the United States would be simply bigger and better than others; it would be radically different. And the QDR's most concrete expression of this commitment to a higher order of qualitative superiority was in its discussion of "transformation." An entire section — by far the longest section in the QDR — is devoted to transformation, a concept that, again, escapes a simple definition in part because "transformation is not an end point."[53] Instead it is a continuous process of adapting the means of warfare to an ever-evolving future resting on four pillars: strengthening joint operations, experimenting with new approaches to warfare, exploiting U.S. intelligence advantages, and developing transformational capabilities through increased research and development.[54] Transformation is a long-term project with many elements. Donald Rumsfeld was the first secretary of defense to center his efforts on transformation and the QDR was intended to be the initial blueprint for that process. An indication of the centrality of transformation to Rumsfeld's goals was the creation of the Office of Force Transformation on October 29, 2001.

The QDR, however, made no tough decisions about what to cut from what it termed the "legacy" forces; that is, what not to "recapitalize" of the traditional array of weaponry in the services to make programmatic and budgetary room for transformative technologies, tactics, and weapons.[55] How to skip forward a generation or how to afford transformation and recapitalization under any circumstances, let alone amid a global war on terror, was left unspecified. As we shall see in chapter 5, Rumsfeld's first attempt to show that transformation was more than a slogan — when he cancelled the Crusader mobile artillery system — caused more consternation in Congress than authorizing war against Iraq.

On to Iraq: The National Security Strategy and Preemption

However innovative or alarming, the Quadrennial Defense Review did not articulate or even hint at what would become the defining and most controversial strategic doctrine of the Bush presidency. The doctrines of the QDR produced a rather open-ended justification for greater military spending. But 9/11 tipped the scales in favor of the superhawks who sought to move beyond such Cold War concepts as deterrence, even with the liberating modifications provided by the QDR. Before the ink was dry on the QDR, and prior to the start of the war in Afghanistan, potential military action against Iraq was widely discussed and debated in the media and within the war councils of the Bush administration.[56] Given that the Iraqi government had not attacked the United States or its vital interests and that there was no immediate (or later) link between that regime and the 9/11 attacks, the unprovoked use of military force for the purpose of, as Under Secretary of Defense Paul Wolfowitz bluntly put it on September 14, "ending states that sponsor terrorism" would require strategic justification.[57] This linchpin of the Bush grand strategy arrived a year after 9/11 in the form of the 2002 *National Security Strategy of the United States* (NSS). Preemption, as it came to be known, was the central concept and innovation in the new strategy, but its appearance in the document did not come as a surprise. The concept had a history that made its prominent place in the post 9/11 national security policy less than unexpected, at least to those attuned to policy debates in Washington.

In the immediate aftermath of 9/11 the president issued various statements about terrorism and the war the United States would be fighting against it. These statements contained the elements of what would quickly be dubbed the "Bush Doctrine." The United States would "make no distinction between the terrorists who committed these acts and those who harbor them." In his first address before a joint session of Congress after 9/11 the president announced one of the most famous of his several post-9/11 binaries: "Every nation, in every region, now has a decision to make. Either you are with us, or you are with the terrorists."[58] Initially such pronouncements focused on those who attacked the United States and those who harbored or aided those who had done so. In this way, the emerging Bush Doctrine could be seen as assertive but focused. But with utterances about "crusade" and a mission "to rid the world of evil," the Bush Doctrine was also grand and open-ended, with an uncertain scope. The United States would take the war to the terrorists and their allies with the goal of fundamentally changing the world.

A refined version of the Bush Doctrine emerged in January 2002 with his first State of the Union address in which the president famously lumped Iraq, Iran, and North Korea together in an "axis of evil." The inaccuracy and strained imagery of an "axis" among nations that either had no relationship with one another or that hated each other did not go unnoticed. Geopolitical accuracy was hardly a consideration in this case. Instead, several implications flowed from this inapt turn of phrase. Suddenly the focus in the war on terror was back on nation-states rather than nonstate actors who had carried out the actual attack. Moreover, the emphasis was not even on terrorism per se as much as on weapons of mass destruction (WMDs) and their proliferation. None of these nations had attacked the United States or its allies, yet the speech implicated that they were to be the focus of U.S. efforts that might not wait for an attack. "We'll be deliberate, yet time is not on our side," warned the president. "I will not wait on events, while dangers gather. I will not stand by, as peril draws closer and closer. The United States of America will not permit the world's most dangerous regimes to threaten us with the world's most destructive weapons."[59] The president did not use any term such as "preemption," but every educated listener knew what he was implying. The United States would unilaterally decide which countries to attack and when, and everyone knew Iraq was first on the list.

This final and vital addition to the muscular set of Bush national security doctrines was tested during the spring and summer of 2002 in various speeches, including Bush's commencement address at West Point.[60] In that address, President Bush made the argument for strategic changes that the post-9/11 world demanded — that the nation should go beyond deterrence and containment. The "war on terror," he said, "will not be won on the defensive. We must take the battle to the enemy, disrupt his plans, and confront the worst threats before they emerge. In the world we have entered, the only path to safety is the path of action." The path of action required that the nation "be ready for preemptive action when necessary to defend our liberty and to defend our lives."

The doctrine of preemptive actions was codified in September 2002 with the release of the NSS. The strategy marked the formal announcement that deterrence, the basic defense strategy of the Cold War, was now outdated. Deterrence, the NSS argued, was still important and useful in many cases but must be supplemented by other measures. In this new age of terrorists and rogue states the necessary supplement to deterrence, according to the NSS, must be military preemption. During the Cold War the United States could depend on deterrence because it "faced a generally status quo, risk-averse adversary." Such a strategy, however, was "less likely to work against leaders of rogue states more willing to take risks." A different kind of policy was required, particularly because of the "overlap between states that sponsor terror and those that pursue WMD." As a result, "to forestall or prevent such hostile acts by our adversaries, the United States will, if necessary, act preemptively" and alone.[61]

The NSS was quick to note that preemption is recognized in international law, that states were justified in defending themselves against an "imminent threat." In the pre-9/11 view of things, an imminent threat implied such things as tangible evidence of forces mobilizing or preparing for an attack. That would no longer do. Instead, "we must adapt the concept of imminent threat to the capabilities and objectives of today's adversaries." This somewhat vague adaptation seemed to open the door to very broad interpretations of both "threat" and "imminent."[62] As one critic put it, "an 'imminent attack' is one for which an enemy has 'capabilities' and that will achieve his 'objectives.' Put another way, an imminent attack could be years away; it might not even be planned. All that is required is that the enemy is capable of the attack and that an attack would meet his objectives; actual plans for an attack, let alone material preparations for one, are not needed."[63] Or as the NSS noted, the United States would take "anticipatory action . . . even if uncertainty remains as to the time and place of the enemy's attack."[64]

The semantics of preemption were thoroughly political and none too subtle. Preemption implied that the initiator knew it was stopping something more or less imminent or inevitable from happening. Many commentators thought the more accurate term for what the NSS was describing was "preventative war," "a war of choice to prevent the emergence of a threat further in the future."[65] Prevention had a potentially more aggressive connotation than preemption as it did not entail definite conclusions about intentions, imminence, or inevitability. Preventative war disguised as preemption dovetailed neatly with the QDR's capabilities-based planning. Just as capabilities-based military planning did not focus on specific manifest threats but on how a potential enemy might be able to fight or threaten U.S. interests, preemption did not require a patent threat, imminent or otherwise. In the case of Iraq, after all, it was not that Iraq definitely had WMDs, had ever sought to provide such things to terrorists, or had any plans to do so. It was enough that Iraq might be able to develop WMDs and conceivably could use them or offer them to terrorists. Whether seen as prevention or preemption, the idea was not wholly new and it had always been an option, implicitly, as a policy. But now preemption was made explicit and defined so permissively as to justify any use of force against a nation that arms itself or acts in any way contrary to U.S. interests. And the aim was not just to protect the United States but also its allies and "friends."

The language in the document also exemplified the kind of irony and tone-deafness about how other countries will hear the rhetoric that has often pervaded American pronouncements. Echoing the president's speeches from the 2000 campaign, the NSS promised not to go it alone because "there is little of lasting consequence we can accomplish without the sustained cooperation of allies and friends," and the United States would seek and obtain that cooperation "with a spirit of humility." Without a shred of self-consciousness or self-reflection, the document also took China to task for "pursuing military capabilities that can threaten its neighbors in the Asia-Pacific region." In so doing, "China is following an outdated path that, in the end, will hamper its own pursuit of national greatness." The same kind of unparalleled military power the United States sought was atavistic and self-defeating in the hands of others. Finally, the "United States will not use force in all cases to preempt emerging threats, nor should nations use preemption as a pretext for aggression."[66] That the United States might not use force in all cases of preemption was a rather roundabout way of saying it would also use diplomacy, which had been used for centuries for true preemptive, or preventative, purposes. And who would judge the nearly indiscernible line between preemption and aggression?

In effect, the more fully articulated Bush Doctrine was a challenge to deterrence and containment, the guiding stars of Cold War security policy. The United States would use force preventatively or preemptively and it would use that force to actively bring about change in nations or regions. Deterrence and containment had not been wholly replaced or eliminated; they had been supplemented, however.[67] For some threats, deterrence was still the appropriate strategy and some problems were more easily contained than directly changed.[68] But the balance had been shifted toward use of force and regime change. This constituted as well a repudiation of the less noted concepts from the Clinton presidency of "engagement and enlargement" discussed in chapter 2. Clinton viewed enlargement — meaning the expansion and greater integration of the family of market democracies — as a replacement for Cold War security doctrines. Engagement and enlargement were related to what later became known as the Clinton Doctrine, which emerged late in his presidency when Clinton sought to justify the use of allied power to intervene in key situations. Clinton argued that the United States and its allies must use their power to prevent the spread of instability. This was enough to alarm people on both sides of the political spectrum. To the left, this opened the door to greater use of military force.[69] To the right, as we have seen, this was a commitment to the quagmire of nation-building. On a superficial level the Clinton and Bush doctrines shared some ends and means. They shared the end of expanding the circle of market democracies and the means of military intervention. The Clinton Doctrine, however, emphasized the use of multinational forces (such as NATO) to intervene (often for humanitarian purposes) in regions where instability might threaten larger war or unrest. The Bush Doctrine, while happy to embrace coalitional support, emphasized unilateral action and the use of military force to change hostile and aggressive regimes, not to stabilize civil wars.

In fact, the links between the Bush and Clinton doctrines are tighter than this comparison implies. Clinton's "engagement and enlargement" was sandwiched between two efforts to make preemption or something quite close to it official U.S. policy. The first effort came near the end of the first Bush presidency in the form of a draft of a new Defense Policy Guidance statement, which are periodic Pentagon exercises to provide overall strategic focus and direction to defense planners. The 1992 draft, directed by then Under Secretary of Defense for Policy Paul Wolfowitz, was the first significant stab at such a framework for the post–Cold War setting. In the leaked portions the concept that touched on preemption was somewhat indirectly stated: "We will retain the pre-eminent responsibility for addressing selectively those wrongs which threaten not only our interests, but those of our allies or friends, or which could seriously unsettle international relations." In the final draft, the relevant paragraph was considerably altered to emphasize international cooperation and unilateral action when U.S. interests were directly at stake. Reports of the parallels between Wolfowitz's initially ill-fated defense guidance statement in 1992 and the policies of the Bush administration a decade later concentrated on the language about unilateral action. This language stated that it would be U.S. policy to maintain the United States' position as the sole military superpower and when and where necessary to be prepared to act independently in a crisis. In some ways, as we saw in chapter 2, the 1992 draft defense guidance statement devoted itself more to the doctrine of dissuasion (without calling it that, at least in the leaked portions) and a general policy of preventing the emergence of a rival comparable to the former Soviet Union. Yet even this relatively measured language was too much for the politics of 1992. After the statement was leaked and publicized, the White House reportedly had Secretary Cheney revise it to deemphasize the unilateralist and imperialist aspects; in the end, it was not so different from what Clinton would later endorse.[70]

The second effort, which can be seen as an attempt to keep Wolfowitz's ideas alive during the Clinton presidency, came in the form of the Project for a New American Century (PNAC), a group composed of what would become known as neoconservatives, including Cheney, Wolfowitz, and Rumsfeld, who as private citizens in the 1990s helped to lead the attack on Clinton's foreign and military policies. Their stated alternative was "a Reaganite policy of military strength and moral clarity," with primacy being given to the "need to increase defense spending significantly if we are to carry out our global responsibilities today and modernize our armed forces for the future."[71] The first major policy statement of PNAC was a 1998 letter to President Clinton on Iraq in which they argued that the policy of "containment" was failing and that stronger action was necessary, including independent military action to remove Saddam Hussein from power. Just as Reagan, in their view, had gone beyond containment during the Cold War to more directly confront the Soviet Union, the United States needed to do more than simply contain Iraq. In this way, PNAC did not directly call for preemption but the desirability of unilateral military action was explicit. The very people who would become the core of the Bush national security team were pushing for something like preemption years before 9/11. The central focus of these calls for unilateral action was not terrorism or terrorist groups but rather Iraq, the nation at the heart of the rogue state doctrine.

Many of the same advocates of preemption were also promoters of the revolution in military affairs and transformation.[72] The two were interrelated means to the larger end of employing U.S. military power to remake the world. Transformation was the route to the kind of military power that would make intervention and preemption easier to do, less costly in both blood and treasure, and therefore more politically acceptable. In a highly ironic fashion, preemption was a "capabilities-based" policy. It was the United States that was basing its policies and the possibilities of using its military force on its own capabilities, rather than the enemy's. As the sophistication and superiority of U.S. military technology grew, the more likely it was to be used in service of an otherwise difficult and dangerous option such as preemption. As soon became evident, war against Iraq was driven in part by this logic of capabilities versus threat. The threat posed by Iraq was rather small, but our capabilities made preemption seem not only feasible but easy. So easy, in fact, that the administration's decision to go into Iraq with a small attacking force, one incapable of managing the subsequent occupation, became in the view of many the fatal flaw in the planning for the Iraq War.[73]

Despite the various changes and pronouncements in military policy including dissuasion and an expanded two-war commitment, public attention was directed toward preemption, and with good reason. Its promulgation as official U.S. strategy was coincidental with and part and parcel of the buildup to the war against Iraq. As we have seen, however, preemption was not only somewhat of a misnomer, it was also part of a larger package of doctrinal innovations and refinements, a package that even absent 9/11 (and therefore perhaps absent an explicit strategy of preemption) would have been remarkable for its aggressive and unilateralist impulses and requirements. Preemption joined with several other factors to create an American national security policy of awesome proportions and ambition combining unilateralism, dissuasion, and a significantly increased forward global presence on land, at sea, and in space, all in service of a nearly bottomless commitment to remaking the world in the American image. The president, in a rather odd juxtaposition with the tragedy of 9/11, put it this way: "The United States will use this moment of opportunity to extend the benefits of freedom across the globe."[74]

With such grand ambitions, could there be any conceivable answer to the central question of military power in national security: How much is enough? Under the Bush Doctrine and its ancillaries, we could never know exactly whom we might be fighting or how. We must be prepared to dissuade, deter, defend, prevent, and preempt. In this, we assume no help from allies; that is, security is in no way collective, even when measuring military strength. Rather we must, on our own, massively out-muscle the rest of the world with a national security state of nearly boundless scope and responsibilities, from protection of the "home-land" to pursuit of the unattainable, if not self-defeating goal, of ridding the world of evil. This transformation of the attacks by a handful of terrorists into an "opportunity" to implement a neo-Wilsonian plan for a new world was breathtaking. As a presidential candidate, Bush had criticized nation-building as a drain on U.S. resources and a diversion of its energies. Yet immediately after 9/11, even with the war in Afghanistan, Iraq was the clear target and focus of the administration's energies. Despite disagreement and concern expressed on editorial pages and within the academy, Congress did not blink and there was no general alarm across the land. Within a month of the release of the NSS, Congress would provide the president, by massive majorities, the blank check authorization for war against Iraq. With that legislation the Bush Doctrine and preemption were transformed from pronouncements into the law of the land.

Nukes for a New World: The Nuclear Posture Review

What role would nuclear weapons play in this brave new world of dissuasion and preemption? The QDR and NSS devoted few words to nuclear weapons in the new doctrines and principles they fashioned to guide American security policy. The role nuclear weapons would play in the post–Cold War world had not been fully resolved in the decade since that era ended, and it was not at all obvious how 9/11 affected further attempts to solve that puzzle. Nothing wrought or implied by the events of 9/11 clearly connoted a larger or enhanced role for nuclear weapons. If anything, September 11 and terrorism were a clarion call for nonproliferation, a redoubling of efforts to ensure the safety and elimination of excess nuclear weapons and materials, especially in the former Soviet Union. While certainly acknowledging such things, the Bush administration planned a rather different future for American nuclear weapons.[75]

As the war in Afghanistan came to its temporarily successful conclusion, the Nuclear Posture Review (NPR) was submitted to Congress on December 31. The NPR, which is still classified, was presented in a declassified fashion on January 9, 2002 in a Pentagon press briefing, and portions were leaked in March.[76] Like the QDR, the NPR was not a new process. The last congressionally mandated review had come in 1994. As Rumsfeld noted in his foreword to the document, the NPR built on the logic of the QDR to put "in motion a major change in our approach to the role of nuclear offensive forces in our deterrent strategy and presents the blueprint for transforming our strategic posture."[77] In fact, the few sentences in the QDR about nuclear forces noted that the forthcoming NPR would take up such questions and hinted at concepts the NPR later elaborated.[78] As with most other elements of the Bush administration's national security doctrines, the NPR had firm intellectual roots and precursors in the work of conservative defense intellectuals and activists in the years and months before 9/11.[79]

The NPR's claim to innovation revolved around the creation of a "New Triad" composed of "Offensive strike systems (both nuclear and non-nuclear); Defenses (both active and passive); and a revitalized defense infrastructure that will provide new capabilities in a timely fashion to meet emerging threats."[80] This triad was new because it replaced, or at the least had to be distinguished from, the former triad of nuclear systems based on land, at sea, and in the air. The Cold War triad of land-based missiles, submarine missiles, and bombers was obsolete, even if U.S. military planners and politicians had never been able to abandon it, and neither did the NPR. The old triad simply became one element of one tine in the new triad. The "New Triad" was a rather strained metaphor, however. To find a third leg the architects of this concept had to use defense infrastructure — in this case a new nuclear weapons complex — instead of a third type of weapon or force. In one sense this inclusion was valid because the part of the defense infrastructure that manufactured nuclear weapons would require a major infusion of cash and resources to be "revitalized." The more accurate characterization would have been "rebuilt." We saw in chapter 3 that the Cold War nuclear weapons complex was shut down and being cleaned up in the 1990s. As far as weapons, the triad was really a dyad. Nuclear weapons were now integrated with conventional strike weapons as part of an offensive strike capability. Defense joined ballistic missile defense with other more passive defensive technologies.

The truly innovative and unsettling component was the offensive strike component, which for the first time since the very early Cold War integrated nuclear and nonnuclear weapons and made them seemingly interchangeable: "Composed of both non-nuclear systems and nuclear weapons, the strike element of the New Triad can provide greater flexibility in the design and conduct of military campaigns to defeat opponents decisively. Non-nuclear strike capabilities may be particularly useful to limit collateral damage and conflict escalation. Nuclear weapons could be employed against targets able to withstand non-nuclear attack (for example, deep underground bunkers or bio-weapon facilities)."[81] In other words, nuclear weapons would be considered as an option in a continuous spectrum with conventional weapons for use in a conflict against a foe that might not even possess nuclear weapons, let alone have used them. This would require, as the NPR notes, new low-yield nuclear weapons—often dubbed "mini-nukes"— that would be capable of penetrating deep underground facilities. In this way nuclear weapons would be fully integrated into the QDR's goals of assurance, dissuasion, deterrence, and defeat. Allies and the American public would be assured that we could not be blackmailed for lack of military options; opponents would be dissuaded from even trying to develop WMD capabilities; the credible threat of nuclear attack would bolster deterrence against rogue states who might consider use of WMDs against the United States or its allies; and finally, smaller earth-penetrating nukes might be necessary to destroy certain hard-to-reach facilities (leadership and/or weapons) of our enemies.[82]

The NPR's brief discussion of what were dubbed "mini-nukes" provoked considerable controversy even with the fallout of 9/11, Afghanistan, and the president's Iraq campaign dominating the news. The leaked portions of the review actually devoted very few words to low-yield or earth-penetrating nuclear weapons, but given that such devices were the only way in practice to interlace conventional and nuclear capabilities—the most provocative implication of the New Triad—such new nuclear weapons took on an importance far greater than the number of words devoted to them. Since 1994 the United States had maintained a legal ban on the development of such low-yield nuclear warheads. In the wake of the Cold War, with nuclear nonproliferation a central policy for the United States and the world, such weapons seemed unnecessary and dangerous. The lower yield of the warheads under discussion was nearly inextricably linked to another characteristic of the new bomb—the ability to penetrate and destroy targets that were deeply buried and hardened against explosions. Informally referred to as a "bunker-buster," the more precise name for this weapon was the "Robust Nuclear Earth Penetrator" or RNEP. Some in the industry suspected a thinly disguised search for a new mission for nukes. A former Sandia lab official called it "outlandish. . . . . It is an effort to maintain a payroll" at the weapons labs. Moreover he was skeptical that anyone "in a uniform" seriously believed we needed such a capability, a view seconded by California Democratic Representative Ellen Tauscher who had talked to such folks. A lab physicist put it more blandly: "I think everyone around here is really encouraged to look at what the actual role is for nuclear weapons."[83] The prospect of using nuclear weapons to attack underground facilities threw up a virtual mushroom cloud of questions. Would this lower the nuclear threshold by keeping the explosion (largely) underground? Could the radioactive fallout be contained? What would world reaction be to U.S. use under any circumstances? Part of the controversy stemmed from the fact that bunker-busting did not necessarily require a nuclear weapon. Given the ability to penetrate hardened bunkers, a large conventional explosion might be able to do the job as effectively, without all the probable physical and political effects of a nuclear weapon.[84]

Before 9/11 and even before Bush became president, congressional Republicans had tried unsuccessfully to remove the 1994 ban on mini-nukes, often referred to as the Spratt-Furse amendment. But in 2003, in the wake of 9/11 and the need to "support the troops" who were by this point in Iraq, Congress complied with an administration request to repeal the ban. The FY 2004 Defense Authorization Act passed in November 2003 authorized funding for research on both the Robust Nuclear Earth Penetrator and Advanced Nuclear Weapons Concepts, in other words, the mini-nukes that might be used in the bunker-busting warhead. Just a year later in fall 2004, amid increasing evidence that the administration, at a minimum, had exaggerated the threat of Iraq WMDs to press its case for war, congressional opposition to the RNEP led in the House by Republican Dave Hobson succeeded in excising funding for the program. In 2005 Congress effectively terminated the program, though research on conventional bunker busters continued.[85] There were some things that even a rather compliant Republican Congress was not willing to do under the guise of war.

The NPR's call for new nuclear capabilities was coupled to another potentially very expensive proposition, "a revitalized nuclear weapons complex that will . . be able, if directed, to design, develop, manufacture, and certify new warheads in response to new national requirements; and maintain readiness to resume underground nuclear testing if required."[86] The most costly legacy of the Cold War was the nuclear weapons complex, which was all but shut down in the 1990s, and parts of which remained open only for the purpose of disassembling nuclear weapons. The NPR called for the reconstruction of the nuclear complex even as the United States was still spending several billion dollars a year cleaning up the old one. The estimates of the cost for such a "revitalized" complex were staggering. In 2003 when the DOE got around to turning this leg of the NPR Triad into an actual program they dubbed it "Complex 2030." The DOE put the cost at $150 billion by 2030, the year designated as the target for completion, but as with any initial cost estimate for such a vast military program this one could be expected to be on the low side.[87]

Turning to the last leg of the New Triad, the NPR completed the doctrinal transition of ballistic missile defense (BMD) from a Cold War pipedream into an ordinary and essential component of national defense. Ballistic missile defense would not serve as just a defensive option of last resort. Instead, "advances in defensive technologies will allow U.S. non-nuclear and nuclear capabilities to be coupled with active and passive defenses to help provide deterrence and protection against attack, preserve U.S. freedom of action, and strengthen the credibility of U.S. alliance commitments." In fact, BMD might reduce the need for offensive nuclear weapons "to hold at risk an adversary's missile launchers." That is, the United States might rely on defense primarily or exclusively, at least in some cases, to deter or prevent the use of an adversary's nuclear missiles. Crucially, in a world devoid of significant nuclear enemies, "missile defenses could defeat small-scale missile attacks intended to coerce the United States into abandoning an embattled ally or friend. . . . . They may also provide the President with an option to manage a crisis involving one or more missile and WMD-armed opponents." But what if the system did not work or was only partially effective? This Achilles heel of BMD was no longer an obstacle because "missile defense systems, like all military systems, can be less than 100-percent effective and still make a significant contribution to security by enhancing deterrence and saving lives if deterrence fails."[88] If this optimistic, or dangerously sanguine, view of BMD's role was unsettling, the claim that BMD would "preserve U.S. freedom of action" was unnerving. This phrase clearly implied that BMD could serve offensive purposes by allowing the United States to take offensive action — perhaps preemptive or preventative action — in the face of a missile threat.

Subject to sharply contrasting interpretations, the NPR was read in two very different ways. Critics saw in the NPR an alarming plan to find ways to make nuclear weapons more usable. The NPR from this perspective seemed to be erasing the bright line between nuclear weapons as a weapon of last resort, as a deterrent, and the actual use of nuclear weapons even in conventional conflict. The Reagan administration had generated a similar controversy with its revision of nuclear doctrine, one that planned explicitly for war-fighting options that would allow the United States to "prevail" in a potentially protracted nuclear war. That was during the Cold War and the opponent was the Soviet Union, when even the most "limited" war-fighting scenario involved hundreds of large nuclear weapons. Now that the Cold War was over and mutual deterrence a thing of the past, the 2001 NPR seemed to be finding a place for nuclear weapons in conventional warfare. As one critic put it, "With the disclosure last weekend of the Nuclear Posture Review, we have learned that our government has redefined our relationship with nuclear weapons. Always a reluctant steward, the United

States now embraces these devices as instruments of war-fighting meant to give us the advantage in an otherwise conventional war."[89]

Others saw something rather different in the document. The NPR, they argued, was nearly the opposite of what critics charged. By emphasizing the potential use of conventional weapons and missile defense to deal with the threat of WMDs, the NPR made the necessary adjustment from Cold War nuclear planning and in many ways decreased the importance of nuclear weapons. The principal threat was the potential use of chemical, biological, or nuclear weapons by relatively weak "rogue" states or terrorists who might not be deterred by the threat of massive retaliation. The NPR sought to provide the United States with a full range of options — nuclear, conventional, and defensive — that would enhance deterrence and the ability to defeat attacks or threats. In this realm, smaller low-yield nuclear weapons play a rather minor role, one that does not violate any long-standing policies of the United States, which had always reserved the right to use nuclear weapons in response to attacks, especially those involving WMDs.[90]

Just as the NPR represented a kind of nuclear war-fighting "lite" for the post–Cold War era, this version of deterrence revised and updated the old worst case scenario regarding the Soviets. Some Cold War nuclear strategists believed the Soviets might not be deterred if the main U.S. option was some form of massive retaliation because massive retaliation lacked credibility. The Soviets might have been willing to roll the nuclear dice, launch a first strike, and then see if the U.S. negotiated instead of retaliated. Even at the time, most analysts thought this an outlandish fantasy, a kind of nuclear gamer's dream-world detached from any sort of political reality. In the new world order, the threat was rogue states or terrorists who were, it was argued, less subject to deterrence, not as "rational" as the Soviet Union in several ways. Many rogues were governed by megalomaniacal dictators, whose rule was often fueled by manipulation of a volatile nationalism. Such leaders might be willing to take great risks. This theory did not have much basis in fact, and the empirical record argued against the alarmist view. In fact, the only significant exceptions were ones in which the United States was complicit in the failure of deterrence by failing to take key steps necessary for deterrence to work. This occurred twice with Iraq, first with its use of chemical weapons in the war with Iran in the 1980s and second with the invasion of Kuwait in 1990. Yet even if one were to grant for the sake of argument that the rogue states were not necessarily subject to rational deterrence because the United States would be self-deterred from responding in kind or with nuclear weapons, it is not clear what the rogue states would expect to happen. After the first Gulf War, it was made clear that the United States was capable of utterly destroying any country's military with conventional weapons alone. If such nations are so irrational that that lesson was not patently clear (and so irrational to believe the United States might not use nuclear weapons if it were attacked with WMDs of any sort clearly traceable to a particular country), then it is certainly not clear why the rather subtle change suggested by the NPR would enhance deterrence. Instead, and insofar as the New Triad was a serious concept, the NPR only enhanced the potential for the use of nuclear weapons in either a counterattack or as part of preemption, which would soon become the Bush administration's most controversial contribution to national security policy. Finally, given the proximity of the NPR to 9/11, the lack of any logical relationship to terrorism is at least curious. This doctrine simply did not apply to terrorists, who were probably beyond the reach and logic of deterrence and whose geopolitical structure was such that retaliatory attack by nuclear weapons was neither militarily practical nor politically possible.

The NPR's somewhat forced use of the image of a Triad, supposedly as a way of showing the break from the Cold War, seemed to reinforce the idea that the thinking here was not really new. Just as the original nuclear triad, conceived as a form of safety through redundancy, became a justification for nuclear overkill, the New Triad had the same potential. Yes, strategic nuclear weapons would be reduced (how could they not be?), but new nukes would be created, along with defenses, and a revitalized nuclear production complex. In a world where some had talked seriously about nuclear abolition, of returning the nuclear genie to its lamp, the NPR appeared to be the best attempt to keep that genie uncorked, to make a few more nuclear wishes, to rethink what had been the unthinkable.

National Security and Presidential Power

The Bush administration arrived in Washington with more than a plan for a military buildup and a desire to use American military power more aggressively. Key actors in the new administration, led by the vice president, intended to reassert and augment presidential power.[91] These goals — military and presidential power — were related and both went to the heart of the Constitution and the separation of powers. Many in and around the Bush administration lamented what they viewed as a long decline in presidential authority and influence. The impartiality of this view was somewhat suspect given the recent ups and downs of presidential power. They clearly lamented the decline of presidential clout amid the Iran-Contra scandal (despite it being an extraordinary abuse of executive authority and despite the timid congressional response), but they were the very same people who less than a decade later welcomed the Republican attempt to use Congress to stymie and end the Clinton presidency. What they supported was not so much general or nonpartisan presidential power but Republican presidential power, especially in foreign and national security policy. Just as crisis and war became the sine qua non of the Bush administration's ability to implement the military policies and, as will see in the next chapter, buildup that the administration planned but otherwise would not have been able to get, the crisis spawned by 9/11 was necessary to translate their particular vision of executive authority into reality. Without 9/11 and Bush's declaration of a war on terror, the nature and consequences of any theories of presidential power held by Bush and his advisors would have remained largely insignificant abstractions.

Instead, 9/11 became the springboard for a series of initiatives: from the expansive interpretation of the first authorization of use of force, to the PATRIOT Act and the executive order creating military commissions for trials of enemy combatants, to the secret NSA wiretapping program and the use of torture. As has been exhaustively explored and documented elsewhere, the administration used 9/11 to enact a virtual rewrite of the Constitution's second Article, much of it based on opinions issued from or through the Office of Legal Counsel in the Justice Department.[92] In matters relating to the president's role as commander in chief, according to these memos and other words and actions from the administration, there were few if any limits on Bush's power. Much of this built on, though went far beyond, the familiar precedents that had accumulated throughout American history favoring presidential initiative in matters of war and peace. The administration's take on the powers of the commander in chief drew upon a broader and hitherto largely academic theory of executive authority.

The neoconservative belief in the assertion of U.S. power went hand in glove with a complementary perspective on presidential authority. Evidence and examples of an imperial president at work during Vietnam, Watergate, and Iran-Contra were seen by the neoconservatives primarily in terms of their negative consequences for presidential power. The reactions to these actions and scandals diminished the power of the presidency. In this way, even the end of the Cold War was a double-edged sword. As it ushered in peace and left the United States as the sole superpower, it simultaneously stripped the president of some of his imperial vestments. Clinton — despite being president — drew conservative wrath in part because he failed to use the moment of U.S. power for the right international causes, or at least that was the nonpartisan rationale. As neoconservatives believed in unilateral use of U.S. military power, so too did they believe in unilateral presidential power. As Vice President Dick Cheney put it, "I believe in a strong, robust executive authority, and I think that the world we live in demands it."[93]

As Cheney's words imply, this concept of presidential power was supposedly motivated by concerns about the world — the world that "demands" presidential power — and the place of the United States in running global affairs. It was a theory based on perceived exigency and historical precedent. Especially in the second half of the twentieth century, as the world got smaller (and the United States larger in power and influence), presidential power grew partly as a consequence of global politics. This state of affairs was not without a constitutional foundation or at least an argument that attempted to provide one. At least from *U.S. v. Curtiss-Wright* (1936) onward, the Supreme Court had generally given the presidency prerogative and latitude in the realm of foreign affairs and national security, power that was fortified by public opinion and congressional deference for much of the Cold War.[94] Vietnam and the imperial presidency tarnished but did not do enduring damage to presidential power in national security.

Nevertheless, as noted earlier, neoconservatives and others, especially at the end of the Cold War, concerted to rebuild support for a robust presidency. In the late 1980s and into the 1990s scholars and practitioners, many of whom found a home in the conservative Federalist Society, began to articulate a theory of the "unitary executive," which had roots in the venerable if mostly defunct doctrine of "coordinate construction." Coordinate construction, with precedents going back at least to Andrew Jackson's bank veto, is the doctrine that the three branches of the national government share in the power and duty to interpret the Constitution and that each has particular authority in assessing the institutional powers given to it. From the start it was a doctrine that favored the president because the court was powerless even to enforce its own rulings. Short of using the power of the purse as a kind of veto, Congress was also quite limited in its abilities to make things happen. Only the president could execute the laws and employ force. If taken seriously coordinate construction meant the president decided what was constitutional and what was not. Updated a bit, the theory of the unitary executive — the name is derived from Federalist 70 — argues that the president has exclusive control over the executive branch and as part of that power he can interpret the provisions of the Constitution and laws that affect his control of the executive. In this revision, however, Hamilton's advocacy of a single (as opposed to plural) presidency for effective and accountable execution is transformed, and the president's duties in Article II become something where the difference between *execution* of the Constitution and the laws and *control* over both is nearly obliterated, especially in the realm of national security.[95]

From the start it was no secret that Bush wished to exercise greater executive powers and that 9/11 was allowing him to do so. Nevertheless, it took several years for some manifestations of this to become public and controversial. The extent to which the 9/11 crisis swept aside other issues is apparent in the fact that the most frequently used assertion of executive power by the Bush presidency did not become news until well after the start of his second term. As support for the Iraq war eroded, Hurricane Katrina devastated New Orleans, and gas prices rose during the fall of 2005, Congress was at work on a defense appropriations bill that was to include a ban on the use of torture. The administration had been dealing with charges of torture especially since the revelations from Abu Ghraib in spring 2004. Things had quieted down before the elections, but then were roiled by statements from Attorney General Alberto Gonzales during his confirmation hearing. Gonzales testified that the administration's position was that antitorture laws and treaties do not restrict what U.S. interrogators might do overseas because the Constitution does not apply abroad.

Republican Senator John McCain, who had been from the outset critical of the administration's failings and claims in this area, attached a new law, to be known as the Detainee Treatment Act of 2005, as an amendment to the FY 2006 Defense Department defense appropriations bill. Passed 90–9 in the Senate, the act specified that "no individual in the custody or under the physical control of the United States Government, regardless of nationality or physical location, shall be subject to cruel, inhuman, or degrading treatment or punishment."[96] President Bush had indicated before the law was sent to him that he agreed to accept a ban on torture. When it landed on his desk, Bush signed the bill including the amendment into law, very quietly, on December 30, 2005. That would seem to have been that. The executive acted; Congress responded; the president agreed by not vetoing the response. Even as he quietly signed the law, however, the president reserved the right to ignore it. As he had before with other laws and without any significant notice, Bush included a "signing statement" with his signature. In language that would be used many times during his presidency, Bush's statement asserted that "the Executive Branch shall construe [the torture ban] in a manner consistent with the constitutional authority of the President to supervise the unitary Executive Branch and as Commander in Chief and consistent with the constitutional limitations on the judicial power."[97] In other words, he could ignore it. His powers as commander in chief and inherent in the unitary executive authorized the president to counteract a direct and explicit law passed by Congress and signed by him.

Presidential signing statements are "official pronouncements issued by the President contemporaneously to the signing of a bill into law that, in addition to commenting on the law generally, have been used to forward the President's interpretation of the statutory language; to assert constitutional objections to the provisions contained therein; and, concordantly, to announce that the provisions of the law will be administered in a manner that comports with the Administration's conception of the President's constitutional prerogatives."[98] The Constitution makes no official provision for the president to issue a statement upon signing a bill. Article I specifies only that a president sign a bill or veto it and return it to Congress "with his objections." Nevertheless, presidential signing statements have a long history, though the vast majority were uncontroversial pronouncements about the bill, not the president's right to ignore it.[99] Bush was issuing dozens of signing statements, many of which contained language similar to the one employed against the torture amendment.

Swamped by the more dramatic events and political aftershocks following 9/11, the president's unprecedented use of the signing statement went all but unnoticed for several years. In fact, in a telling reversal of standard practice for such current events, a political science professor, Phillip Cooper, published a scholarly article in 2005 on the import of Bush's signing statements well before it became a topic in the mainstream press.[100] The McCain amendment, however, finally shed a little more light on signing statements. In late April 2006 an article in the *Boston Globe* became the first extended treatment in the mainstream press on the topic. It informed Americans that "President Bush has quietly claimed the authority to disobey more than 750 laws" and that he had asserted the authority to "set aside any statute passed by Congress when it conflicts with his interpretation of the Constitution."[101] The statutes affected by such signing statements involved, in addition to the ban on torture, military rules and regulations; the gathering of military intelligence; affirmative action provisions; requirements that Congress be informed about certain executive actions including financial diversions "from an authorized program in order to start a secret operation, such as the 'black sites' where suspected terrorists are secretly imprisoned"; INS requirements; military funding in Colombia; and "whistle-blower" protections for nuclear regulatory officials. By 2007 Bush had issued 152 signing statements. It was not a record; Clinton, for example, had issued 381. However, 78 percent of Bush's statements challenged one or more provisions signed into law. In fact, those 118 signing statements challenged over 1,000 individual provisions of laws. No president had ever used signing statements in this way.[102] Bush's use of presidential signing statements caused some to reconsider what had been described as Bush's "failure" to utilize the presidential veto power. According to a 2006 *New York Times* editorial, "President Bush doesn't bother with vetoes; he simply declares his intention not to enforce anything he dislikes."[103] Presidency expert Phillip Cooper agreed, arguing that those who focused on a Bush-Cheney "failure" to use the veto were "quite wrong" as signing statements were being used as a "very effective and substantive line-item veto to effectively nullify a wide range of statutory provisions even as he signed the legislation that contained them into law."[104]

This use of signing statements was finally revealed, however, along with many other examples of Bush's use and abuse of presidential power, which have been well documented by the press and academics. This use and abuse was made possible by the politics of 9/11 and employed primarily to advance his foreign and military policy agenda, including the expensive and aggressive military doctrines examined in this chapter, such as preemption and its application in Iraq, the war which ultimately would become the expression of presidential power that would define and haunt his presidency and the nation. One side of this agenda, however, stayed largely opaque to the American public. Bush's plans for national defense, from transformation to BMD and the substantial increases in spending they would require, were in doubt before September 11, 2001. As we are about to see, after that date, the subsequent wars and the policies behind them made possible, and at the same time obscured, a massive military buildup that had next to nothing to do with a war on terror.

CHAPTER FIVE

HIDDen In PLaIn SIGHT
The Bush Military Buildup

The Bush administration took power with plans for a more assertive national security policy backed by a transformed and rearmed military, all of which would require substantial increases in military spending. Prior to September 11, 2001, however, the administration lacked the necessary political leverage to bring these plans to full fruition. The Republican Congress seemed ready to support some of the administration's plans for military transformation and recapitalization, which included fabulously expensive programs such as ballistic missile defense and the F-22 fighter, but there is every reason to doubt the administration could have sustained a major buildup in the absence of 9/11. Largely because of the way the Bush administration interpreted those attacks for the American public and the world, an immediate war and the longer term equivalent of the Cold War were launched. The United States was not only targeting and attacking specific actors such as Al Qaeda and the Taliban, who were implicated in the attacks, but also launching a war on terrorism in general, to be fought anywhere, much as had been done in the Cold War against communism.

In chapter 2 I discussed the parallels between the political impact of the Korean invasion in 1950 and Iraq's invasion of Kuwait in 1990. The events of 9/11 brought that parallel to mind once again. Much as the North Korean invasion of South Korea in June 1950 allowed the hawks in the Truman administration to implement the more aggressive and expensive policies advocated in NSC 68 (most of which had little to do with Asia, let alone Korea), the attacks of

September 11 provided the political power to automatically realize the expansive plans for increases in military budgets, transformative programs, and security policies based on concepts such as dissuasion and preemption. Even without 9/11, the doctrinal changes presented in the Quadrennial Defense Review (QDR) and Nuclear Posture Review (NPR) were forthcoming. More aggressive strategies coupled with more generous budgets, provided by a relatively compliant Republican congressional majority, would have produced at least a modest military buildup, but not one approaching the peacetime buildup under President Ronald Reagan. With 9/11 and the wars that followed, however, the sky was the limit for defense spending as the Bush administration proceeded to implement a massive military buildup nearly without debate or controversy. The attacks and the wars that followed not only displaced other issues and conflicts to the distinct advantage of the administration, they even masked central aspects of national security policy. September 11 provided the political cover for massive increases in military spending to furnish the martial muscle for a new grand strategy premised on unprecedented military superiority.

Changes in Proposed Military Spending after 9/11

As we saw in chapter 4, President George W. Bush's first budget proposed a modest increase in military spending of $14.2 billion, or 4.8 percent over 2001, in line with other increases since 1999, but the administration added another $18.4 billion to that for a total of $32.6 billion, or 11 percent over 2001. Bush proudly announced that this would be "the largest increase in military spending since Ronald Reagan was the president and commander-in-chief."[1] This increase did not face a test in Congress prior to September 11. After that date, there was no stopping it.

"On September 10, 2001, Rumsfeld faced a totally invidious choice," as one analyst and former Office of Management and Budget official put it. "He had to choose between the present and the future, and he knew it. . . . The Pentagon planning system was in a crunch. The budget was in severe stress." But September 11 "completely changed the planning horizon for defense. . . . The floodgates opened. Everything was a priority."[2] Bush and Secretary of Defense Donald Rumsfeld had begun 2001 by pledging to reform and spend wisely. Even as late as August 2001, Bush noted that his "administration is going to have to winnow them [military spending priorities] down" because "we probably cannot afford every weapon system."[3] As we have seen, the administration had floated ideas about skipping a generation of weapons, which was essential to military transformation but also partly a bow to fiscal reality. Following 9/11 such tradeoffs and choices seemed to vanish, at least temporarily.

The political impact of September 11 was quickly confirmed by congressional action. Amid the expressions of outrage and calls for justice and vengeance, the most frequently voiced sentiment on the House and Senate floors was that Congress would do what was necessary to fund the incipient conflict. During the limited floor debate over the 2002 defense budget, while a few Congress members urged attention to careful and wise spending, more commented on the fact that this budget was just a start, that we needed to spend more, or that this budget was just a down payment. During the November 28, 2001 debate in the House on the defense appropriations bill, the bill generated so little controversy that not many spoke either for or against. Washington Democrat Norm Dicks thought that the amount of money in the bill "is the right direction, but we have not done nearly enough." Republican Ray LaHood of Illinois urged his colleagues to "pass it to send a signal that the Congress is really behind having a strong defense." A few raised questions and concerns. "Where is the transformation?" asked California Democrat Jane Harmon. "The Quadrennial Defense Review," she continued, "talked grandly about progress but put its money into funding the status quo." Nevertheless, she supported the bill.[4]

Even amid the crisis and war in Afghanistan, members of Congress interlaced their approval of greater military spending with diligent efforts to secure other things they wanted from the defense budget (no matter how parochial or marginally related to the attacks or a rational response to them). During the same debate Republican Representative Doug Bereuter was quick to thank the committee for including $3.8 million for an Air National Guard program that directly benefited his state of Nebraska. Likewise another Republican, J. C. Watts, used his time to call the bill an "important first step in both waging the war on terrorism and addressing readiness shortfalls that have been years in the making" and to add that he was pleased to inform his constituents that more than $52 million in military construction projects had been passed to help installations in the Fourth District of Oklahoma that "are on the front lines of the war against terrorism." Watts was followed directly by Democratic Representative Corrine Brown, whose first priority was to thank the committee for not including another round of base closures in the legislation — Brown's Florida district, not coincidentally, contained or was near several military installations — because that "would have closed military bases at a time when we all can agree that we need a strong military."[5] In fact possible base closings seemed to the major concern for more than a few members of Congress, some of whom, like Republican Senator Jim Bunning of Kentucky, argued that "now more than ever we should hold off further downsizing of our military infrastructure as we analyze how to fight the first war of the 21st century."[6]

Members of Congress showed little hesitation in forging their particular district and state needs into vital weapons and shields in the new war. Before the end of September 2001, the House and Senate passed the military construction bill, adding $700 million in new projects not requested by the White House or Pentagon. Not surprisingly most of these additions happened to be in the home states of leading members of the appropriations committees and had very little to do with the fight against terrorism. As part of this process, Rumsfeld had to threaten a presidential veto to get Congress to back away from a legislatively mandated pause in further base closings. The defense authorization bill, also considered in September, attracted seventy-nine amendments, only fifteen of which could be charitably related to a response to the ground-shifting reality of 9/11; most were related to the district or state of the author. The annual defense appropriations bill and first emergency supplemental spending measure for the global war on terror followed the same pattern. Despite declamations by Senator John McCain about the $2.1 billion in earmarks in the regular bill and $1.46 billion in the supplemental, Congress was not deterred. Over 100 amendments were passed in "managers' packages" that grouped many amendments together, thus shielding the particular authors and their wishes from direct votes and scrutiny. Nearly all were pork or even completely irrelevant.[7] The fall of 2001 was just an indication of what was to come as far as congressional irresponsibility. Instead of chastening Congress to behave and mind the store, the attacks gave greater leeway for congressional parochialism and pork-barrel politics.

The political aftermath of September 11 had the impact as well of brushing aside opposition to some of Bush's highest defense priorities, including ballistic missile defense (BMD). "Days after the terrorist attacks, Senate Democrats dropped their effort to limit program tests that would violate the 1972 Anti-Ballistic Missile (ABM) Treaty," and House Democrats abandoned their efforts to make significant cuts in BMD funding.[8] This raised some important questions. What changes and cuts, if any, would be made by the president, the Pentagon, and Congress to pay for the additional fiscal burden of the global war on terror? Or did even the earliest actions of the Congress and the president point to a somewhat different way of phrasing the question: Was 9/11 going to have the effect of making any cuts or changes politically unnecessary? As we shall see, even the powerful and unflappable secretary of defense would have trouble getting past Congress with the one bit of "transformation" that required cutting something from the budget. Just days after September 11, Democratic Senator Joseph Lieberman said that Congress's job was to "lock arms in support of the commander in chief," but someday in the future "we're going to need to talk about funding and how it's carried out."[9] That day, as we shall see, would never come.

Aside from the supplemental budgetary requests to meet the emergency of 9/11 and the military response to it (including operations in Afghanistan), the Bush administration did not reveal the impact that the QDR or 9/11 would have on the bottom line until its FY 2003 budget request made in February 2002. By this time, major combat operations in Afghanistan were (temporarily) over, but the president had declared a global war on terror; labeled Iraq, Iran, and North Korea an "axis of evil"; and begun the campaign that would lead to war with Iraq. During his 2002 State of the Union address Bush also made an easy and imprecise political link between "this war" and military spending:

> It costs a lot to fight this war. We have spent more than a billion dollars a month —
> over $30 million a day — and we must be prepared for future operations. Afghanistan proved that expensive precision weapons defeat the enemy and spare innocent
> lives, and we need more of them. We need to replace aging aircraft and make our
> military more agile, to put our troops anywhere in the world quickly and safely. Our
> men and women in uniform deserve the best weapons, the best equipment, the best
> training — and they also deserve another pay raise. My budget includes the largest
> increase in defense spending in two decades — because while the price of freedom
> and security is high, it is never too high. Whatever it costs to defend our country,
> we will pay.[10]

President Bush did not explain that the costs of the war were being handled by emergency supplemental appropriations separate from the regular budget requests. Seventeen billion dollars for the war on terror had been appropriated in 2001; another $14 billion was requested for 2002; 2003 would require nearly $70 billion. The "largest increase" in two decades referred to the military budget *independent* of the emergency and war. This means that the 2003 budget request reflected almost exclusively new spending over and above the costs of the war on terror. It represented what the Bush administration had planned to do regardless of 9/11.

The proposed changes to the military budget were substantial (fig. 5.1). Figure

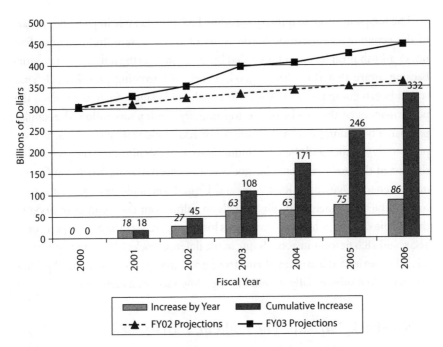

Fig. 5.1. Projections of Military Spending before and after September 2001. *Source:* Office of Management and Budget.

5.1 compares the five-year projections for defense spending made in the Bush administration's 2002 and 2003 budget proposals. Bush made rather modest projections for military spending increases in his budget for 2002 (put together months before September 2001), estimating only a 16.4 percent increase from 2001 to 2006 (2.7 percent per year). The fiscal 2003 request, from February 2002, was radically different. With an average annual increase of 6.7 percent, the military budget would grow 47 percent in six years, a cumulative addition of $332 billion dollars to the pre-9/11 plans for the defense budget. These projections proved quite accurate, as we shall see. Even as over $600 billion in war supplementals were added, the increases in military spending, apart from the war, followed the path laid down in the 2003 request. The members of the Bush administration who pushed for preventive war with Iraq had embraced Ronald Reagan's national security policy and worked for decades to excise the specter of the American failure in Vietnam. Perhaps ironically, the United States was about to combine the difficulties and expenses of a protracted war with a Reagan-sized military buildup.

The incipient surge in military spending had a predictable impact on one part of the economy. Anticipation by investors of an increase in military spending under a Bush presidency had preceded his election. "As the public and investors became aware that Bush had a good chance of becoming president, defense stocks began going up right away," observed one business analyst.[11] Indeed the performances of the stocks of the top military contractors followed a similar pattern: a bottoming-out in the summer of 2000 followed by increases in 2001 prior to September and then continuing into 2002, significantly outperforming the rest of the stock market. The stocks of Lockheed Martin, Northrop Grumman, General Dynamics, Raytheon, and United Technologies — five of the six top contractors — increased substantially in value from the summer of 2000 to the middle of 2002, while the Dow Jones lost 6.18 percent in 2000, 7.1 percent in 2001, and 18.8 percent in 2002. Some of the defense stocks fell around mid-2002, but all experienced a sustained rise from 2003 into 2008, outpacing the Dow average, often substantially, as military spending increased each year.[12]

No Shock, No Awe: The Buildup, 2001–2008

The wars and the military buildup grew simultaneously. The administration, with the support of Congress, was able to exceed its revised projections for the regular defense budget even as war spending quickly surpassed the largest prewar estimates (fig. 5.2).[13] The politics of war obscured the size of the buildup by concentrating congressional and public attention on the conflicts in Afghanistan and then Iraq, making potential criticism of arguably unnecessary or wasteful military spending politically unattractive if not dangerous. This simultaneous expansion of the war budget and the regular military budget was aided, as we shall see later in this chapter, by the fact that the wars continued to be funded by supplemental appropriation bills, which were not subject to the regular budget process and spending restrictions. Tough choices could be evaded. Money for the conflicts was not in direct competition with money for research, development, and procurement of new weapons systems that were largely unrelated to the wars.

Within a few years, the Bush administration's total military spending reached and then exceeded the peak spending (adjusted for inflation) of the Cold War era, including the Korean War, Vietnam, and the Reagan buildup (fig. 5.3).[14] By 2005 and 2006, however, the Iraq war dominated the news. Little notice was given to the fact that the regular defense budget was growing an average of nearly

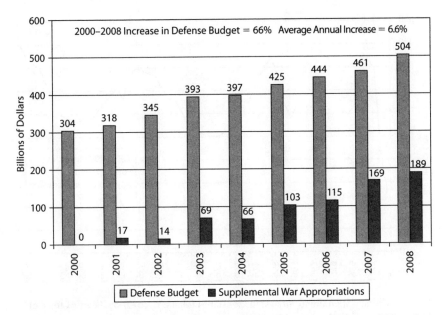

Fig. 5.2. Defense Spending versus Supplemental War Appropriations. *Source:* Office of Management and Budget.

7 percent per year. Military spending had climbed from its post–World War II low of 16.1 percent of the federal budget in 1999 back up to 21 percent by 2008. This 5 percent increase equaled the combined budgets of several cabinet-level departments—for example, the total of Homeland Security, Interior, Justice, State, and Labor. In conjunction with the tax cuts of 2001 and 2003, the rapid rise in military spending was making a substantial contribution to the return of large deficits and an increase in the national debt from about $5.6 trillion in 2000 to about $9 trillion in 2007, which in turn led to increases in interest payments as a portion of the federal budget. As a percentage of the economy, military and war spending combined grew from 3 percent to just over 4 percent of GDP over the same period. Four percent was still a historically low figure for the defense burden. While in no way a measure of what should actually be spent on national security, the relatively low percentage helped politically and was often cited by the Pentagon and the administration as an alternative perspective on how much was being spent on national security and the wars.[15]

Despite the unprecedented size of the supplemental appropriations to cover, supposedly, the extra costs imposed by the wars, and despite the substantial

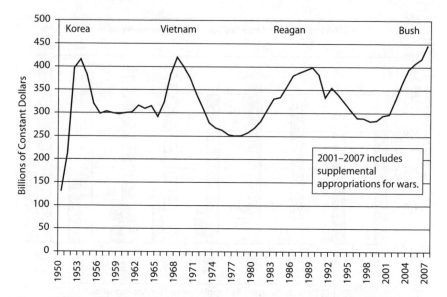

Fig. 5.3. Military Spending (Outlays) in Constant Dollars, 1950–2007. *Source:* Office of Management and Budget.

annual real increases in the regular defense budgets, the dominant impression at least until early 2007 was that the wars were leaving little money for the Pentagon's other needs such as procurement, research, and operations. Indeed the Defense Department seemed willing to foster this belief. As one skeptical reporter wrote, "Amid one of the greatest military spending increases in history, the Pentagon is starved for cash."[16] Little was done by Congress or anyone else to unravel this paradox despite the obvious contradiction and implausibility. Reports surfaced from late 2004 onward that showed the Pentagon was bracing for budget reductions and program cuts, but then nothing happened. And the next Pentagon budget arrived with a comfortable real increase, soon followed by another record supplemental request.[17] Another measure of the scale of the buildup separate from the wars is the amount of money spent on uniformed personnel *excluding* the war supplementals. In 2006 the Pentagon was spending nearly $350,000 for each man and woman on active duty and reserve, about $100,000 more per capita than in 2000 or a 40 percent increase.[18] A funding crunch was not plausible, but few were paying attention. In fact, as we shall later see in chapter 6, the irony became clear when the quagmire in Iraq led many, including Democrats, to call for more military spending to "rebuild" the army that had been degraded by the wars.

The mythology about the military's financial woes took other forms as well. A corollary distortion breathed new life into the Pentagon's classic interservice rivalries. The wars that were taking up so much money and being fought almost exclusively by the army and marines, which would have to be rebuilt as a result of the wars, meant that the other services — the air force and the navy — would pay the price in terms of reduced budgets. For example, in October 2007 National Public Radio reported that "while the Army and the Marines are now awash in extra funds, the Air Force faces severe cutbacks."[19] "The Air Force," continued the story, "is the second-largest service branch, accounting for about one-quarter of all active-duty military. But airmen make up only about 5 percent of the total troop presence in Iraq. And the numbers have prompted Pentagon bean counters to shift Air Force money away to the other service branches." In some respects such stories suffered from distortions or sins of omission. For example, "cutbacks" and "to shift" referred, as is often the case, to reductions in planned or expected growth. For example, the air force might have been planning for a 20 percent increase over three years, but would now get only 12 percent. In Washington, a reduction in growth is often portrayed as a cut, and in this case, as in many others, the reports did not clarify the true character of the reduction.

Unfortunately, seeing such distortion as a mere sin of omission hardly represents the magnitude of the distortion. Such claims of "severe cutbacks" failed to take account, once again, of the fact that the wars were being funded by massive supplemental appropriations, larger in 2007 alone than the combined military budgets of Great Britain, France, and Japan, three of the top five military spenders in the world.[20] Moreover, Bush's 2008 defense budget proposed an 11 percent increase, separate from the war funding. The evidence for severe reductions was severely lacking because it did not exist. Instead the military services all enjoyed extravagant growth during the Bush years (fig. 5.4). Figure 5.4 shows the total and capital (procurement combined with research and development) budgets for each service and defense-wide programs in 2008 and the corresponding percentage of growth since 2000, before the addition of any war supplemental funding.[21] If cutbacks were involved, they need to show up here, in the regular military budget. They do not. The army grew faster than the other services overall and as far as procurement and research and development (R&D), but it still lagged well behind in total spending.

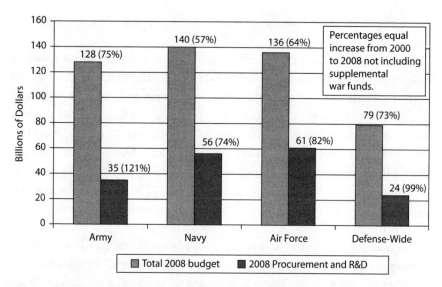

Fig. 5.4. Spending and Percentage Increases by Military Service, 2000–2008, Excluding War Funding. *Source:* Department of Defense, Comptroller.

One could argue that the army was the most overdue, war or no war, for transformation and recapitalization. Nevertheless, the air force, navy, and defense-wide programs hardly suffered with overall increases since 2000 of 57, 64, and 73 percent, respectively. The capital budgets of the air force and navy still swamped the army's budget, with defense-wide programs growing nearly as quickly as those of the army. The remarkable growth of procurement and R&D budgets shows the extent to which the wars were not a barrier to the separate military buildup. This expansion of capital programs, large as it was, was significantly augmented by the "backdoor buildup" contributed by the supplemental war funding.

The Bush Buildup in Historical Perspective

More insight into the size, composition, and politics of the Bush buildup comes from a closer comparison with the military spending of previous administrations. Prior to the Bush presidency, the last three periods of major increases in military spending came under Truman with the Korean War, Johnson during the Vietnam War, and Reagan as part of the Cold War; two as a direct consequence of war and the other in the absence of war.[22] As we have seen, just as the Korean War made possible the implementation of NSC 68, 9/11 did the same for the Bush administration's aggressive national security strategies and doctrines. The parallels carry over into the material consequences as well. The military buildup during the Korean War was overwhelmingly capital-intensive, with procurement and R&D increasing over 1,000 percent in just a few years while personnel and operations and maintenance (O&M) increased about 150 percent. Important differences were at work, however. When the Korean War began in 1950, U.S. military power was greatly diminished after the demobilization from World War II, whereas 9/11 occurred when the United States was the world's undisputed military giant, especially in qualitative terms. The Truman administration had been pushing for a major buildup even before North Korea crossed the 38th parallel. Korea provided the war and ideological bludgeon to produce a buildup that was ultimately aimed more at the defense of Europe than victory in Asia. Military spending, though decreasing with the end of the war, stabilized at a higher plateau that in real terms was nearly three times the level before the Korean War.

The next Asian war, in Vietnam, produced a rather labor- and operations-intensive increase in military spending. Spending for operations and maintenance (O&M) shot up dramatically in comparison to weapons procurement and R&D. Even during an era with conscription, and therefore low labor costs, and a war that consumed considerable equipment, personnel costs outpaced procurement and R&D (fig. 5.5). Figure 5.5 compares the buildups during the Vietnam War under President Lyndon Johnson with those under Ronald Reagan and George W. Bush by showing the percentage of real increase in the major components of the military budget (personnel, O&M, and procurement combined with R&D) from the year before each buildup started to each peak year of budget authority. Under Reagan, the military budget increased nearly 50 percent when adjusted for inflation, and the core of that increase was radically capital-intensive. Procurement and R&D increased by 100 percent as the Reagan administration sought first and foremost to modernize most major weapons systems and invest in new technologies, including ballistic missile defenses. Operational funding increased significantly (34 percent) but paled by comparison. The personnel budget barely grew in real terms.

The combination of war and vast increases in the regular military budget under Bush surpassed previous real spending and percentage growth. Remarkable and largely unrecognized is the extent to which the Bush administration was able to combine war spending with a very capital-intensive buildup (represented in the third set of columns in fig. 5.5). The massive spending on the various post-9/11 conflicts, especially Iraq, produced tremendous increases in personnel and O&M expenditures. Not only had labor become generally more expensive, with an all-volunteer and skilled armed services competing against a fairly successful economy, the war prompted even higher pay, including extensive use of such things as reenlistment bonuses and high salaries for civilian contractors. At the same time, American war-fighting had become more capital-intensive because of a higher ratio of costly weapons and equipment per uniformed personnel, which also added to O&M expenses. And yet, much of the increase in both O&M and personnel were covered in the supplemental or emergency appropriations for the wars, not in the regular Pentagon budget. Nevertheless, it is remarkable that when supplemental war spending is combined with the regular defense budgets, procurement and R&D went up 92 percent in real terms from 2000 to 2009 and still outpaced personnel (45 percent) and even O&M (80 percent) costs. Part of this increase was due to the fact that the "emergency" supplemental appropriations for the wars contained a great deal of funding for procurement and R&D, much of which could not be categorized as emergency funding or directly war-related.

Apart from the supplemental war spending, President Bush did not quite match the percentage increase in military spending achieved by Reagan. But his buildup — with eight straight years of real increases — was more sustained than any previous administration, whether at war or peace. Prior to 9/11 the Bush administration planned a Reaganesque capital-intensive buildup (the essence of "transformation"), such that, even if it could not match the scale of the Reagan-era increases, it could mirror the major goal of next-generation rearmament. The capital-intensive character of the Bush buildup separate from funding for the wars is represented in the fourth set of columns in figure 5.5. Without counting a dime of the $750 billion in war supplementals appropriated through 2008, Pentagon budgets for procurement and R&D increased 63 percent in real terms, far outpacing the 28 percent increase in personnel spending and the 19 percent increase in O&M. The war allowed Bush to mirror Reagan's research- and procurement-intensive buildup without Reagan's emphasis on nuclear weapons programs.

The Bush administration had little trouble funding dozens of weapons projects that had little or nothing to do with fighting and winning the struggles of the first decade of the twenty-first century. What weapons might be useful or essential in a long-term war against terrorism is debatable, of course. But most of the

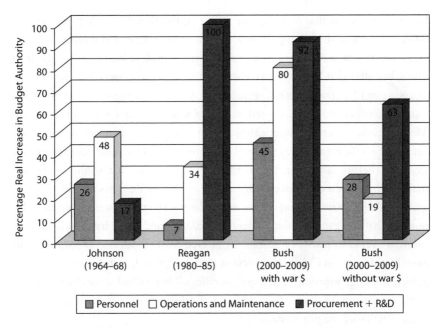

Fig. 5.5. The Bush Buildup Compared (with and without War Spending). *Source:* Department of Defense, Comptroller.

big-ticket programs to be discussed below (the F-22, the Joint Strike Fighter, ballistic missile defense, and much of the navy's ship-building program) were based on conflicts with nation-states. The buildup, or much of it, was a solution in search of a problem. The Department of Defense needed, as one critical commentator put it, "a 'peer' competitor like China worthy of our weaponry. We have the hammer. Now all we need is the right nail."[23]

This comparison of military buildups is not just about how much was spent; it also points to the politics of defense policy. In stark contrast to the Bush years, the military buildup of the early 1980s became one of the principal controversies of the early Reagan presidency. Reagan's buildup and military doctrines were subject to vigorous opposition from Congress and the public and spawned a substantial peace movement even though the nation was not at war. Centered on opposition to his nuclear weapons programs and strategy, this movement converged on the nuclear freeze proposal as a positive alternative to Reagan's policies. The movement grew quite rapidly, producing one of the largest political rallies in American history (500,000 in Central Park) in June 1982. It culminated in the spring of 1983 when the House voted 278–149 for a somewhat diluted nuclear freeze amendment that would go on to die in the Republican Senate. Despite public concern in the late 1970s about the decline of American might and influence, the threat was elusive and evanescent—it had helped get Reagan into office, but after that Reagan's own rhetoric and policies, especially about nuclear weapons and Central America, seemed to many more dangerous than the Russian bear, which was preoccupied with its Central Asian version of Vietnam. Moreover, there were no American troops in harm's way.[24] Instead, many Americans were confused and alarmed by the combination of hawkish (and sometimes cavalier) rhetoric about nuclear conflict and programs that would seemingly make such conflicts more likely. One could argue that Reagan's military policies generated a peace movement at least in part *because* the nation was not at war. The point is that Reagan's buildup, despite initial support, never had leverage from external events to justify or sustain it. In fact, many moderate Democrats and even Republicans in Congress criticized the waste, fraud, and abuse that accompanied the huge infusion of defense spending. They rallied around a banner of "military reform," a nonpartisan package of reforms aimed at ensuring that our defense dollars were not wasted.[25]

Bush's buildup, on the other hand, was made possible by the crisis of 9/11. Few Americans were aware of the scale and scope of the nonwar defense budgets. The impact of the global war on terror was to silence virtually all resistance to a militaristic response. The opposition that did finally arise was focused on the threat of war against Iraq and then the actual war once it started. The buildup, which proceeded rapidly, went all but unnoticed. As one measure of this phenomenon, in 2005 the *New York Times* unsurprisingly featured at least 126 articles, editorials, and opinion pieces on the subject of the conflict in Iraq, nearly all of which were about the U.S. role in that war. That same year the *Times* had 10 articles or editorials on the subject of military spending, and at least 3 of those had some link to war spending as well. Contrast that with the 62 articles and editorials on military spending from 1985 at the height of the Reagan buildup (nearly all of which were about some controversy regarding the size and future of the Pentagon budget).[26] Under Bush the public was not well informed, and Congress was compliant and complicit. Some part of congressional behavior can be explained by a Republican majority in the House, but the Senate was evenly divided.[27] So partisanship is, at best, a partial explanation. Instead the answer lies in a combination of ideological conviction and political acquiescence. The events of 9/11 reaffirmed and empowered the hawkish convictions of many members of Congress, convinced some who had not been of that mindset, and cowed others

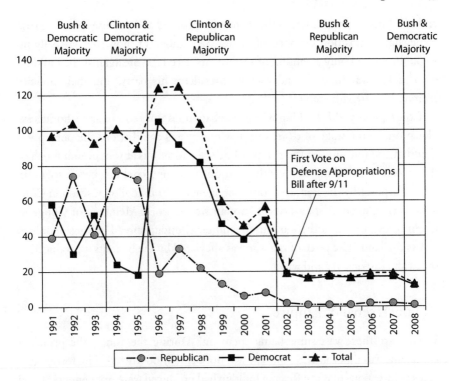

Fig. 5.6. Votes against Defense Appropriations Bills in the House, 1991–2008. *Source:* Library of Congress, THOMAS.

into submission regardless of their sincere beliefs about the buildup and its relation to a war on terror.

Congressional votes on defense appropriations bills — funding for the military *separate from* the supplemental war appropriations — provide evidence for the level of compliance, even after public support for the war collapsed along with President Bush's popularity. Voting against defense appropriations bills by members of either party, common if not prevalent in the 1980s and 1990s, utterly disappeared after 9/11 (fig. 5.6). As figure 5.6 shows, the partisan source of opposition shifted with circumstances throughout the post–Cold War period. Under President George H. W. Bush, partisan positions were mixed as the defense budget was decreasing. Republicans counterattacked under President Bill Clinton by voting against Democratic military appropriation bills in fairly large numbers, but then Democrats voted in even larger numbers against defense spending bills produced by the new Republican majority after 1995. Toward the end of Clinton's presidency, as the deficit disappeared and defense spending rose somewhat, opposition dropped off. After September 11, however, virtually no Republicans and only a handful of Democrats dared to vote against the buildup, even as the war in Iraq rendered the president, his party, and their policies seemingly quite vulnerable.

Consequently, this buildup without debate does not require an elaborate explanation. In the wake of 9/11, very few politicians could afford the perception that they did not support the troops while the nation was at war, even if much of the money had nothing to do with a war on terror and could be better spent on other purposes by the Pentagon or other agencies. Potential opposition in Congress was stymied. Also, a cynical bargain was at work. Members of Congress might be queasy about the war, but the military buildup spread billions of dollars across the land. The price of the war was alleviated by the benefits it produced in states and districts far and wide.

The Arsenal of Empire

What were these vast sums being spent on? During the 1990s, the principal complaint was that the U.S. military was not being modernized. The formidable stocks of weapons that the Reagan buildup had produced were not being replaced rapidly enough. The lag time between weapon development and production had been extended by the relatively lean military budgets in the first decade after the Cold War. Some components of the Reagan-era arsenal were aging and no replacements were heading down the assembly line. George W. Bush campaigned on the need to modernize (and transform), and though he often dealt more in slogans ("help is on the way") than specifics, those who followed this area of public policy knew the Republican Party was united behind more money not just for defense in general but for weapons development and procurement in particular. It was time to produce the arsenal for the twenty-first century.

As far as procurement and R&D, the Pentagon had a massive wish list. In 2004 the Pentagon was working on seventy-seven arms programs with "a collective price tag of $1.3 trillion."[28] Prior to 9/11 the administration's highest-priority weapons program appeared to be ballistic missile defense (BMD). As we shall see, it remained a high priority even after 9/11 and was the most expensive weapons program overall in the military budget. After 9/11 the administration worked hard to make the argument that the relevance of BMD only increased in the wake of the attacks. Whatever the merits of the administration's position on BMD, many other programs sought by the army, navy, and air force seemed much more suited for interstate warfare on a massive scale. Nothing embodied the tension between programs rooted in the Cold War and the kind of transformative weapons required after 9/11 more than tactical fighter and attack aircraft.

Tactical fighter and attack aircraft are fixed-wing aircraft used by the air force, navy, and marines to destroy enemy aircraft and attack ground targets. From the late 1970s to the Bush presidency, such forces were represented most prominently by the F-15, F-16, F-14, and F-18. In the 1990s, in anticipation of the earlier models reaching the end of their life spans, three new fighter programs were underway, with production slated to begin in earnest in the first decade of the new century. The F-22 or Raptor was the air force's stealthy air-superiority fighter designed to replace the F-15. The air force originally planned to acquire 750 of them by 2010. For the navy, the F/A-18E/F would supplant older F-18 models, with a goal of 1,000 over the period of 1997 to 2015. The largest program was the Joint Strike Fighter (JSF), later designated the F-35. Designed as a replacement for the F-16, the JSF would comprise the bulk of the air force tactical air command, with the air force getting about 2,000 of the 3,000 projected JSFs. The marines would get about 640 and the navy about 300, with production running from about 2005 through 2030. As was noted in chapter 3, this is one of the most expensive cans that Clinton was able to kick down the road as all three programs entered the new century behind schedule. By 2000, the F-18 had commenced a modest level of production, but the F-22 and JSF were still being refined, prototyped, and tested. Near the end of the Clinton presidency all three programs had been cut back. Already down to 438, the F-22 was cut to 339, the F-18 from 1,000 to 548, and the JSF less dramatically cut from 2,978 to 2,852 aircraft.[29] Reductions notwithstanding, the Bush administration arrived on the scene eager for recapitalization but facing what still appeared to be unsustainable demands from this one sector alone—all together, over 3,700 aircraft at an estimated cost (in the late 1990s) of over $350 billion.[30]

Despite being the smallest program in terms of numbers of aircraft to be produced, the F-22 Raptor best exemplified the three-dimensional tensions between "legacy" programs—those with roots during or near the end of the Cold War—transformation, and the putative demands of a global war on terror. Started in the 1980s and epitomizing the search for supremacy for its own sake, the Raptor could have been the poster child for "dissuasion," the doctrine of radical superiority discussed in chapter 4. As one Washington consultant put it, "It's a plane that sends a message to the world, 'Don't even think about competing with the

U.S.' "[31] After the Cold War, when no potential foe would dare to take to the sky against U.S. Air Force and Navy aircraft, the F-22 was the air force's highest priority. Not only was the F-22 arguably unnecessary, it was also an extravagantly expensive and troubled program. Prior to the election of a Republican president in 2000 and before 9/11, many Republicans in Congress were willing to question the wisdom of a commitment to the F-22. In 1999, Republican Appropriations Committee Chair Jerry Lewis led an effort to cut procurement funding for the program. The cut passed the House but not the Senate, and ultimately a compromise was reached, one that still cut the president's $1.9 billion F-22 request by about $900 million.[32]

The plane's designation, in fact, became an indicator of its politics. The F-22 Raptor briefly became the F/A-22 when it was modified to have some ground attack capability in part to overcome the criticism that a purely air-superiority fighter might not be practical.[33] Even as the air force settled on the F-22A as the final designation and production was underway, the program continued to have problems. One plane inexplicably crashed on a test flight on December 20, 2004. At this late date, the air force was still arguing for 381 F-22As, but Rumsfeld was holding the line for a lower number. The defense secretary's plans near the end of 2004 for at least $30 billion in cuts in unnecessary programs put the F-22 front and center with a reduction to 179. With about $40 billion in research and development costs spread over fewer units, the cost of an individual Raptor rocketed skyward faster than the plane. With a production run of 179, each plane's total cost was in the range of $350 million, about ten times the cost of the fighter it was replacing, the F-15. The development of the F-22 paralleled the other "plane to end all planes" from the end of the Cold War, the B-2 stealth bomber, which like the F-22A was intended to be invisible to radar. The original goal of 132 B-2s was slashed to 21 due to budgetary concerns and the end of the Cold War, making the bomber's cost per plane about $2.1 billion.

As the potential number of F-22s plummeted, pork barrel politics once again kicked in, covered by a thin gloss of national security rhetoric. The state of Georgia, with Martin Marietta one its major employers, led the way. The two Georgia Senators, both Republicans, and thirteen other members of Congress wrote the White House in defense of the Raptor, arguing that cuts to the program put the "nation's global air superiority requirements" at risk.[34] That the nation and its allies had total global air superiority and that it was hardly at risk did not seem to enter into the debate; instead curious arguments held sway that reflected contemporary fashion about who should be in charge of military decisions, civilians or generals. Phil Gingrey, whose district held the Marietta F-22 plant, argued that Congress "can't let civilian bureaucrats under the current Secretary of Defense make decisions that could harm the protection of our nation. We should listen to our military commanders and our warfighters."[35] The disparaging references to Rumsfeld as the "current" secretary of defense and to other bureaucrats who were not to be listened to — the same tough-guy neoconservatives who had knocked heads only two years earlier to get the military brass ready to fight the imperial wars and embrace transformation — signaled that times had changed politically. The generals were once again the ones to back, at least when they wanted to buy more weapons. As with nearly any large weapons platform project, Georgia and Lockheed Martin were not alone in this fight. The often quoted statistic was that the Raptor had over 1,000 subcontractors in forty-three states.[36]

Fighter aircraft were far from the only major weapons systems awaiting full-scale development or production after the election of 2000. The navy wanted more than F-18s and some JSFs. What it really wanted amounted to having a new navy. Just as stealth had come to be the defining feature of modern strategic and tactical aircraft, the navy was working on new ships and submarines that were stealthy in a nautical fashion — but the justification for this was rather strained. If possible, here was an area where the United States had even greater superiority than in fighter aircraft. The United States possessed the only truly global naval force in the world, and only our closest allies had comparably modern, if rather more modest, navies. The Russian navy, the only conceivable exception, was run down, radically downsized, and largely dormant even into the new century. Nevertheless, the U.S. Navy looked forward to the production of several new classes of combat vessels, including the Virginia-class attack submarine and the DD-21 Zumwalt-class land-attack destroyer, both with stealthy characteristics and designed to assist with littoral military operations (that is, to provide land attack support to ground forces), with an estimated 170 vessels to be produced between 2000 and 2020.[37]

The most pedestrian service, the army, had equally expansive and in some ways more revolutionary projects, but it was playing a game of catch-up. At the end of the Cold War the army had plans for a series of follow-on replacement programs for major weapons systems, including the Crusader mobile artillery system and Comanche helicopter. Some of those plans seemed rather out-of-date, a replication of the kind of heavy armor tactics that were to be used in Central Europe against the Soviet Union and which did not clearly fit a post–

Cold War environment, even though the 1997 QDR deemed both weapons "necessary to the Force XXI concept" (then the designation for transformation and the Revolution in Military Affairs [RMA] as applied to the army) to result in a digitalized and more agile force. War games in the mid-1990s and events in Kosovo in 1999 confirmed the need for a new approach. From this movement toward more nimble and digitalized forces emerged Future Combat Systems (FCS), which by the middle of the Bush administration could be described as a "family of 14 weapons, drones, robots, sensors, and hybrid-electric combat vehicles connected by a wireless network." It was the most expensive army program ever.[38]

All three services were doing their best to retain and complete Cold War legacy systems like the F-22 and also hitch a ride on the train of transformation. But the original path to transformation would be complicated by preemption and the global war on terror. The combination of exacting tasks for national security set by the administration — deterrence, defense, dissuasion, preemption, and transformation — expanded nearly every avenue for growth in the means of warfare. In such an environment, no potential technology was too sophisticated or expensive. Transformation in particular, which involved at least some version, however compromised, of skipping a generation of weapons to get to the future of warfare, was by necessity a very research-intensive project. Could the great leap forward be made, however, while fighting what turned out to be two protracted wars dominated by counterinsurgency and nation-building?

Rumsfeld and others would point to Afghanistan as an indication of the potential of transformational tactics and weaponry, even if the budgets and programs that would produce full-scale transformation were just getting under way. For example, the United States was using Predator drones in Afghanistan and elsewhere to help fight the war on terror. The Predator, an unmanned aerial vehicle (UAV), was originally built for reconnaissance. Relatively inexpensive UAVs could fly for hours on end over critical areas feeding real-time video and data back to battlefield commanders. This kind of high-tech force-multiplier was a cornerstone of transformation. The Predator was itself quickly transformed, however, by both the air force and the CIA into a battlefield weapon. The air force added a laser targeting capability so that the drone could not just detect and report targets, it could direct laser-guided bombs from other aircraft onto the target. Additionally, the CIA put a small air-to-ground, anti-armor missile on board its Predators. The CIA's armed drone was used in Afghanistan extensively, but its role as a weapon became widely known only after one flying over Yemen in late 2002 fired and killed six people traveling in a car, reportedly Al Qaeda operatives.[39] Whether or not the six were terrorists, the Predator had killed and would go on to kill innocents in Afghanistan and elsewhere.[40] The war on terror was by definition going to involve unconventional warfare, but the robotic summary execution of suspects in a country with which the United States was not at war raised all sorts of issues of international law and pragmatic concerns about U.S. policy. The United States could kill at a distance by remote control, which might be safe and cost-effective, but would it ultimately help or hurt the larger war on terror? Other strikes in Afghanistan and Pakistan would show that transformation did not necessarily harmonize with winning hearts and minds in a counterinsurgency, a problem that would immediately confront and confound President Bush's successor.[41] Unmanned aerial vehicles such as the Predator, whatever their merits and despite their problems, were just the most prominent element in a robotics revolution involving many programs and weapons that was a mostly quiet but increasingly important component of the capital-intensive Bush buildup.[42]

In some respects Rumsfeld tried to implement the transformation-in-progress in Iraq by limiting the force size for the invasion and by applying some transformational doctrines and force elements in advance of the final product. In Iraq, transformation and preemption would *initially* coincide. Later, this combination would prove an embarrassment and disaster, and Rumsfeld would disingenuously argue, regarding Iraq, that "you go to war with the Army you have . . . not the Army you might want."[43] Instead, as Iraq bogged down into a protracted and costly conflict, preemption, which had morphed into nation-building, and transformation, which was about building the nimble force of the future, began to collide in theory and practice.

Though never really a part of public debate about the war, the gap between the nascent revolution in procurement and the conditions of war was glaring to those paying attention. The most public manifestation came in the form of complaints largely from the families of soldiers who said that their sons and daughters were being sent into combat without adequate equipment (including rather prosaic items such as body armor or properly armored vehicles). These were the problems that prompted Rumsfeld to make his poorly received remark, "You go to war with the Army you have," in front of an audience of soldiers on duty in Iraq. The conflict between procurement and the conditions of war was also implicit in the whole concept of an overextended army—the long tours of duty and heavy use of reserves. How could the United States be in this position when it accounted for half of the world's military expenditures and was not even involved by this point in major combat operations, the main enemy having been defeated? No one in Washington seemed interested in finding an answer to this question.

The long-term commitment to the awkward synthesis of nation-building and counterinsurgency produced other problems for transformation as well. For example, with American troops sustaining heavy casualties from improvised explosive devices (IEDs), the army engineered a crash program to produce Mine-Resistant Ambush Protected (MRAP) vehicles — not something anyone had anticipated as part of a revolution in military affairs. In the 2008 budget Congress authorized $17.2 billion (in the supplemental war funding appropriations) for the production of 15,000 MRAP vehicles, and over 3,500 were delivered to Central Command in one year.[44]

All the while, the president was requesting and Congress providing for technologies and weapons that were not just transformational but potentially revolutionary. Early in the post-9/11 era the administration got into some hot water when it was revealed that one program, accurately but inaptly named "Total Information Awareness," established in January 2002 within the Defense Advanced Research Projects Agency (DARPA), was being run by John Poindexter, former Iran-Contra culprit convicted of lying to Congress. The focus of the program was on stupendously powerful and advanced computing programs to process and analyze unprecedented amounts of information with unparalleled sophistication, ostensibly to catch terrorists. Concerns were raised that the program could result in uncontrolled surveillance of millions of innocent American citizens, particularly through the integration of commercial and governmental databases. Congress deauthorized the program in 2003, but aspects of it survived in other DARPA programs.[45]

Later, and without any controversy whatsoever, a program named "Prompt Global Strike" was initiated. The term "global strike" referred to several futuristic weapons programs under development that would allow the U.S. military to attack targets nearly immediately anywhere on the globe, primarily with non-nuclear weapons and preferably from controls or weapons based in the United States.[46] "Prompt and high-volume global strike" was necessary, the 2001 QDR argued, "to deter aggression or coercion, and if deterrence fails, to provide a broader range of conventional response options to the president." This could come in the form of a highly accurate warhead on what was once a nuclear ballistic missile, a hypersonic cruise missile, or perhaps super-velocity rods sent from outer space. This same report then noted dryly that the potential employment of global strike "will require broader authorities from the Congress."[47] In other words, the Constitution's grip on the war power became even more uncertain once conventional war could be initiated and conducted entirely from within the country on a moment's notice. This and other such wonders were under development as the public and politicians focused on the increasingly discouraging developments in Iraq and Afghanistan.

Ballistic Missile Defense

As we have seen, one of the few specific military programs that Bush mentioned in his run for the presidency was ballistic missile defense (BMD). Bush and the Republican Party had promised to deploy a national missile defense system as soon as possible. In the words of the 2000 platform, "America must deploy effective missile defenses, based on an evaluation of the best available options, including sea-based, at the earliest possible date. These defenses must be designed to protect all 50 states, America's deployed forces overseas, and our friends and allies in the fellowship of freedom against missile attacks by outlaw states or accidental launches."[48] The platform called as well for revision of the Anti-Ballistic Missile (ABM) Treaty, "an obsolete treaty signed in 1972 with a Soviet Union that no longer exists," to allow this deployment. What this meant, without saying so explicitly, was the termination of the treaty. In the new president's first address to Congress in February 2001, the need to develop and deploy BMD was the focus of his few comments on military security, aside from announcing a pay and benefits increase for the troops and a brief reference to transformation. In a speech that May the president made it clear that he and the Republican Party meant what they said about the ABM agreement. We "must move beyond the constraints of the 30-year-old ABM Treaty," he said, a treaty that "prohibits us from exploring all options for defending against the threats that face us, our allies and other countries." This speech emphasized a potential renegotiation of the pact to allow for cooperation and greater flexibility.[49] BMD was also the principal beneficiary of the biggest increase in the 2002 defense budget, a $2.6 billion boost in research and development money for a variety of advanced technologies. Several months later the QDR provided a strong indication of the scope of the administration's commitment to BMD:

DoD has refocused and revitalized the missile defense program, shifting from a single-site "national" missile defense approach to a broad-based research, development, and testing effort aimed at deployment of layered missile defenses. These changes in the missile defense program will permit the exploration of many previously untested technologies and approaches that will produce defenses able to intercept missiles of various ranges and in various phases of flight. These defenses will help protect U.S. forward-deployed forces. Moreover, they will provide limited defense against missile threats not only for the American people, but also for U.S. friends and allies.[50]

As with other elements of Bush's national security agenda, BMD would get a critical boost from the attacks of September 11. Despite the irony that the United States was attacked by its own airliners, the proponents of BMD focused on a different type of attack. Terrorists and rogues, they argued, could surprise us by using missiles against us, much as they shocked us with the use of suicide pilots on commercial aircraft. Bush and company quickly shifted the narrative of 9/11 from the perpetrators — agents of a stateless organization — back to a struggle against nation-states in an axis of evil. They also began to emphasize possession of weapons of mass destruction by rogue states instead of the kind of asymmetric attacks launched by Al Qaeda. Taking advantage of the strong public support for the president in the first months following 9/11, Bush announced on December 13, 2001 that he was notifying Russia of the United States' intention to withdraw from the ABM treaty effective, per treaty requirements, six months hence in June 2002. "I have concluded," said Bush, that "the ABM treaty hinders our government's ability to develop ways to protect our people from future terrorist or rogue state missile attacks."[51] Absent 9/11 such an action would have been much more controversial, if not impossible politically.

Withdrawal left the Bush administration free, with the support of Congress, to pursue a multifaceted BMD program. The short-term goal was the deployment of a limited national missile defense (NMD) system, one capable of defending much of the continental United States against an attack from a small number of missile warheads. Although the term "Global Protection against Limited Strikes" (or GPALS) was no longer used, the concept was the same — to combine a limited NMD system with other forms of BMD, including theater and battlefield systems such as the Terminal High Altitude Area Defense program (THAAD) and the Patriot, in order to achieve global coverage. Later in a policy statement from May 2003 the administration eliminated the distinction between national and global as "artificial." Also gone was any requirement that these systems be fully tested and operationally effective prior to deployment. The NMD system would be phased and evolutionary, and the United States would build and deploy each component or layer as it was ready. In this approach there was no clearly defined end point or "final, fixed . . . architecture" for the program; additions could be made as technology improved. The system did not have to be perfect from the outset because it would be altered and improved in an ongoing process.[52] This approach complemented the latitude provided by the Nuclear Posture Review's reassurance, discussed in the last chapter, that a BMD system did not have to be 100 percent effective to enhance deterrence and save lives.

That the administration meant what it said in this regard was proven by the alacrity with which it began digging silos in Alaska as withdrawal from the ABM went into effect and before the boosters and hit-to-kill warheads, along with the radars and software involved, had passed, by many interpretations, any realistic tests. The initial system had no new missiles of its own — though it was supposed to get them — and relied instead on old Minuteman IIIs. This was sometimes referred to as a "test bed" deployment. It would have the convenient political benefit of allowing the president to claim he had deployed defenses even though it was at best a partially successful testing ground. Regardless, the president directed the Pentagon to have an initial system fielded by fall 2004.[53] In fact, Bush announced that goal in December 2002 less than a week after a failed test of the core system, when the hit-to-kill warhead failed to separate from the booster, one incident in a long series of less than reassuring test results. Even once the first six missiles were installed at Fort Greely in Alaska, a 2004 test from the Marshall Islands in the Pacific failed when the interceptor did not launch. By the Missile Defense Agency's accounting the ground-based interceptor system failed five out of ten tests from 1999 through early 2005, and knowledgeable analysts were critical of most of the successful tests because the conditions were so unrealistic.[54] During these ups and downs, the Pentagon cancelled several planned tests. This led some experts to conclude that "they are having trouble trying to deploy and test at the same time" and that political considerations regarding the risk that more failed tests might have on deployment were affecting the test schedule.[55] The lack of steady progress is probably one reason that in spring 2002 the possibility briefly surfaced of using nuclear-tipped interceptors — the same rather hazardous and technologically crude form of interception deployed on the short-lived ABM system of the late 1960s — instead of or in addition to kinetic kill vehicles. Congress quickly rejected this back to the future approach.[56]

Regardless, by 2005 the United States had a limited NMD capability in place and, to whatever extent, it was operational. This was just a starting point, albeit a rather expensive beginning. By the time President Bush had his chance to bring BMD to fruition, the United States had spent nearly $58 billion on national missile defense systems in the seventeen years from 1985 through 2001. In the seven years from 2002 through 2008, Bush and Congress would commit another $58 billion. Even with a partial and only partially successful deployment of a handful of missiles, it was, by far, the most expensive program in military history.[57] The Bush administration refused to put a price tag on its plans because, conveniently, it had not decided what to build. In 2008 the Congressional Budget Office projected that spending on all BMD programs would peak in 2018 at between $15 and $20 billion annually, depending on cost increases, and decrease thereafter, adding well over $100 billion more across the decade after Bush left office to the total cost of the administration's "layered" missile defense, assuming his successor followed the same path.[58] The nation's commitment to such an exorbitantly expensive project — especially one that combined dubious effectiveness against a rather remote threat — was hardly debated and never challenged during Bush's presidency. One might have expected that wars costing over half a trillion dollars would have prompted a search to economize elsewhere. Instead the wars and the politics they produced masked and protected the drive for missile defense. Such as it was, what started as Reagan's dream was by 2008, twenty-five years later, at one and the same time much less (in terms of what had been built) and much more (in its costs) than its early proponents might have imagined.

Supplemental War Appropriations and the Backdoor Buildup

By the summer of 2007, supplemental funding for the war on terror had reached over $550 billion. Despite criticisms of the use of putatively emergency supplemental appropriations and despite recommendations that the administration integrate war spending into the regular military budget, these practices continued.[59] In 2006 Senators John McCain and Robert Byrd authored an amendment to the 2007 defense authorization bill mandating that future war funding be made part of the regular budget process. Although Bush signed the bill with the McCain-Byrd amendment, he did so with a signing statement specifying that he could, in effect, ignore it.[60] Although the main purpose of this chapter is to show the size of the military buildup separate from the war funding, no account could ignore the remarkable ways in which the supplemental war funding also became part of the buildup.

Before passage of the McCain-Byrd amendment, evidence had emerged that the supplemental requests were taking advantage of the politics of war to exceed what was required for ongoing operations in Iraq and Afghanistan. Reports showed that some of the funding for procurement and research involved weapons systems and equipment that was either inappropriate or, in some cases, would not be available for several years. These things should have been in the general defense budget and in no way qualified for emergency or supplemental spending. The army's Modularity Program included in supplemental requests for fiscal years 2005 and 2006 is an example of a regular modernization/transformation program that was funded via emergency supplemental requests.[61] Such additions were sanctioned and encouraged in October 2006 when Deputy Secretary of Defense Gordon England sent a memo to the services announcing the expansion of supplemental funding to include efforts outside of Iraq and Afghanistan. This raised concerns that virtually anything even tangentially related to the war on terror could be funded through emergency supplemental appropriations.[62] A congressional staffer concluded that the services "are using the availability of the supplementals to finance virtually all of the shortfalls they can identify."[63]

The latitude taken by the administration was demonstrated by "replacement of old equipment with new models—actions historically subject to the normal budget review process."[64] For example, the 2007 supplemental contained money for twenty-two new C-130J Hercules cargo planes. It also included a $400 million request for two F-35 fighters, which would not be combat ready for at least three years. Another $300 million was requested for seven of the new (and controversial) V-22 Osprey transport planes, another system that was arguably not ready for deployment let alone war. There was even considerable money for the research and development of such things as a new unmanned aerial vehicle.[65]

It is important to note the inconsistencies in the administration's rhetoric supporting the use of emergency supplementals for funding the wars in Iraq and Afghanistan. On one hand, the administration argued that the immediate and urgent need for repairs and replacement of equipment necessitated emergency supplemental requests. On the other, billions of dollars were requested for equipment that might not be available for years or would never be used in Iraq. These requests should have been included in the general budget, as they failed to satisfy an immediate need. In addition to purchasing new or nonexistent items, much of the existing equipment was being modernized and upgraded with new technology

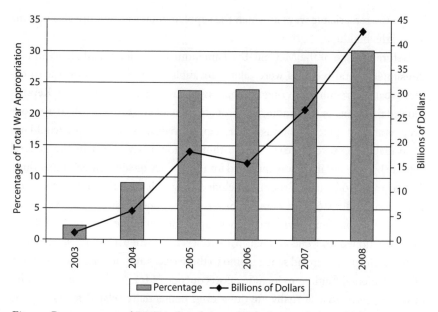

Fig. 5.7. Procurement and R&D in Supplemental War Appropriations. *Source:* House and Senate Defense Appropriations Conference Reports and Department of Defense, Comptroller.

rather than simply being restored to its previous condition. Budget documents indicated that the M1A1 Abrams tank would receive an "unspecified systems enhancement program." The army and the marines in particular came to view the supplementals as essential to their plans for modernization and transformation.[66]

Whether this use of the supplemental process was an abuse or not, the result was a backdoor addition to the military buildup. Before 9/11 emergency supplementals composed a few percent at most of total defense spending. In 2007 about 28 percent of military spending was in the form of supplemental funding.[67] In particular, the supplemental appropriations beefed up the capital-intensive aspects of the military budget. Procurement and R&D have composed over 20 percent of the supplementals since 2005 and would reach 30 percent with the 2008 supplemental (fig. 5.7). That 30 percent translated into $42.8 billion for procurement and R&D, more than the entire defense budgets of all but a few nations. Even ignoring the direct evidence that the supplementals contained new, nonwar procurement, it was self-evident that the United States was not expending or degrading nearly $43 billion worth of equipment annually in Iraq and Afghanistan.

The extraordinary thing is that this backdoor buildup proceeded at the same time as the regular Pentagon budget — particularly procurement and R&D — was increasing rapidly. In effect, projects that could not be advanced with nearly 7 percent growth each year in the regular military budget were wedged into the supplementals. Aside from the soon to be irrelevant McCain-Byrd amendment, congressional resistance to the abuse of supplemental spending was negligible, given the generally solid partisan support for the administration through the elections of 2006 and the ongoing fear of any perception of not "supporting the troops." The use of supplemental spending prevented Congress from being forced to balance increases with cuts for other projects, which would likely have been done if the money for the backdoor buildup was reflected in the official budget.[68]

Congress in the Shadow of Tragedy, War, and the President

Congress was not minding the store. Members were paralyzed by the politics of supporting the troops at the same time that they were too busy shopping along with the White House, generals, and admirals. As the president was protecting and expanding the power of his office, Congress went down a rather different path. Neither defending its institutional powers nor in any way rising to the occasion produced by 9/11, Congress capitulated to the presidency and redefined collective irresponsibility. Earlier in this chapter we noted briefly that parochialism was evident even in the weeks following the attack of September 11. Despite conditions that would seem to preclude overtly or patently parochial behavior, members of Congress were quite capable of doing the unexpected. In social science terms this could be seen as a "least likely" test of a hypothesis; that is, conditions under which one least expects the type of behavior or outcome predicted by the hypothesis. If the behavior or outcome is observed, it can be seen as strong evidence in support of the hypothesis. If under the circumstances of a dire national security emergency, Congress nevertheless indulges in parochial behavior and pork barrel politics, it strengthens the theory about the power of those tendencies. Congress did its best to confirm the theory.[69]

The global hunting license furnished by 9/11 provided the justification for the preplanned massive increases in military spending, but there were limits. Even before Iraq, the expense of the global war on terrorism in Afghanistan and elsewhere was coming into conflict with the general buildup. Moreover, as we have seen, there had been a great deal of rhetoric about transformation. One use of transformation was as another slick justification for more spending on new weapons systems. Another face of transformation, however, was that old ways of doing business had to change. This implied that some hardware planned during and for the Cold War did not harmonize with revolution in military affairs and would be cancelled. A year into the Bush administration, however, even with the toughest secretary of defense in memory, nothing had been transformed in this second sense of the concept.

With the war in Afghanistan costing around $1.5 billion per month,[70] and a rapidly rising deficit, transformation was feeling the pinch. "Those transformation investments cannot be made," argued Secretary Rumsfeld, "without terminating some programs and finding other savings."[71] In effect, Rumsfeld needed a sacrificial lamb to show that transformation meant something besides additional funds, and that the war coupled with what in 2002 could still seem like impending budgetary restrictions demanded some degree of military reform. The easiest target proved to be a piece of army artillery with the unfortunate name of "Crusader," which Rumsfeld announced he was cancelling in May 2002. Just as President Bush was forced to retract his image of the war on terror as a "crusade," the army would have to sacrifice the Crusader as one of its weapons of the future. Nevertheless, this was hardly a given. The Crusader was fully supported in the 2003 budget that President Bush had presented to Congress only a few months earlier. Moreover, reports indicated that Rumsfeld's decision was up for grabs almost until it was announced.[72]

The Crusader was a classic Cold War–era program. It was a self-propelled howitzer, essentially a cannon on a tank chassis, being developed to replace its vintage but much updated predecessor. The army's original plans in the 1990s called for the production of over 800 Crusaders. That was reduced by the end of the decade to 480 but still at a projected cost of over $11 billion, and the program had been considered for termination before Rumsfeld returned to the Pentagon.[73] The problem was that artillery was looking less and less necessary in warfare where American aircraft were unopposed and could serve as artillery for the army, especially with the increasing precision of air-dropped munitions. The Crusader, whatever its other technical merits, was heavy, difficult to transport, and expensive.

Not surprisingly, opposition to Rumsfeld's cancellation of the cannon came from the army, the program's allies in Congress, and the affected contractors. In classic bureaucratic fashion, the army was not persuaded by arguments about air power because that was controlled by the air force and navy. It was, moreover, a threat to one of the traditional army skills and missions — the artillery. In fact, a small scandal ensued when a "talking points" memo in defense of the program was discovered to have been faxed to congressional aides by a civilian army bureaucrat. The army was accused of going "behind Rumsfeld's back to lobby for the Crusader."[74] Many members of Congress did not need prompting as they leapt to criticize Rumsfeld's decision. Much of the carping was predictably and neatly linked to the geography of the Crusader's commercial contracts, including Oklahoma where the Crusader would be assembled. Senators James Inhofe and Don Nickels and Representative J. C. Watts (whose district would be most affected) fought to preserve the program and pointed to the recent change of mind by the administration as an indication that the Crusader was being singled out for political reasons.[75] Even a few liberal Democrats such as Carl Levin (from Michigan, where six companies were affected by the cancellation) had to question the decision at least by saying the process was flawed.[76] Something called the "Crusader Industrial Alliance" ran hyperbolic ads in such insider publications as *Congressional Quarterly Weekly Report* that warned, among other wild distortions, that the Crusader was "the only sure thing between our soldiers and the enemy" and that eight other countries "can easily outgun our current artillery systems."[77] If wars involved Olympic-like competitions within categories of weapons, this argument might have made some sense. They don't, and the argument was ludicrous.

Bush went so far as to warn Congress — in the first such budget threat of 2002 — that a veto might await any defense authorization bill that contravened the cancellation.[78] The fight in Congress that summer was bitter and at times it appeared that legislators might overrule Rumsfeld and the Commander in Chief. Congress seemed poised to provide an unwelcome answer to Rumsfeld's less than rhetorical question addressed to the Senate Armed Services Committee: "Is there nothing we're doing that we can ever stop?"[79] Finally, at the end of the summer, Congress ratified the Crusader's cancellation, but only after Rumsfeld and Congress had agreed to significant funding for developing the next generation of artillery as part of the Future Combat System program. If nothing else, this cushioned the blow to the contractors, principally United Defense Industries, stung by the termination of the Crusader, and much of the congressional action was an effort to save as many jobs as possible. For the first year at least the cancellation was not going to save any money.[80] The Crusader's status as a sacrificial lamb was reinforced as time went on and no other programs were cancelled. A year and a half later the Crusader was finally joined by another army program, the Comanche helicopter, which was cancelled in February 2004 after about $7 billion in expenditures. The army planned, however, to use the more than $14 billion that would have been spent on over a hundred Comanches instead to purchase and upgrade hundreds of existing models, including Black Hawks.[81] Later in 2004, under some political pressure from the Iraq war and record deficits, Rumsfeld proposed other programmatic reductions in high-profile weapons platforms, but no outright cancellations.

The extraordinary perception of the sanctity of military spending was manifest in unintentionally revealing comments made on Capitol Hill on a regular basis. Not long after Rumsfeld announced the cancellation of the Crusader, two Republican hawks, Representatives Duncan Hunter and Curt Weldon, held a press conference in part to express their dismay at the low levels of procurement funding in the president's military budget request for 2003. More money was required to avoid decisions like that which cancelled the Crusader and those funds would only come through increased political support, which the Armed Services Committee needed to foster. As Weldon saw it, the committee needed to get contractors and their dependents to bring pressure to bear in support of more defense funding. Weldon argued that "they [defense contractors] want us to plus up more funding . . . but they don't want to take the extra step to educate and sensitize their work force, their subcontractors and suppliers. . . . We understand that to fight this overall battle, we've got to . . . take on the whole mind-set of America."[82] This was an extraordinary argument given the actual prowar mind-set of America at the time (and given that Weldon and friends had supported huge tax cuts), but it was even more extraordinary that Weldon felt no compunction about arguing that the most self-interested state-sponsored industries should actively lobby on their own behalf (probably with the use of federal dollars).

Although under the circumstances congressional action on the Crusader could be considered scandalous, it was not a scandal because, aside from the brief flare-up over the army's lobbying, there were no violations of ethics rules and no laws were broken. Congress was, however, at least knee-deep in one of the few procurement scandals to emerge during the Bush presidency that was not related to the wars in Iraq and Afghanistan. The main aerial refueling tanker used by the air force, the KC-135 Stratotanker, was showing its age — the last one was delivered to the air force in 1965, though substantial modifications had been made to the fleet. Nevertheless, the air force, which had some newer tankers too, was not pushing for a replacement.[83] Members of Congress were looking for one, however, and they produced an unusual arrangement for the Pentagon to lease rather than purchase new tankers. In 2004 McCain described for the Senate the origins of the tanker deal:

Nearly 3 years ago, behind closed doors, the [Senate] Appropriations Committee slipped a $30 billion rider in the fiscal year 2002 Defense appropriations bill. This rider authorized the Air Force to lease from Boeing up to 100 767s for use as aerial refueling tankers. Before the rider appeared in the bill, Air Force leadership never came to the authorizing committees about this issue. In fact, tankers have never come up in either the President's budget or the Defense Department's unfunded priority list. The Air Force's tanker lease program was born of a virgin birth.[84]

John McCain called the proposed contract "war profiteering" that "borders on gross negligence" and voiced concern that four of the planes would be leased for travel by Bush administration officials.[85] His accusations were not hyperbole. By this point, a former high-ranking procurement officer for the air force had been convicted of public corruption for her actions on the tanker deal, and the secretary of the air force, also deeply implicated in the scandal, had submitted his resignation three days before McCain spoke on the Senate floor. The air force might not have requested new tankers, but when Congress put together the tanker-leasing deal, some air force officials were caught trying to get a good deal for themselves rather than the American taxpayer.

In September 2003 the Pentagon launched an investigation into the actions of Darleen Druyun, the former deputy assistant air force secretary for acquisition and management who had overseen the tanker negotiations before she left the Pentagon earlier that year for a job with Boeing. Boeing was the manufacturer of the planes picked for the lease deal. She was investigated for "passing information to The Boeing Co. about a rival's bid for a $21 billion contract to lease aerial tankers." Based on recovered email communications between senior Boeing officials, Druyun appeared to have given the information to Boeing in exchange for a high-paying, senior-level position. Druyun agreed to serve a nine-month federal sentence and admitted to "inflating proposed payments to Boeing." Boeing executive Michael M. Sears (who offered Druyun a $250,000 position) was also sentenced and the CEO of the corporation resigned.[86]

Despite what was then an emerging scandal, members of Congress had pushed hard for the deal. While "ultimately nothing divided House and Senate conferees as much as the tanker program" during the FY 2004 defense authorization conference, a hybrid version was signed into law on November 24, 2003 just as the air force discussed publicly for the first time a "serious corrosion problem in the tankers."[87] Early backers of the deal in Congress, particularly those from the state of Washington where the planes would be built, remained supportive of the measure despite the controversy. Senator Maria Cantwell cited post-9/11 concerns, arguing that "we cannot afford to ignore the need to modernize our tanker fleet — unlike other planes in our arsenal, there is simply no replacement to tankers. Put simply, without a modern tanker fleet, our nation's air power could be crippled."[88] Senator Ted Stevens, who claimed the leasing plan was his idea, said there was not enough money to buy the planes outright and he "just [did] not understand why we should put people to fly planes in combat that were made before their grandfathers were in the military."[89] Senator Pat Roberts argued that cost should not be an issue in matters of national security; to prove his point, he held up a "piece of fuselage from a tanker, showing a layer that was peeling away from the plane's surface."[90]

The controversy notwithstanding, with congressional approval the Pentagon in early November 2003 finalized a compromise $27 billion plan to lease twenty Boeing 767s and buy eighty more before 2014. Among others, the Washington state congressional delegation was ecstatic. Senator Patty Murray praised the deal at a press conference with Senator Maria Cantwell and Representatives Norm Dicks and Rick Larsen because it would "be a real shot in the arm for our economy and for you young men and women who protect our country."[91] Only two weeks later, however, Boeing announced the firings of Sears and Druyun and "almost immediately" Defense Secretary Rumsfeld suspended the tanker program while the Pentagon investigated its own business practices. Among others, House Speaker Dennis Hastert, who "fought to the last minute for the original lease proposal," was unhappy with Rumsfeld's decision and lamented the fact that "each day we wait is another day we don't have the tankers being built . . . the bottom line is we need the tankers . . . this is a national security issue." Republican member Todd Tiahrt, who represented Wichita, Kansas, where the planes built in Washington state would be converted, said, "It feels like we've been running a race and they keep moving the finish line."[92]

Despite House and Senate attempts to resurrect the program, the tanker agreement was dead. In June 2005 the Pentagon's inspector general issued a 270-page report that detailed how rules were violated in a rush to bypass procedure. The inspector general also noted that Druyun "did not operate in a vacuum" and that, in addition to members of Congress, officials at the air force, Pentagon, and possibly the White House helped push the deal.[93] In April 2006, the Pentagon gave the air force the authority to start a competition for tanker production, this time for purchase, not lease, with the intention of awarding the contract by summer 2007. This led, in turn, to more turbulence when Boeing successfully protested the award to a bid by Northrop Grumman and the European Aeronautic Defence and Space Company. The future of military aerial refueling was still undetermined by the end of the Bush presidency after Defense Secretary Robert Gates cancelled further competition over the program in September 2008, calling for a "cooling off" period.[94]

Hitching a Ride(r): The Pork Barrel of National Security

Despite the fact that the Crusader was ultimately canceled and the tanker lease deal stopped, these cases evinced just how far members of Congress would go and how much cover the war on terror would provide. Nearly anything could and would be linked to "supporting the troops" and "winning the war." But much did not have to be because Congress, even in the face of what would become an increasingly expensive and unpopular war in Iraq, was still adept at the kind of relatively quiet distributive politics that function so well in flush times. During the years after 9/11, Congress produced a significant increase in "earmarks" in the military budget. When the defense budget was climbing at an average of 7 percent a year not counting the hundreds of billions in war-funding supplementals, who was going to quibble over minor changes and additions?

Earmarks (sometimes called "member projects") refer to items added by members of Congress that are not requested by the administration or the relevant bureaucracy that typically "target benefits to a particular company, organization or locality."[95] Moreover, these items would not have been added by the relevant congressional committee were it not for the particular request by an individual member or small number of members. Earmarks are commonly associated with pork barrel spending and waste. Whether wasteful or not, billions of dollars in military earmarks were doled out after 9/11, often in increments between $1 million and $3 million, and usually directly benefitting interests in the state or district of the sponsoring member. During the FY 2007 appropriations process, Senator James Talent of Missouri led an effort to add $2.1 billion for ten C-17 cargo planes, a program the Pentagon wanted to discontinue. Alaska Senator Ted Stevens included $1.2 million for prostate cancer research. For 2008, Representative Solomon Ortiz of Texas attached $3 million in funding for something called a Virtual Clinic Learning Lab at the University of Texas, Corpus Christi.[96]

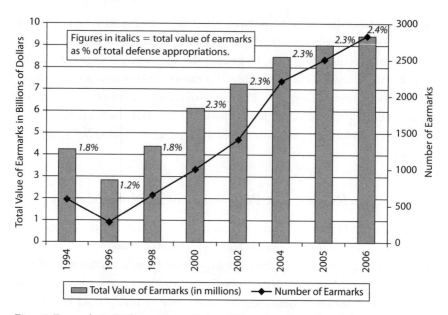

Fig. 5.8. Earmarks in Defense Appropriations Bills, 1994–2006. *Source:* Congressional Research Service.

Relevant or ridiculous, earmarks in defense appropriations bills shot up with the Bush buildup. According to studies by the Congressional Research Service, the dollar value of military earmarks increased steadily from 2000 to 2006, increasing by 54 percent over that period, faster than the increase in the overall (nonwar) defense budget. The number of earmarks grew by 186 percent from 997 in 2000 to 2,847 in 2006 (fig. 5.8).[97] On the one hand, rising from just 2.28 percent to only 2.36 percent of total defense appropriations, earmarks can be seen as insignificant because they constitute such a small percentage of the total budget. On the other hand, by 2006 such add-ons totaled $9.43 billion and collectively exceeded the annual spending on any individual weapons system, such as the F-22 fighter or a new aircraft carrier, and even the total annual spending for the Ballistic Missile Defense program (which consists of many individual elements and contracts).[98]

The academic literature on Congress often finds its place and purpose in correcting or modifying popular — read unfavorable — perceptions or conventional wisdoms about congressional action. For example, campaign donations by special interests, generally thought to influence the behavior if not the votes of members of Congress, are often shown to have generally benign or ambiguous effects. In this vein, earmarks or pork barrel projects have sometimes been cast in a more positive light by demonstrating, for example, how they are used to build legislative majorities for legislation that benefits the general public.[99] This argument is at once strange and unremarkable. If anything it reinforces the view of Congress as parochial and self-centered insofar as legislative leaders have to bribe members with distributive goodies even to pass major policy issues on their merits. In any event, this cautiously positive perspective on pork has little to say about congressional action on military appropriations in the wake of 9/11. The money being spent on national security in such a crisis and during war qualifies as legislation in the general interest. With so many lives and the security of the nation supposedly at stake, these military appropriation bills did not need earmarks to gain legislative support. In fact, it was quite the reverse. The massive money train was going to leave the legislative station unimpeded, so it was time to get on board. With all this funding going to support the war and the troops, there was plenty of room. These bills attracted virtually no scrutiny and few negative votes as the earmarks were loaded aboard the money train.

Congress Swings Briefly into Action: The Dubai Port Incident and the Winds of Change

Despite hundreds of signing statements, proof of torture, prisoner renditions, and revelations of illegal wiretaps, congressional parochialism and complicity in and subservience to presidential power remained the rule through the 2006 elections. The fight over the Crusader, the only instance in which Congress directly confronted and tried to veto a somewhat significant administration decision in the area of national security, was eclipsed, in irony if nothing else, four years later in February and March of 2006 by a brief eruption over the corporate management of U.S. ports. A decision by the Bush administration to allow operational control of some major U.S. ports by a firm based in Dubai and owned by the government of Dubai, part of the United Arab Emirates, elicited a sharp and politically effective congressional response. In a matter of days Bush confronted and capitulated to the most significant congressional threat to his control of issues related to national security after 9/11.

The UAE firm, DP World, wanted to purchase the British company that had the job of managing six major U.S. ports and various other terminal facilities.

Such an arrangement required review and approval by a relatively obscure inter-agency panel called the Committee on Foreign Investment in the United States, which is chaired by the secretary of the treasury and reviews foreign acquisitions that could impact national security.[100] The panel approved the acquisition, but reports in mid-February about the change created a media and political fire-storm, even though, relative to major actions the administration had taken, this was a tempest in a teapot. Because the issue involved a company controlled by a Middle Eastern government with potential control over port security, one of the focal areas of post-9/11 homeland security, opposition to the administration's move was cost free and nearly reflexive. Many Republicans and conservatives came out against the deal, including the Republican speaker of the House and the Senate majority leader, as did prominent Democrats and liberals. At first, Bush fought back in characteristic fashion and threatened to veto any congressional attempts to overturn the acquisition, but then he backed off when informed by congressional leaders from his own party that the votes were there to override a veto. The strength of congressional opposition was later evinced in a 348 to 71 vote in the House on an amendment to prevent the deal. Such legislation would prove unnecessary when DP World announced that it would put its recent ac-quisition up for sale to an American concern. This diffused the crisis, but the rapidity and forcefulness of the congressional reaction was without parallel in the Bush presidency. The relatively disproportionate reaction spoke volumes about the perverse politics of national security.[101]

The Dubai ports episode was a harbinger of change. No matter how trivial the substance might have seemed when compared to so many other things on which Congress might have challenged the president, the unprecedented reaction indi-cated that the winds had shifted. Bush no longer had firm control over the Republican majority that had served his administration with all but unquestion-ing obedience for five years. The year 2005 had been a very bad one for the war in Iraq, and 2006 would be a nightmare, beginning with a sharp upsurge in sectarian violence and civilian casualties following the bombing of a mosque in Samarra. The administration and U.S. military had lost control of the conflict. Public support for the war and the president were sinking rapidly. The politics of crisis and war that had been the foundation of the Bush presidency was crumbling. Democrats looked forward to the midterm congressional elections as circum-stances began to augur a reversal of fortune. Iraq was the signal issue and the Democratic majority would have its hands full trying to change the direction of the war. Even if increasingly unpopular, Bush was still president and commander in chief. That the Democrats might have the time, energy, or inclination to confront the buildup under such circumstances looked unlikely. They would have the opportunity, however. Despite the setbacks, President Bush early in the new year and in the face of the new Democratic majority would submit his largest defense budget alongside the largest single supplemental war request.

CHAPTER SIX

PAYING THE PRICE
From Bush to Obama

Not long after the attacks of 9/11, the nation learned that for the Bush administration the crisis was not really about Al Qaeda and Afghanistan but about Iraq. In some important ways, as we have seen, the crisis was not really about Iraq either but rather about rearmament and unprecedented military superiority. Well into his second term, despite the rising unpopularity of the war and his presidency, President George W. Bush and his administration retained a cavalier adamance about the wars and the wider project of global domination. The Democratic Congress was confounded in its brief attempts to change the course of the war and went back to signing off on the endless bills for it with hardly a protest. Soon the 2008 campaign for the presidency would reveal, in spite of the gravity of events, how shallow the national dialogue could be on national security.

The Bush presidency and the campaign to replace him would be whipsawed by parallel crises in energy and the economy, crises that should have indicated to everyone involved just how misguided and dangerous the national obsession with military power had been. Barack Obama, whose election provided a brief respite from the economic storm, would begin his presidency amid a crisis that threatened to eclipse his historic victory. Abraham Lincoln took office just in time for a war that would define his presidency from start to finish, and Franklin Roosevelt inherited a depression and later led the nation into war. Obama's presidency commenced with two protracted wars and an unfolding economic disaster. Added to this daunting set of challenges were the costs and legacies of the Bush military buildup.

Not Ready to Make Nice, Not Ready to Back Down

On February 6, 2006, the Pentagon released the second Quadrennial Defense Review (QDR) Report of the Bush administration. A month later, the 2006 National Security Strategy (NSS) of the United States appeared. The 2001 QDR, with its doctrines of dissuasion and capabilities-based planning, along with the 2002 National Security Strategy and its declaration of preemption and articulation of the imperial mission, can be seen as the founding documents of the functional equivalent of a new cold war. Four years on, as the first implementation of preemption was looking a lot like a quagmire, would the Bush administration reassess? In many ways, 2006 was the turning point in the Iraq War, and so documents written toward the end of 2005 and the early weeks of 2006 might not have fully reflected the implications of the downward spiral in the conflict as well as the accompanying decline of American public opinion. Nevertheless, the sanguine formulations of the two newer documents were breathtaking. If the founding documents from 2001 and 2002 were astounding for their breadth and boldness, the 2006 reports were remarkable for their myopic persistence in the face of grim realities.

"America is at war." Thus began the president's letter presenting the 2006 NSS.[1] This was a deceptively simple, at some level undeniable, observation, one that could serve as an opening to an acknowledgement of lessons learned, adjustments, and tradeoffs. But the first sentence of the NSS proper quickly clarified the implication of the president's introduction. The crusade would continue: "It is the policy of the United States to seek and support democratic movements and institutions in every nation and culture, with the ultimate goal of ending tyranny in our world."[2] If not quite "rid the world of evil," it was a grand ambition nevertheless. Stated in this way, it elided and evaded the overwhelmingly military character of the war on terror. The means to the end might be varied — indeed the 2006 NSS, much like its predecessor, devoted considerable space to free trade, diplomacy, and all sorts of nonmilitary initiatives — but within the context of American actions over the preceding years it probably struck the few who were paying attention to the new document as either unconvincing or too little too late.

Instead, the martial elements of the 2006 NSS sounded tragically familiar and in some cases were unintentionally defensive. For example, "The place of preemption in our national security strategy remains the same." This would be an odd statement to make unless it was a response to the obvious conclusion already reached by many Americans that Iraq proved preemption to be a very dangerous and flawed strategy, especially when based on inflated threats and questionable handling of intelligence data. The closest the document came to an acknowledgement of how the path to preemption was paved with faulty or false claims — "pre-war intelligence estimates of Iraqi WMD stockpiles were wrong" — was immediately turned into a positive lesson for next time: "We must learn from this experience if we are to counter successfully the very real threat of proliferation." Moreover, after admitting that Saddam Hussein was being coy about his weapons of mass destruction (WMD) program and making suppositions about its status as a deterrent against Iran, the NSS concluded that "Saddam's strategy of bluff, denial, and deception is a dangerous game that dictators play at their peril." In other words, even though the United States was paying a very high cost for its actions, it served as a warning for others.[3]

If the 2006 NSS was not ready to make nice, it was ready to use false dichotomies in service of its political ends. Written at a time when the war was getting increasingly unpopular and the president's approval was dropping steadily, Bush dared to claim that "America now faces a choice between the path of fear and the path of confidence. The path of fear — isolationism and protectionism, retreat and retrenchment — appeals to those who find our challenges too great and fail to see our opportunities." Even for an administration steeped in ironic doublespeak, this was a remarkable statement — first, for its claim that the Bush administration represented confidence rather than fear; and second, for the sophomoric dichotomy between the path of confidence and its contrast, an abyss of retreat and retrenchment. The "path of confidence" in the 2006 NSS remained an open-ended commitment to global restructuring and wars of expansive scope and indefinite duration.[4]

The Quadrennial Defense Review Report of 2006 opened on a similar bellicose note with the claim that the "United States is a nation engaged in what will be a long war." But this long war was no longer the all-encompassing Global War on Terrorism; instead, the new QDR offered a somewhat awkward reformulation of the grand cause. The United States was in "a global war against violent extremists who use terrorism as their weapon of choice, and who seek to destroy our free way of life." This was a version of the "struggle against violent extremism" (SAVE) that Rumsfeld trotted out in 2005 in part to escape the criticism that the global war on terror was a war against a tactic, not an enemy or ideology. But this new version was no less global or expansive.[5] The 2006 QDR reasserted the primacy of capabilities-based planning and dissuasion in addition to the entire project of global hegemony on land, at sea, in the air, and in outer space. In fact, this QDR put some emphasis on the need for even more capabilities to shape, dissuade, and deter, including global strike, discussed in chapter 5, with its attendant requirement of "broader authorities from the Congress." Despite some language about limits, like its predecessor the new QDR made no tough decisions about resources. Nearly any weapon or technology was essential because the commitments were likewise all but boundless, with the retention of the inevitable, seemingly immortal, two-simultaneous-war requirement, backed by the option of decisive defeat in one war and the ability to mount lesser contingency operations at the same time.

The reality of conflicts over the intervening years was recognized, much as in the 2006 NSS, in a somewhat backhanded manner. The QDR noted that "in this era, characterized by uncertainty and surprise," one example of the "new strategic environment" is a change from "conducting war against nations — to conducting war in countries we are not at war with." The novelty of this is at best questionable. Vietnam, for example, comes to mind, not to mention the fact that most of World War II was fought outside Germany and Japan. That a preemptive attack on Iraq was not a war with Iraq is a conceptual leap of considerable magnitude, as was the claim that such a preemptive attack is somehow connected to an era of "uncertainty and surprise," unless the authors were talking about U.S. policy and preemption itself. In the context of discussing the two-simultaneous-war requirement, the report noted that "operational end-states defined in terms of 'swiftly-defeating' or 'winning decisively' against adversaries may be less useful for some types of operations U.S. forces may be directed to conduct, such as . . . conducting a long-duration, irregular warfare campaign against enemies employing asymmetric tactics." This might be thought of as a way of describing the "long war" but in another sense it seemed to be a way of describing, after the fact, what was happening at the time in Iraq, which was fighting a "long-duration, irregular warfare campaign" in a "country with which we are not at war," as though that had been the plan all along. A cliché about military planners throughout history is that they often made the mistake of forging plans for the war of the future by basing their strategy and tactics on lessons from the most recent conflict; that is, they plan to fight the last war all over again. In 2006 the Pentagon, it would seem, was planning to fight the last war before it was even over.[6]

The parallels between the long war and the Cold War were not lost on the authors of either document, though they invoked them in a positive and assertive fashion. "The United States is in the early years of a long struggle," the 2006 NSS noted, "similar to what our country faced in the early years of the Cold War."[7] Likewise the 2006 QDR opened by reminding Americans that when President Bush took office, "the country was . . . still savoring victory in the Cold War — the culmination of that long struggle that occupied generations of Americans." These were not lamentations; they were, rather, somewhat hollow attempts at Churchillian exhortation. Instead of bemoaning the fact that we had created the moral, political, institutional, and fiscal equivalent of a new Cold War, we were to embrace it as a new challenge. By 2006 this call to arms failed to resonate. What sounded new and robust to some in 2001 and 2002 appealed now to very few beyond the remaining diehards in the administration and some unrepentant neoconservatives and Republican pundits.

Just as the wisdom of preemption was in doubt as a result of Iraq, another Bush doctrine — dissuasion — was being discredited around the globe. Unwittingly, one assumes, Secretary of Defense Donald Rumsfeld, who first advanced the doctrine of dissuasion, later revealed the extent of its failure. Commenting on China's military spending at a regional security conference in Singapore in early June 2005, Rumsfeld posed what he probably thought were probing questions. "Since no nation threatens China," he began, "one must wonder: Why this growing investment? Why these continuing large and expanding arms purchases?" Later that year during his first visit to China, Rumsfeld raised concerns about that nation's level of military spending, claiming it was much higher than reported by that country's government.[8] Although Rumsfeld meant these comments clearly as a criticism of China and as a rhetorical attempt to put pressure on China to justify its actions, his remarks revealed something else altogether — the failure of dissuasion. As one of the few nations on earth toward which the policy of dissuasion could have been directed (assuming it was a sincere policy in the first place), China would be the key test of the doctrine in action. In fact, the significant and sustained acceleration in China's military expenditures and modernization programs did not come until the Bush administration and its buildup, a fact documented and highlighted by the Bush administration's own reports.[9] If by mid-2005, a few years into a massive U.S. buildup, the secretary of defense felt compelled to draw attention to significant increases in Chinese efforts and expenditures, then something was not quite right with the policy. Rumsfeld and the Pentagon may never have believed China could truly compete with the United States, but they could sincerely think that the increases in China's military efforts, even if trivial in comparison to the U.S. budget, still mattered as far as regional security. If that is true, it then points to the absurd nature of the doctrine — it was addressed to no one (except perhaps to those who supply funds to the Pentagon).

As pointed out in the discussion of dissuasion in chapter 4, it was easy to guess that many of our closest friends and allies would be the ones dissuaded insofar as they could take a free ride on American military excess. As things turned out, with the exception of the United Kingdom, whose decision to join the United States in the war on Iraq contributed mightily to a 25 percent real increase in its military budget between 2000 and 2005, Europe did not step up defense spending to join in the long war and struggle. Military spending in Western Europe, including Great Britain, increased a rather modest 4 percent in real terms between 2000 and 2004 and then dropped a bit in 2005 and 2006 to a 2.5 percent increase overall. Great Britain's budget even decreased slightly after peaking in 2005. Excluding the United States and Canada, expenditures by the original sixteen NATO nations on military personnel and equipment barely moved between 2000 and 2005. Germany's military spending dropped 10 percent by 2007. Japan's national security budget increased just over 2 percent in real terms between 2000 and 2003 before dropping back to the level of 2000 by 2006. In contrast, sustained real increases did occur in the Middle East (36 percent) and East Asia (35 percent) where some nations were generally less friendly toward the United States.[10]

Whether or not the putative enemies of the United States were spending more, some indisputably decided or discovered that the quickest fix and cheapest path to keeping the United States at bay was through the acquisition of nuclear weapons. The basic premise of dissuasion was correct. The United States was so far ahead that relatively poor countries such as North Korea, Syria, Iran, and Iraq could never hope to compete with the United States in military power. Recognition of this reality, however, predated the doctrine of dissuasion and its use as a justification for getting even further ahead by spending still more. It is implausible that these countries had not premised their security policies on some sort of asymmetrical strategy, however deluded or mistaken in some cases.[11] That is, they would not, or could not, try to match the United States but they could seek some way to offset or mitigate the advantages of U.S. superiority. The use of WMDs was one such avenue; North Korea, for example, was able to use nuclear weapons as effective leverage against U.S. power especially after the invasion of Iraq.

By this point, in spite of the confident rhetoric pervading the administration's statements of national security policy, Iraq was taking almost everything in the wrong direction. In the shadow of that war, the conflict in Afghanistan drew less attention from the media and American public for some time, long enough for it to be frequently labeled the "forgotten war" by journalists and others.[12] As in Iraq, things were not going well in the forgotten war, and heading into 2006, an election year, the news from both countries would only get worse.

The New Democratic Majority: Not Ready to Step Up

By the start of 2006, support for the Iraq War was heading toward 40 percent in most polls. That figure would decline, depending on the exact form of the question polled, to near 30 percent by the fall and the eve of the congressional elections. Predictably, Bush's handling of the war received equally poor ratings, and approval of his overall job performance was tightly linked to opinion on the war (fig. 6.1). The war was the signal national issue heading into the elections. In polls before the election the vast majority of Americans said that the Iraq War would be extremely or very important in their vote (82 percent).[13] Other issues, including corruption from lobbying scandals and resulting Republican resignations, shaped the elections and some specific races.[14] Regardless, with the winds of war now in their favor, Democrats gained control of both chambers of Congress for the first since 1994, with net gains of thirty-one seats in the House and six seats in the Senate.

Nevertheless, the elections did little to disturb the buildup that was proceeding without a debate. The Democrats owed much of their victory to the state of the war, but once in power they had a tough time end-gaming Iraq without undermining their fragile credibility on defense; all the more reason to turn a blind eye to the overall military budget no matter how large and arguably unjustified. In fact, just after the Democrats took control of Congress, the February release of the president's proposed 2008 budget revealed how little had changed politically. "This is a huge number," said House Speaker Nancy Pelosi, presumably referring to the nearly $650 billion that the administration was requesting to fund both the Pentagon's regular budget and the war. As the administration was asking for several large appropriations all at once, there were several figures that

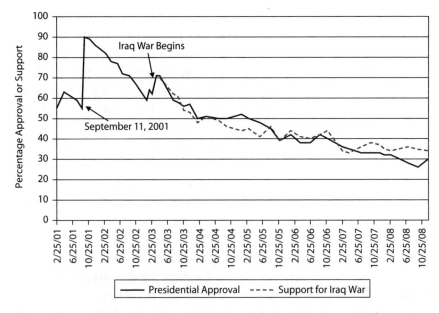

Fig. 6.1. Support for President George W. Bush and the Iraq War. *Source:* Washington Post/ABC News Polls. Support for President Bush was gauged by the question: Do you approve or disapprove of the way George W. Bush is handling his job as president? Support for the Iraq War was measured by the question: All in all . . . do you think the war with Iraq was worth fighting, or not?

might be considered "huge." First there was the extra $100 billion war supplemental for 2007 (to supplement the $70 billion already appropriated that year). Next was the $142 billion war supplemental for 2008. And last, but certainly not least, was the approximately $504 billion for the regular military budget, about a 10 percent increase from the year before. All together the president was asking for three-quarters of a trillion dollars, and this did not include funds for the Department of Homeland Security. Even these extraordinary numbers generated little outrage or even inquiry and failed to pierce the shroud that had all but enveloped the massive military buildup that proceeded apart from and in addition to the war on terror. Like Pelosi, some Democrats expressed alarm at the astronomical figures presented, but that was about it. Instead, Democrats were quick to note that in spite of their concerns, "we clearly want to make sure our troops have everything they need."[15] "Democrats pledge," said Senate Majority Leader Harry Reid, "that our troops will receive everything they need to do their jobs."[16]

Spending for the war was vaulting past the half-trillion mark on its way toward exceeding the total real spending on the nearly ten years of the Vietnam War. Simultaneously, the regular defense budget was increasing by over 10 percent the same year the Democrats took over Congress. War spending and the military budget were increasing independently and by leaps and bounds. This was another indication of just how much the politics of 9/11 was alive and well despite the sea change in the fortunes of war and the tide of public opinion. The new Democratic majority, joined by an increasing number of disillusioned Republicans, would concentrate on changing policy in Iraq. Whether they could "support the troops" by bringing them home as soon as possible was very much in question. Far more certain was that supporting the troops meant neither the supplemental war appropriations nor the Pentagon budget was seriously questioned or challenged. As we will soon see, even the campaign to see who would replace George Bush and inherit his legacy in national security and military spending would not trouble these waters. Until the end of Bush's presidency, his buildup would remain just below the surface, largely out of view.

If the buildup was conspicuous by its absence as an issue, the Iraq War was front and center. And yet despite the message sent by the voting in November, the congressional elections were followed by developments and decisions that indicated how little change might come of it. Much of the news focused on the seemingly abrupt resignation of Donald Rumsfeld the day after the elections, but that was rather unsurprising in substance if not timing. As embarrassing as it might seem for the administration to risk the appearance that the resignation followed the election results, it at least flowed logically from the outcome. Amid the postelection turmoil, with the resignation of Rumsfeld and the release of the Iraq Study Group report (which was very critical of the handling of the war), the nation anticipated a new plan for Iraq. The president, however, informed the nation and the world that he was "not going to be rushed" into making his decision. Given that decisions about the war never should have depended on an election or a study group, many might have wondered at the concept of being "rushed" when in late November 2006 the U.S. "cakewalk" in Iraq had just eclipsed in duration the U.S. involvement in World War II. The president spoke as though the war were some sort of surprise that had only recently come to his attention.

The first change was Bush's decision to send more troops to Iraq in an effort to gain control of Baghdad. The so-called surge — not an escalation — enjoyed few vocal supporters outside of Bush and Senator John McCain, who had been calling for more troops for several years. The top uniformed military advisors to the president, the Joint Chiefs of Staff, did not ask for the troop surge and favored instead a change in strategy to provide greater support to Iraqi units. Bush also replaced the military commanders in charge of operations in Iraq with those who were more supportive of the surge.[17]

Secondly, on December 19, 2006, the day after Robert Gates was sworn in as secretary of defense to replace Donald Rumsfeld, President Bush announced that he asked Gates to make a recommendation on a permanent increase in the size of the army and marines.[18] The timing and irony were self-evident. Rumsfeld, the advocate of a transformed military that would rely less on troops and architect of an Iraq invasion with fewer troops than the army wanted, was barely out the door before the administration performed a quick about-face and pushed for a substantial increase in ground troops. Instead of realizing that the war was a mistake and that the policy of imperial overreach had failed, the elite response (and a bipartisan response at that) was to intensify the war and increase the national military capacity for intervention abroad. After all, if the surge in Iraq was temporary, and everyone agreed that the permanent troops would come on too slowly to help in that regard, then what was the permanent increase for? If the public was rejecting nation-building and other imperial projects unrelated to a war on scattered groups that did not control particular states, then what would a permanent increase in the size of the armed forces accomplish?

Several years earlier, Congress had authorized a supposedly temporary increase of 30,000 in the size of the active-duty army as a response to the attacks of 9/11, which took the army from about 484,000 to 514,000. That temporary increase was not even complete by the end of 2006, but by that point army officials were treating 514,000 as a permanent floor.[19] Prior to Bush's announcement, permanent increases had been endorsed by Democrats and others often critical of the administration's policies in Iraq and elsewhere, including the *Washington Post* and *New York Times*, which called for an increase of between 75,000 and 100,000.[20] Another effort, coordinated by the neoconservatives who had spearheaded the cause of regime change in Iraq since the 1990s, concluded that the United States "should aim for an increase in the active duty Army and Marine Corps, together, of at least 25,000 troops each year over the next several years."[21] In January 2007 Gates recommended to the president a permanent increase of 92,000, with 65,000 more soldiers for the army and 27,000 additional marines.

The Four Percent Fraud

As the administration was preparing to add thousands of new soldiers — another expensive and unnecessary element to the buildup — Bush and his allies were trying to promote a view of military spending that made the record-setting military budgets seem reasonable. In 2007 as Bush prepared the largest defense budget and war-spending requests of his administration, public debate was being shaped by conservatives and defenders of the administration to view things in a rather different manner. Proponents of high military spending began to talk about the right level of military spending almost exclusively in terms of its percentage of the economy. This legerdemain turned the elephant of the largest military buildup since World War II into a mouse. In a short time it would become a mantra, repeated incessantly by key actors on this side of the debate, if debate is even a fair way to characterize what became essentially a one-sided conversation. Almost any form of governmental spending — military or otherwise — looks small when compared to the largest economy in the world, especially if that economy is growing. Government spending can increase significantly in real dollars without appearing to grow at all if measured by its relation to the size of the economy, typically measured as its gross domestic product. Even modest economic growth can obscure major increases in actual spending. Given the hundreds of billions that were added to the military budget, both because of the wars and otherwise, this particular measure became the only way to make the military budget look smaller and manageable.

But mere reasonableness and perspective — as in "this is simply an important way to think about the relative burden of the military budget" — was never the goal. Instead, measuring the military budget as a percentage of the economy was elevated to the status of principle — it was touted as the central measure of the national commitment to security. In early 2007, the conservative Heritage Foundation started a campaign called "Four Percent for Freedom."[22] The nation, the argument went, should commit itself to an absolute floor of 4 percent of GDP for national defense. The rationale consisted of several points, but it was anchored to an argument about the historical relationship between the size of military spending and the size of the economy. Otherwise, how would one know whether 4 percent is a lot or a little? Even with the war and significant increases in ordinary military spending, by 2006 military spending represented 4 percent of the fabulously large U.S. economy. When compared to the years of the Cold War from

1950 through 1990, during which military spending averaged about 7.6 percent of the economy, 4 percent was a small share. The advocates of this way of looking at things wanted policy- and opinionmakers to draw the conclusion that 4 percent would not be a burden to the economy and would represent a sustainable floor below which military spending should not drop. This would allow for stable planning and progress at home and consistent calculations by potential enemies abroad about our commitments.[23]

By this logic, national security spending would not have to be justified by facts on the ground, by demonstrated need, but rather by its relatively light burden on the economy and the fact that the future would be more stable and knowable. Did it matter that national security needs might have no relationship to the size of the economy? The advocates of this view would never, of course, have agreed to a similar percentage-based proposition about education or welfare or anything else unconnected to national security. Arguments about whether national security deserves a special status notwithstanding, this campaign reeked of political convenience. September 11 had become the fulcrum with which to reintroduce Reagan-sized defense budgets and a way had to be found to sustain this tactic as the emergency faded and the war ground its way toward an uncertain conclusion. The Four Percent for Freedom campaign was an attempt to elide arguments about missions, burdens, and need and simply emplace a rather lofty floor. If taken seriously, however, strict adherence to such a policy could produce some interesting consequences. If the economy were to grow at a rapid pace, then would military spending increase accordingly without any reference to threats or requirements? What if the economy actually shrank? Such considerations aside, even if the campaign succeeded on a mostly rhetorical or symbolic level, which was probably the main goal, it would make anything less than 4 percent seem questionable.

All too quickly, that is what began to happen. Republican presidential candidates discussed defense spending almost exclusively in terms of its percentage of GDP, and some leading contenders referred to or explicitly endorsed the 4 percent concept.[24] The GDP measure was used by members of Congress as a way to make the astounding budgets seem reasonable. For example, at an October 2007 hearing before the House Budget Committee, the CBO projected that the long-term total costs of the wars in Iraq and Afghanistan could reach $2.4 trillion dollars. Democrats were already stunned by the size of the 2007 supplemental war request, which totaled $190 billion. To rebut the testimony about the skyrocketing costs of war, the ranking Republican Representative Paul Ryan argued

"that the costs of the wars in Iraq and Afghanistan, when measured by the percentage of the gross national product going to defense-related spending, is low
compared to previous conflicts and the average during the Cold War."[25] That
same month at a press conference with Defense Secretary Gates, the new chairman of the Joint Chiefs of Staff, Admiral Mike Mullen, noted that while the
defense budget was "higher now than it's ever been," it was about 4 percent of
GDP, "and I would see that in the future as an absolute floor."[26] A *New York Times*
reporter, covering Mullen's remarks, then went on to devote an entire paragraph
in the article to making the point that 4 percent was historically on the low side,
with no other context or qualifications. Marine Commandant General Conway
also used the historical comparison to 4 percent as a way to put the buildup and
war in perspective.[27] Secretary Gates himself defended the high level of spending
in February 2007 by arguing that "the amount of money the United States is
projected to spend on defense this year is actually a smaller percentage of GDP
(gross domestic product) than when I left government 14 years ago following the
end of the Cold War." A year later as part of presenting the FY 2009 military
budget, the Pentagon press secretary said that the "secretary believes that whenever we transition away from war supplementals, the Congress should dedicate 4
percent of our GDP to funding national security. That is what he believes to be a
reasonable price to stay free and protect our interests around the world."[28]

Notice what this line of argument implied. It was all but an admission that the
wars did not cause the increase in the regular military budget, and that the war
funding, in fact, was being used to supplement the separate buildup. The wars
were there for the buildup far more than the buildup was there for the wars. Why
else, as we "transition away from war supplementals" and the wars wind down and
end, would Congress have to increase defense spending to 4 percent of GDP? It
would be hard to imagine something closer to an official confirmation, however
unintentional, of the central argument this book makes about the Bush buildup.

Just at the GDP could help make military spending look small, the Iraq War —
whatever its impact on the economy — was used to make the Pentagon's material
needs substantial and urgent despite the record levels of funding. The allegedly
"broken" or "nearly broken" or "breakable" armed forces, which were claimed to
be near, at, or beyond the breaking point because of the war in Iraq, became
another justification for more defense spending over and above the vast increases
for the wars. The Heritage Foundation in 2007, as part of the Four Percent for
Freedom campaign, was anticipating yet another hollow force. This one, they
argued, could follow the disengagement (victorious or otherwise) from Iraq, as

the support for military spending waned and the pressure from mandatory programs such as Social Security increased. Indeed, the conjurers of this specter had the audacity to use a baseless analogy to the U.S. military in 1950 at the start of the Korean War, going so far as to argue that "today, our military faces similar obstacles."[29] The wars that helped hide the huge increases in military spending were by 2007 doing double-duty, producing the messy fallout and consequences that justified the maintenance of very large Pentagon budgets once the wars were winding down or over. As we will see, these specious perspectives on defense spending became important elements in what little debate there was on this subject during the 2008 presidential campaign.

By early 2008 the downward spiral in the economy had replaced the Iraq War as the major issue on the minds of Americans. This raised the question of whether the war (not high military spending in general) was contributing to the bad times at home.[30] The president himself rejected this possibility on more than one occasion. During a February TV interview while in Africa, President Bush stated that he did not think the "economy . . . is suffering because of this war." "I don't agree with that," stated the president. "I think, actually, the spending on the war might help with jobs . . . because we're buying equipment, and people are working. I think this economy is down because we built too many houses."[31] In an early April national poll in 2008, 67 percent of respondents "said that the war had contributed 'a lot' to American economic problems."[32] Also in April, in prepared remarks in defense of the war, the president put the cost of the conflict into what was becoming an all-too-familiar context:

> Some in Washington argue that the war costs too much money. There's no doubt that the costs of this war have been high. But during other major conflicts in our history, the relative cost has been even higher. Think about the Cold War. During the Truman and Eisenhower administrations, our defense budget rose as high as 13 percent of our total economy. Even during the Reagan administration, when our economy expanded significantly, the defense budget still accounted for about 6 percent of GDP. Our citizens recognized that the imperative of stopping Soviet expansion justified this expense. Today, we face an enemy that is not only expansionist in its aims, but has actually attacked our homeland — and intends to do so again. Yet our defense budget accounts for just over 4 percent of our economy — less than our commitment at any point during the four decades of the Cold War. This is still a large amount of money, but it is modest — a modest fraction of our nation's wealth — and it pales when compared to the cost of another terrorist attack on our people.[33]

At about the same time the president was expressing his opinion on the relationship between the war and the economy, Nobel Prize–winning economist Joseph Stiglitz published a co-authored book entitled *The Three Trillion Dollar War*.[34] The authors argued that supplemental appropriations to cover the immediate costs of the war, while enormous, did not reflect the full, long-term cost of the conflict. Major costs such as significant increases in veteran benefits and the interest on the debt attributable to the war added considerably to the present and future burden. The budget for the Department of Veterans Affairs (VA), for example, grew faster than nonwar Pentagon spending, increasing by 85 percent, from $47 billion to $88 billion between 2001 and 2008, with the president and Congress rapidly adding over 10 percent to the VA in 2008 in response to the scandal about sordid conditions and treatment of wounded veterans at facilities such as Walter Reed Army Medical Center.[35] The admonition to "support the troops" had enabled military spending and a buildup that had little to do with that honorable but increasingly jaded sentiment, and now it was revealed that, despite the hundreds of billions for war and the Pentagon's other priorities, there had not been enough to pay for decent treatment and facilities.

Moreover, the authors showed that the macroeconomic costs to the economy (including high oil prices and opportunity costs) far outweighed the war-related "jobs" cited by the president. Americans were misled twice on the issue of costs. First, the administration fostered and defended unrealistically low estimates of the costs, and then it allowed the mounting expenses of the war to be deficit-financed. In fact, instead of a tax increase to fund the war, Americans received more tax cuts. As the authors argue, this masked the cost of the war and lowered potential opposition to it, because Americans did not bear any increased financial burden. But the obligation was just delayed. The hundreds of billions added to the debt would, at the very least, increase U.S. government interest payments for years to come. In this way, the money, unavailable for more productive purposes, would be twice wasted.

The Costs and Consequences of Privatization

As part of this actuarial assessment of the Iraq War, we may ask how privatization fared. As noted in chapter 3, the first Bush presidency and the Clinton administration implemented policies that increased the use of private contractors to handle many basic and essential military functions, not just those at home on bases and in depots. Reliance on private contractors was structured into the Pentagon's ability to use force abroad for any extended period of time. The extent to which this was true became apparent to many Americans only well into the Iraq War. The abuses by private contractors in Iraq has filled several volumes, and I will only touch on some aspects relevant for the purposes of this analysis.[36]

Defense Secretary Rumsfeld, along with others in the administration, believed that the Iraq invasion would mirror the Gulf War of 1991, a quick, decisive action relying on the vast superiority of U.S. military might and technology. The war, Rumsfeld said, "could last six days, six weeks. I doubt six months."[37] As part of this belief in a short, decisive conflict, Rumsfeld insisted on keeping initial troop levels low. The use of private contractors enabled the Pentagon to carry out its mission while keeping the number of troops well below what otherwise would have been needed, offering "the potential backstop of additional forces but at no political cost."[38]

However brief the initial invasion, it was not decisive. With the protracted occupation and grind of the insurgency, the increasingly massive use of contractors soon became part of the controversy surrounding the war. Investigations into waste, fraud, and abuse by private contractors in Iraq would proliferate, and some would be implicated in the deaths of Iraqi civilians. To a lesser extent, the sheer size and extent of the private side of the war effort would become the story. In 2007 the State and Defense departments' data showed there to be more contractors (approximately 180,000) than troops (around 160,000) in Iraq, and that might have been an underestimation.[39] Moreover, an estimated 20 percent of the total amount spent for the war was on private contractors operating in the Iraq theater, about $85 billion between 2003 and 2007.[40] This was not just Pentagon money at work. Contract spending by the State Department increased from $1.2 billion to $4.7 billion, an increase of over 280 percent at a time when the budget for core operations of the State Department was about $10 billion.[41] The war made Halliburton the sixth-largest corporate contractor with the U.S. government in 2006 (it was twenty-eighth in 2000).[42]

As noted in chapter 3, one of the primary justifications given for the move toward privatization after the Cold War was to save money. However, whether outsourcing is cost effective depends on a number of factors, and the evidence indicated that, rather than saving money, contracting had inflated the already exorbitant costs of the Iraq War.[43] One reason for this is that many of the largest contracts in Iraq were awarded without competitive bidding. For example, just before the start of the war Halliburton received a $7 billion, no-bid contract from the Pentagon to put out oil well fires and provide other undisclosed services despite the fact that a number of other companies were interested in the contract.[44] Although the lack of competitive bidding was defended as a necessity of war,[45] it brings into question the market justification of outsourcing as a method of cost savings. According to an investigation by the House Committee on Government Oversight and Reform, between 2000 and 2006 federal spending on contracts awarded without full and open competition grew from $67.5 billion to $206.9 billion, with the military accounting for nearly all of the increase.[46]

In addition, cost-plus or cost-reimbursement contracts, the most common kind of contracts under LOGCAP, were accused of contributing to increasing costs. Under this type of contract the government agrees to pay the contracting company the cost of the service plus a fixed fee above these costs, which will be the company's profits, usually 1 to 3 percent. These are considered the most useful kind of contracts when the overall cost of the project is unknown and there is ample room for government oversight to ensure that cost-control measures are undertaken.[47] However, critics asserted that such war-related contracts lacked sufficient oversight and that they created an incentive for companies to inflate their costs, thereby fattening the fee they received for the services.[48] Halliburton and its subsidiary Kellogg, Brown & Root (KBR) came under particular scrutiny for the alleged abuse of no-bid and cost-reimbursement contracts. In mid-2005 an internal Pentagon review found nearly a billion dollars of "questioned" costs billed by KBR, meaning the costs had been investigated and found to be higher than necessary. These costs included bills for meals that were never delivered to soldiers, the purchase of half a million dollars of unneeded heavy equipment, and extremely high fees charged to the military for fuel imports in 2003.[49]

Closely related to the controversies surrounding no-bid contracts is the issue of fraud and mismanagement. The media and GAO reported on problems throughout the war, but government inquiries increased once Democrats took back control of Congress in 2007.[50] Concerns included overbilling, fraudulent account practices, and failure to deliver services that were paid for.[51] Inadequate oversight was one of the sources of this problem. Despite the significant increase in government monies dedicated to procurement since 2000, the number of federal employees charged with overseeing these contracts had been virtually stagnant, and private contractors were being substituted to oversee other private contractors.[52] Various contractors, especially Halliburton — the very name became a shorthand for waste, fraud, and abuse in Iraq — faced accusations and even penalties for overcharging and other shortcomings. The firm Blackwater provided armed guards, employed primarily by the State Department, who likewise became symbols of how much money was being spent on private contractors whose work in some cases risked undermining the U.S. operation in Iraq. Report after report dissected the manifold problems with how money was being spent in and around Iraq. The irony, of course, is that while billions of dollars were being given to Halliburton and other private contractors and overall defense spending was reaching unprecedented levels, the military struggled to maintain its equipment and provide troops with necessary protective gear.[53]

Even when public opinion about the war in Iraq had shifted decisively in a negative direction, it remained politically dangerous to go after defense spending. It was one thing to object to war policy, but quite another to question, let alone endanger, any of the spending on support for the troops. In fact, as we have seen, the dire consequences of the war were being touted as a justification for increasing military spending to "reset" the army and marines. Investigations of unjustifiable and unpatriotic examples of waste, fraud, and abuse by military contractors — nearly inevitable amid the Bush spending spree — were all but limited to war-related contracts in Afghanistan and Iraq.[54] It was unlikely that the vast sums being spent on the Bush buildup had not produced some of the same problems that came to plague the Reagan Pentagon and weapons contracting in the 1980s, which culminated in Operation Ill Wind, the largest investigation and prosecution in U.S. history of federal contracting fraud.[55]

Studies such as *The Three Trillion Dollar War* sought to put a more accurate price tag on the war. With numbers on such a monumental scale, was it even rational to ask whether the extensive use of private contractors had saved American taxpayers any money? Even if so inclined, would the American government be able to answer such a question given the size, complexity, and loose practices of the Iraq War? Would this debacle even prompt a reassessment of the benefits of privatization? The probable costs of this policy went beyond waste, fraud, and abuse. Privatization had done precisely what a few scholars had warned about before it was applied to the war on terror — it substituted private interests for public power in places it did not belong and it lowered barriers to the use of force.[56] By hiding costs and displacing some of the risk, and by adding another set of corporate interests and the profit motive, privatization made it that much easier to go to war early and easily only to learn the bad news when it was too late.

The Road Not Taken: Energy Policy 1988–2008

Meanwhile the United States did little to mitigate, let alone solve, the other problems it confronted in nearly every arena of public policy. The wars and accompanying politics displaced many other issues and complicated potential solutions. For example, the money and talent that went to the wars and the military buildup might have been put to use in financing a "war" for energy independence. In 2001, the attacks of 9/11 gave the president the extraordinary opportunity to rally the nation behind that kind of effort, which could have been, as many put it, a modern Manhattan Project. Bush showed no interest in such a crusade. Though it is unfortunate that the president did not exploit the moment for this purpose, his inaction was nothing new. The nation had done virtually nothing to end its dependence on foreign oil or fossil fuels more generally since the late 1970s. As the United States was winning the Cold War, spending trillions of dollars on defense and building every conceivable weapon, it was losing the war for energy independence by doing very little during years when inaction was politically safe but otherwise irrational.

While President Reagan waged a cold war by credit card, his administration did not build on some of the gains in energy efficiency made during the 1970s. This could be demonstrated in several areas of public policy, including government R&D in alternative energies. But perhaps the area of greatest importance in substance and symbolism is automotive gas mileage. Spurred by the rising power of OPEC and the crisis in oil and gas prices, Congress passed the Energy Policy and Conservation Act of 1975, which mandated among other things increases in the average mileage of new automobiles sold in the United States. The resulting Corporate Average Fuel Economy (CAFE) standard was set at 18.0 miles per gallon (mpg) for those cars manufactured for model year 1978. This was to increase incrementally until the average fuel economy standard reached 27.5 by 1985. With support from Reagan and in spite of some congressional resistance, the Department of Transportation lowered the standard to 26 mpg and kept it at that level until 1989, when the standard was raised to 26.5 and then 27.5 in 1990. It would go no higher. And this was just for passenger vehicles, not trucks and the new category of vehicles known as Sport Utility Vehicles or SUVs. The requirement for "light trucks," which was the designation given by regulators to vans, pickups, and SUVs, was only 20.5 mpg. In 1987 and 1988, the average fuel

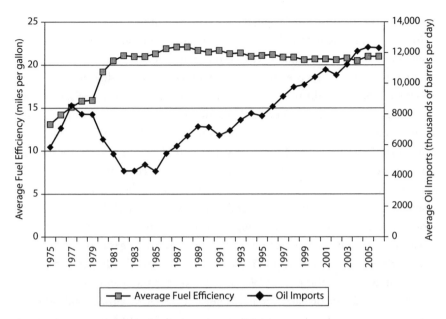

Fig. 6.2. U.S. Vehicle Gas Mileage and Oil Imports, 1975–2006. *Source:* Environmental Protection Agency and Department of Energy.

economy for new vehicles sold in the United States, including light trucks such as pickups, the very popular minivans, and the emerging market of SUVs, peaked at just over 22 miles per gallon (fig. 6.2).

As the Cold War ended at the start of the 1990s oil was plentiful and cheap, and gas prices in the United States would decline in real terms throughout the decade. Popular concern over U.S. reliance on oil imports had largely been forgotten, and nothing was done by Congress to promote fuel efficiency in transportation. Average mileage of vehicles on the road would gradually decrease to under 21 miles per gallon by the late 1990s, with the rise of pickups and SUVs playing an increasingly prominent role in this decrease.[57] During these years of stagnation, as the EPA would report, car manufacturers would devote the bulk of their technological gains for efficiency to offset significant increases in vehicle weight, horsepower, and acceleration. The nation would spend the 1990s driving heavier and faster cars propelled by gasoline that reached historically low real prices by the middle of the decade. A disciplined energy policy was another battle Clinton was unwilling to fight, particularly after Republicans took control of

Congress in 1995. Instead of using the good times to impose even modest energy reforms, the president and Congress would allow the economy and Americans' addiction to huge trucks and SUVs to grow in unison.

Energy is of course a premier issue of national security. Adequate and secure sources of energy for the nation are among the foremost concerns of state policy. The frequent necessity of securing those supplies and sources, in turn, often becomes a raison d'être, either directly or indirectly, for the scope and scale of the national military apparatus. In a country the size of the United States, the military apparatus can be so large that it becomes a significant consumer of what it is, in part, constituted to secure. The need for energy, if far from deterministic, becomes yet another bias in favor of a globe-spanning military. This brief examination of energy policy serves to highlight one of the more important opportunity costs of the nation's preoccupation with a war on terror. These points also show the relationship between the politics, both high and low, that functioned to preserve as much as possible of the Cold War military apparatus and the politics — all too low — of inaction on energy policy. The same forces that pushed and pulled on military spending during the transition after the end of the Cold War also kept down the chances of any serious attempt to lessen the nation's dependence on foreign oil. For example, the deficit politics of the early 1990s coupled with a sluggish economy made any energy taxes or regulations politically unpalatable. Later, when the good times of the late 1990s kicked in (aided considerably by low oil prices), the effect was to take the pressure off military spending and the perceived need for an energy policy. A few years later, President Bush not only failed to use the crisis and war to change course in this vital area, he encouraged greater irresponsibility. As was widely noted at the time, after September 11 the president and some other leaders did not call for sacrifice; instead their appeal for a return to normalcy at times sounded like an exhortation to consume. Americans were urged to travel and shop as their contribution to the cause.[58] Less noted was the fact that October 2001 set a record for sales of SUVs and pickups (as well as cars in general) that would stand until June 2005.[59] The subsequent wars would make the gas-guzzling Hummer quite popular, and it was not difficult to make other psychological links between SUV sales and the heightened sense of insecurity after 9/11.[60]

Bush's failure to exploit the 9/11 moment for the benefit of the same cause is hardly shocking given the ideology of his administration and its fixation on 9/11 as the opening for war in Iraq and a new global order under the "adult supervision" of the United States. It remains, nevertheless, one of the greatest lost opportunities in the history of the American presidency. Presidents cannot create the social or global circumstances that will validate and translate their grander visions into policy. They either are elected to office riding the wave of such circumstances or once in office a major event or crisis presents an opening. Had steady progress been made from the 1980s onward, perhaps some sort of Manhattan Project for energy independence would not have been necessary. Even a tiny adjustment of the imbalance between governmental spending on military research ($73 billion in 2006) and energy research (less than $1.2 billion) might have helped. Instead, two decades of neglect had left the United States in such a position that any serious effort to deal with the problem would have to be on an immense scale to overcome the years of detrimental policies and the deadweight of consumer choices.

By the end of the Bush presidency gas prices had gone through several upward surges. The war that was or was not about oil had certainly done nothing to help the American consumer. In 2006, in one of the least insightful moments in the history of State of the Union addresses, President Bush revealed that "we have a serious problem: America is addicted to oil, which is often imported from unstable parts of the world." But it was not until the next such address, a year later, that Bush announced a series of potentially meaningful initiatives on energy, including a proposal to "reform and modernize" gas mileage standards. His presidency would end with only the most modest and tentative beginnings toward reversing the damage done by years of willful neglect.

Bipartisan Negligence: The Presidential Campaign

When the president released his FY 2009 budget proposal, a few headlines and editorials took note of the fact that the request for Pentagon funding — not counting any separate appropriations for the war — would mark the eleventh straight year of real increases in the defense budget and, along with outlays for the war, take military spending to its highest level since World War II.[61] Later that year the GAO released reports that revealed some of the effects of the largely unsupervised and unrestricted boom in weapons research and production. The Pentagon's planned investment in weapons programs had ballooned from $790 billion in 2000 to $1.6 trillion in 2007 with over $850 billion of that commitment still outstanding. Acquisition costs had skyrocketed and the performance on the contracts appeared to be "increasingly suboptimal."[62] In short, the Pentagon had committed itself to more programs than it could manage well or support financially over the long run.

These alarming facts disappeared, however, amid the news of a faltering economy and the contest for the presidential nominations. The size and merits of the Bush buildup, or its relation to a post-Iraq national security policy, failed to penetrate the primary election campaigns of either party, and nothing would change in the general campaign between John McCain and Barack Obama. In fact, one could be forgiven for concluding from the candidates' rhetoric that defense spending was too low. Insofar as the subject was mentioned at all, the frontrunners among the Republicans all endorsed higher military budgets and the Democrats talked about having to rebuild our armed forces in the wake of the war. The costs and consequences of the Bush buildup remained unquestioned and unexplored.

Even well-read citizens and policymakers could be excused for being unaware of this product of the Bush presidency. The tenor of the news coverage and rhetoric of politicians on both sides of the aisle probably left most Americans believing that the wars have left little money for other aspects of military power. Neither political party drew attention to the buildup, and the presidential campaign epitomized the politics that had hidden it in plain sight. Any hopes that the start of the presidential campaign might spark a debate about the scope and purpose of the Bush buildup were dashed immediately. Candidates were compelled to either reject or embrace the "troop surge" but there was still, apparently, no wiggle room in either party to question the flood of money disappearing into the Pentagon. The campaign, insofar as the issue of military spending was discussed at all, featured nearly unanimous bipartisan agreement among the major candidates that their administrations would increase military spending in the wake of the Iraq War.

Early Republican frontrunner Mitt Romney, the ex-governor of Massachusetts whose foreign policy credentials amounted to his work on the 2002 Winter Olympics in Salt Lake City, not surprisingly supported high levels of military spending. In an April 2007 address, his earliest effort to articulate his views on the war and national security policy, Romney made two explicit proposals: to increase the size of the military by 100,000 troops and to increase defense spending to at least 4 percent of the U.S. GDP. As for the problems to be fixed by the greater number of troops and more money, Romney blamed them on Bill Clinton, who in 1993 "began to dismantle the military," not on Bush or the war.[63] Romney, as might be expected, was not alone. His call for 100,000 troops was echoed by candidates John McCain and Rudolph Giuliani. The former mayor of New York wanted even more, however: "at least another 10 new combat brigades above the additions that are already proposed by President Bush."[64] According to Giuliani the United States "must rebuild" its military force, and this rebuilding "will not be cheap." McCain, the eventual nominee, echoed this by calling for an increase in the army and marines from "the currently planned level of roughly 750,000 troops to 900,000 troops."[65] Like Giuliani, McCain wanted tens of thousands more troops than even the Bush plans. McCain also endorsed a larger defense budget, using the 4 percent figure as his benchmark of affordability.

Mike Huckabee, who vaulted from obscurity to frontrunner at the Iowa caucuses, also agreed with the increase of 92,000 troops, and this was one reason "why we must increase our military budget." By how much? Here Huckabee actually departed from his colleagues, not in the extent of his analysis of the problem, which was nonexistent, but in his readiness to throw money at it. Instead of echoing the 4 percent mantra, Huckabee harkened back to Reagan and 1986 when the military consumed about 6 percent of GDP. "We need to return to that six percent level," noted Huckabee, without further elaboration or justification, and without any indication that he understood that a 2 percent increase in the percentage of GDP devoted to defense translated into an increase from about $500 billion to $750 billion dollars for the Pentagon — a 50 percent increase.[66]

On the Democratic side, the commitments on military spending were in general less hawkish but hardly a frontal challenge to the Bush legacy. The original frontrunner, Senator Hillary Clinton, promised to "rebuild our armed services and restore them body and soul" after their having been "stretched . . . to the breaking point" by Iraq. She promised "to work to expand and modernize the military so that fighting wars no longer comes at the expense of deployments for long-term deterrence, military readiness, or responses to urgent needs at home."[67] Barack Obama, who early in his campaign said that he would probably increase defense spending at least initially, endorsed an increase of 92,000 soldiers and marines.[68] Only John Edwards, at least among the major contenders, resisted the temptation for the candidates to, as he put it, "outbid" one another on the number of troops they would add. Edwards also rightly wondered what the rationale would be for adding thousands of troops even as we prepared to withdraw from Iraq.[69] Edwards's point, however obvious, stood out for its incisiveness on a subject otherwise bereft of insight during the campaign. If the war in Iraq must and should end, then what would we do with 100,000 more soldiers and marines that wouldn't be available for several years? Was the plan to be involved in another disastrous quagmire by then? Even Obama's attempt at an explanation was rather mystifying. "The war in Afghanistan and the ill-advised invasion of Iraq," argued the Illinois Senator, "have clearly demonstrated the consequences of underestimating the number of troops required to fight two wars and defend our homeland."[70] From someone such as Obama, who was against the Iraq War from the start and planned to end it as soon as possible, this kind of comment was unsettling. Nearly all the comments by the candidates, Democrat and Republican alike, implied that details and substantive arguments were unimportant and to be avoided because they tended to undermine the sloganeering that was disguised as policy. Things did not improve during the fall battle between Obama and McCain. The economic crisis took up much of the first presidential debate that was to have focused on foreign and national security policy. No questions in any of the debates were asked about military policy apart from the wars, and even the skirmishes over particulars of foreign policy sometimes descended into the ridiculous. The two candidates offered nothing of substance about the future of military spending.[71]

Thus emerged the subtle partisan distinction on defense. If a Republican, one's task was to criticize the handling of the war but surpass the president on the size of the permanent military you would seek to fight the war on terror. If a Democrat, one could go as far as calling the war a mistake that should never have been made but also outdo the president on the number of troops you plan not to use in the misguided way that resulted in the call for more soldiers in the first place. The irony of this was not evident in the debates or coverage of the candidates. A debacle from which everyone in theory was seeking to extract the nation, one that would sooner rather than later have to end, somehow supported an argument for military spending and forces beyond what Bush had produced by the last year of his presidency.[72] Barack Obama had run and won on a platform of "change we can believe in." Like the congressional Democratic majority that had preceded him, Obama had no public plans for bringing military spending under control. He would face a difficult task in trying to change the course of the wars, and he also was confronted with a rapidly escalating economic crisis that would overwhelm everything else before he even had taken the oath of office.

Legacy, Crisis, and Change?
The New President and the Future of Military Policy

In late July 2008, the White House projected that 2009 would see a $490 billion deficit, up from $407 billion predicted when the budget was first released in February. The new estimate reflected the worsening economy and the cost of another fiscal stimulus in the form of tax rebates. The costs of the wars were routinely mentioned, but almost in passing, as a given. Five years into the Iraq War, the president and Congress passed nearly $200 billion in "supplemental" war funding (which made it by a huge margin the second largest discretionary government program next to the regular defense budget). This increase was on top of a postwar record defense budget, but somehow it seemed secondary, old news, even though most Americans still had no idea how much the war was costing. Bush was ending his presidency where it began, with recession and war. The energy crisis and gas prices were still dominating the news when the mortgage finance debacle emerged to displace nearly everything else with what many were quickly calling the worst economic crisis since the Great Depression. The government responded immediately with a rescue plan to bail out the credit industry that could commit up to $700 billion for various purposes, including the possible purchase of so-called toxic assets held by private firms.

While everyone was upset and unsettled by this plan, many in Washington felt something along these lines had to be done. But many members of Congress, including the majority of Republicans and a significant percentage of Democrats in the House, voted against the first version of the legislation, with public opinion polls evincing considerable anger among Americans about a policy that could be seen as rewarding reckless practices by Wall Street firms while doing nothing directly for average Americans, especially homeowners, who were suffering. Seven hundred billion dollars — a stunning sum to all involved — was about the same amount of money the president and Congress had appropriated and spent on the wars in Iraq and Afghanistan, not including the hundreds of billions of additional dollars devoted to the buildup under the political cover of those wars.

When Barack Obama took office his first order of business was the completion and passage of an economic stimulus bill. Initially totaling over $800 billion in spending and tax cuts, the eventual $787 billion package was as spectacular as the bailout had been only weeks earlier. The bailout and stimulus (along with the wars and military buildup) produced truly jaw-dropping deficits. The shortfall for fiscal year 2009 was projected to reach nearly $1.85 trillion, four times the formerly mammoth $459 billion deficit of 2008.[73] While many congressional Republicans voted against the stimulus, Democrats and the public, by and large, supported the president.[74]

And what of national security and defense policy? Here, Iraq and Afghanistan remained the focus. Much was made of Obama's plan to send 17,000 more troops to the latter even as the withdrawal from the former would proceed rather slowly.

Other defense priorities and spending separate from the war were not addressed in the early weeks of the new presidency. The president would have to submit his first budget proposal, however, in February. As if to symbolize the Democrats' lack of an alternative vision or program for national security or the political dangers represented by the wars and buildup, the lone holdover from the Bush administration was Defense Secretary Robert Gates, the man brought in to clean up the mess left by Donald Rumsfeld. Gates could be viewed simultaneously if somewhat incongruously as a form of continuity but also as the ideal "tough love" messenger to the Pentagon that times were changing. "One thing we have known for many months," Gates told members of Congress, "is the spigot of defense funding opened by 9/11 is closing." "We must have the courage to make hard choices," he added, knowing full well that his audience was infamous for its lack of valor on this front.[75]

Under the leadership of Obama and Gates, however, the spigot would turn slowly and, at least initially, in the wrong direction. Lost in news of the record spending and deficits contained in the president's February budget proposal for the fiscal year 2010 was the fact that the Pentagon's nonwar budget would increase about 4 percent, an echo of Bush's first defense budget request in early 2001. Perhaps unsurprisingly no hard choices accompanied this budget increase. Several weeks passed before the next shoe dropped, and when it did people interpreted or reacted to the sound in very different ways. On April 6 Defense Secretary Gates, in an unusual move, held a press conference in advance of the formal submission of his defense budget request to announce the major elements contained in it. Gates said his proposals would "profoundly reform" and "fundamental[ly] overhaul" business at the Pentagon, and his list of cuts in and changes to specific major weapons programs lent credence to his claims.[76] Nevertheless, some reporters seemed to accept the rhetoric at face value by leading the story with references to "sweeping budget cuts," "Pentagon budget cuts," even "huge slashes" and "deep cuts."[77] And yet the Pentagon budget, the one Gates was previewing, was for $534 billion, and the 4 percent increase over 2009. In his remarks Gates emphasized some reductions and adjustments to expensive high-profile programs, but the full array of changes contained both subtractions and additions. Much was made of his decision to stop the F-22 at 187, but 183 or thereabouts had been the target number for a few years already. Instead, the air force would concentrate on the Joint Strike Fighter (JSF), and several billion more was in the budget to accelerate production, but production of over 2,000 JSFs had been planned for years. Yes, the Army's Future Combat System vehicle program would be revisited and modified, but billions would be added for more troops and special forces. Production of one type of naval combat vessel would be halted but another would be accelerated. Ballistic missile defense programs would be trimmed and refocused, but funding for theater missile defense would be augmented. The spigot was not being closed as much as the flow was being redirected, all in all in a rather modest fashion.[78]

Moreover, two days later Obama announced his plans for an $83.4 billion supplemental spending bill for the wars. This was for the remainder of 2009, however, on top of $66 billion already allocated by Bush and the previous Congress. This nearly $150 billion would bring the total for the two wars to about $1 trillion. Moreover, about $600 million in the supplemental was for the last four F-22s.[79] Obama was, on the one hand, ending this exorbitantly expensive weapons program but, on the other, extending Bush's practice, discussed in chapter 5, of putting nonemergency, nonwar spending in the supplemental appropriations.

In response to a question about the likely congressional reaction to his plans, Gates said, "I hope that the members of Congress will rise above parochial interests and consider what is in the best interest of the nation as a whole."[80] In anticipation of the end of F-22 production and weeks before Gates's announcement, Lockheed Martin had started an advertising campaign claiming that up to 95,000 jobs were at risk.[81] It took many members of Congress only hours to respond to Gates's proposed cuts. The Connecticut congressional delegation wrote a letter to President Obama decrying the F-22 termination and calling for protection of the industrial base for fighter production.[82] Republican Senator Johnny Isakson of Georgia joined his Connecticut colleagues, finding it "unacceptable that this administration wants to eliminate 2,000 jobs in Marietta and potentially 95,000 jobs nationwide at a time when unemployment rates are rising across the country."[83] Republican Senator Chris Bond joined with Boeing workers from his state of Missouri to argue that "our nation needs more St. Louis–made fighter planes so our military can continue to meet current and emerging threats."[84] In short, it was the early 1990s all over again. While not featuring anything like the scale or certainty of the post–Cold War cuts, the politics were the same. The economy was foundering just after a huge buildup made reductions in defense spending logical, even urgent. Economic woes were being used to justify the production of weapons that had no other purpose. While hoping that money would be saved somewhere and fiscal discipline be imposed by someone, members of Congress would resist wherever and whenever they felt the pinch.[85]

It was déjà vu in another unfortunate respect as well. Many Republicans did not need state jobs as a motivation to criticize Gates or the president. "I cannot believe what I heard today," responded Senator James Inhofe of Oklahoma in a video from Afghanistan. "President Obama is disarming America. Never before has a president so ravaged the military at a time of war." "Our sons and daughters," continued Inofe, "are risking their lives fighting an enemy whose sole purpose is the destruction of our country and our way of life, while their President disarms America. And all this to support his welfare state."[86] Inhofe also joined Senators Lisa Murkowski (R-AK), Joe Lieberman (ID-CT), Jon Kyl (R-AZ), Mark Begich (D-AK), Jeff Sessions (R-AL) in sending a letter to Obama complaining about cuts to ballistic missile defense.[87] "This is not the time to go cheap on defense," argued Senator Lindsay Graham. The South Carolina Republican added that Obama's "budget is really heavy on butter and short on guns."[88] That the military budget was actually increasing and that nearly $150 billion more in war funding was on its way was apparently irrelevant. A Democrat was in the White House once again at a time when difficult decisions about defense had to be made; that was enough. Some, including Obama's former rival Senator John McCain and Senator Jim Webb, issued more measured statements backing Gates's efforts.[89] The same month it was reported that the Department of Homeland Security, invoking parallels to the early 1990s, had issued a report warning of the possible resurgence of domestic right-wing extremist groups fostered by the recession and the election of Obama.[90] In a final ironic echo, like Clinton before him, candidate Obama had said he would work to end the ban on gays in the military, but he and Secretary Gates made it clear that they had other priorities for at least the first year and that reform in this area would happen slowly and carefully.[91]

In the first chapter, I outlined the elements behind what I argue is the bias in national security policy toward hawkish policies, including the distribution of the costs and benefits of many military policies and defense spending; the organization and relative power of social forces arrayed for and against militaristic policies; the nature of two-party competition and the separation of powers; and other characteristics of the issue such as its tendency to evoke the jingoistic but powerful tropes and rhetoric of national strength and weakness. We saw these forces operating during the 1990s and throughout the presidency of George W. Bush, pushing in the earlier period against further reductions in the military, and after 9/11 facilitating an essentially uncontrolled and sustained explosion of defense spending. And while it was too early at the time of writing—a few months into

Obama's presidency—to predict whether these forces would yet again prevail, they were already at work, complicating the young president's efforts to control and reform this immense and powerful legacy.

If things went well with the bailout of the financial sector, the U.S. taxpayer might end up paying very little; a profit was remotely possible depending on how the money was used. It was at least plausible that the stimulus package could rescue the economy. At the very least it would generate jobs and help many Americans. The military buildup that was hidden in plain sight had created jobs, but that is not what it was for. What it actually was for, and the price Americans were paying for it, had never been debated or decided on in any meaningful way. What was America's return on this investment when weighed against all the other vital problems the nation faced, many of which had a great deal to do with national security? Above all else, the lives and money in Iraq and Afghanistan were not coming back in any way, shape, or form. All things considered, the possibility of a return on the nation's investment in those conflicts disappeared years earlier, and all Americans were left with was hollow rhetoric about the need to come home with "victory." The United States entered the eighth year of the war on terror, and the new president inherited a country in economic crisis, bereft of an energy policy and facing formidable and expensive problems, from national infrastructure to health care and social security. But the United States had, if nothing else, the finest military on earth. The nation would be paying for that unique privilege for years to come.

NOTES

CHAPTER 1: Irrational Security

1. For exceptions see, inter alia, Ira Katznelson and Martin Shefter, eds., *Shaped by War and Trade: International Influences on American Political Development* (Princeton, N.J.: Princeton University Press, 2002); and Aaron L. Friedberg, *In the Shadow of the Garrison State: America's Anti-Statism and Its Cold War Grand Strategy* (Princeton, N.J.: Princeton University Press, 2000). More generally, there is a relatively small but notable school of scholarship on the politics of national security policy, stretching from Samuel Huntington's *The Common Defense* (New York: Columbia University Press, 1961) to some recent works, a few of which I cite in this chapter. For a discussion of the methodological debates at the intersection of domestic and international politics, see Daniel Wirls, "APD, IR and the National Security State," paper presented at the annual meeting of the American Political Science Association, Philadelphia, August 31–September 2, 2006.

2. For one of the more recent takes on this debate, see Kevin Narizny, *The Political Economy of Grand Strategy* (Ithaca, N.Y.: Cornell University Press, 2007). Although my thinking has evolved and incorporated various formulations such as social constructivism, I adhere to the main principles of the argument I made in the early 1990s about the relationship between domestic politics and military policy; see *Buildup: The Politics of Defense in the Reagan Era* (Ithaca, N.Y.: Cornell University Press, 1992), 1–9.

3. The most important exception is Derek Chollet and James Goldgeier, *America between the Wars: From 11/9 to 9/11* (New York: PublicAffairs, 2008), which covers some of the same politics and debates in chapters 2 and 3 of this volume. Another is Andrew Bacevich, *The New American Militarism* (New York: Oxford University Press, 2005). Bacevich provides an analysis of the deeper roots of Bush's militarism in such things as neoconservative ideology, the consequences of the Vietnam War, and Reagan's revival of the Republican Party. One of the most detailed studies of the evolution of military policy from the late 1980s through 2001 is offered by Richard A. Lacquement Jr., *Shaping American Military Capabilities after the Cold War* (Westport, Conn.: Praeger, 2003), but his study ends just as the Bush administration is commencing the war on terror and before the Iraq War. Another study that traces the ideological linkages between the 1990s and the Bush administration is Tony Smith, *A Pact with the Devil: Washington's Bid for World Supremacy and the Betrayal of the American Promise* (New York: Routledge, 2007). Another critical analysis that roots Bush's post–9/11 policies historically without losing sight of their novel features is Mel Gurtov, *Superpower on Crusade: The Bush Doctrine in U.S. Foreign Policy* (Boulder, Col.: Lynne Rienner, 2006). Edward Haley, *Strategies of Dominance: The Misdirection of U.S. Foreign Policy* (Baltimore: Johns Hopkins University Press, 2006) focuses on foreign policy but covers from the first Bush presidency through the first years of the second.

4. Bob Woodward produced four volumes after 9/11 on the Bush presidency and the wars: *Bush at War, Plan of Attack, State of Denial,* and *The War Within* (all Simon and Schuster, 2002, 2004, 2006, 2008); see also Thomas Ricks, *Fiasco: The American Military Adventure in Iraq* (New York: Penguin, 2006); Michael R. Gordon and Bernard E. Trainor, *Cobra II: The Inside Story of the Invasion and Occupation of Iraq* (New York: Pantheon, 2006); George Packer, *The Assassins' Gate: America in Iraq* (New York: Farrar, Straus, and Giroux, 2005); Ron Suskind, *The One Percent Doctrine: Deep Inside America's Pursuit of Its Enemies since 9/11* (New York: Simon and Schuster, 2006); Charlie Savage, *Takeover: The Return of the Imperial Presidency and the Subversion of American Democracy* (New York: Little, Brown, 2007); Jane Mayer, *The Dark Side: The Inside Story of How the War on Terror Turned into a War on American Ideals* (New York: Doubleday, 2008).

5. Among many others are Stephen M. Walt, *Taming American Power: The Global Response to U.S. Primacy* (New York: W. W. Norton, 2005); Stephen G. Brooks and William C. Wohlforth, *World Out of Balance: International Relations and the Challenge of American Primacy* (Princeton, N.J.: Princeton University Press, 2008); Robert Pape, *Dying to Win: The Strategic Logic of Suicide Terrorism* (New York: Random House, 2006); John A. Nagl, *Learning to Eat Soup with a Knife: Counterinsurgency Lessons from Malaya and Vietnam* (Chicago: University of Chicago Press, 2005); Niall Ferguson, *Colossus: The Rise and Fall of the American Empire* (New York: Penguin, 2005); Amy Chua, *Day of Empire: How Hyperpowers Rise to Global Dominance — and Why They Fall* (New York: Doubleday, 2007); and Michael Hardt and Antonio Negri, *Multitude: War and Democracy in the Age of Empire* (New York: Penguin, 2005). This is also the perspective that dominates the pages of journals such as *Foreign Affairs, Foreign Policy,* and *International Security,* which have published hundreds of articles on these topics since the end of the Cold War.

6. Dana Priest, *The Mission: Waging War and Keeping Peace with America's Military* (New York: Norton, 2003); David Halberstam, *War in a Time of Peace: Bush, Clinton, and the Generals* (New York: Scribner, 2001); Ryan C. Hendrickson, *The Clinton Wars* (Nashville: Vanderbilt University Press, 2002). An important exception is Michael Klare, *Rogue States and Nuclear Outlaws* (New York: Hill and Wang, 1995), which parallels the kind of critical analysis of policy formation in this volume but ends in Clinton's first term.

7. Jack Snyder, *Myths of Empire* (Ithaca, N.Y.: Cornell University Press, 1991).

8. For two recent works that support this line of analysis, see Jeffrey M. Cavanaugh, "From the 'Red Juggernaut' to Iraqi WMD: Threat Inflation and How It Succeeds in the United States," *Political Science Quarterly* 122, no. 4 (winter 2007–2008): 555–84; Christopher J. Fettweis, "Credibility and the War on Terror," *Political Science Quarterly* 122, no. 4 (winter 2007–2008): 607–33.

9. For a contrasting perspective based on the history and importance of economic sectionalism in U.S. history, see Peter Trubowitz, *Defining the National Interest* (Chicago: University of Chicago Press, 1998).

10. Anatol Lieven, *America Right or Wrong: An Anatomy of American Nationalism* (New York: Oxford University Press, 2004); Paul T. McCartney, "American Nationalism and U.S. Foreign Policy from September 11 to the Iraq War," in *The Meaning of American Democracy,* ed. Robert Y. Shapiro (New York: Academy of Political Science, 2005), 89–113; Tony Smith, *A Pact with the Devil* (New York: Routledge, 2007); Bacevich, *American Militarism,* 9–33.

11. There is also a substantial literature on masculinity and manhood that speaks to their implications or consequences for military policy. A powerful analysis of manhood

(and antifeminist) politics in the wake of 9/11 is offered by Susan Faludi, *The Terror Dream: Fear and Fantasy in Post–9/11 America* (New York: Metropolitan Books, 2007). Also see Michelle Swers, "Building a Reputation on National Security: The Impact of Stereotypes Related to Gender and Military Experience," *Legislative Studies Quarterly* 32, no. 4 (November 2007): 559–95; Jennifer Lawless, "Women, War, and Winning Elections: Gender Stereotyping in the Post–September 11th Era," *Political Research Quarterly* 57 (2004): 479–90.

12. *Youngstown Sheet & Tube Co. v. Sawyer*, 343 U.S. 579 (1952).

13. Cecil V. Crabb Jr. and Pat M. Holt, *Invitation to Struggle: Congress, the President, and Foreign Policy* (Washington, D.C.: Congressional Quarterly Press, 1980).

14. State of the Union Address, January 19, 1999.

15. Eugene Gholz and Harvey M. Sapolsky, "Restructuring the U.S. Defense Industry," *International Security* 24, no. 3 (winter 1999–2000): 14.

CHAPTER 2 : After the Cold War

1. An account that covers many of the same issues and events through 1993 is Michael Klare, *Rogue States and Nuclear Outlaws* (New York: Hill and Wang, 1995). Covering the entire decade (and therefore overlapping with chapter 3 as well) is Derek Chollet and James Goldgeier, *America between the Wars: From 11/9 to 9/11* (New York: PublicAffairs, 2008). Although done for the air force, the following contains a good history and analysis of the Base Force and Bottom-Up Review to be discussed in this chapter: Eric V. Larson, David T. Orletsky, and Kristin J. Leuschner, *Defense Planning in a Decade of Change: Lessons from the Base Force, Bottom-Up Review, and Quadrennial Defense Review* (Santa Monica, Calif.: RAND, 2001). See also James Lebovic, *Foregone Conclusions: U.S. Weapons Acquisition in the Post–Cold War Transition* (Boulder, Col.: Westview Press, 1996).

2. The amounts fell by −4.4% in fiscal 1986, −3.0% in 1987, −1.9% in 1988, and −.9% in 1989, adjusted for inflation. Defense spending as a percentage of GNP was also falling after 1986.

3. For Reagan's remarks and other information on the veto see Pat Towell, "Veto of Defense Bill Ups the Political Ante," *Congressional Quarterly Weekly Report*, August 6, 1988, 2143–45.

4. Ibid., 2143.

5. Lou Cannon and R. Jeffrey Smith, "President Blames SDI Delays on Hill's 'Irresponsible' Cuts," *Washington Post*, March 15, 1988.

6. Stephen Skowronek, *The Politics Presidents Make* (Cambridge: Harvard University Press, 1994), 429–30.

7. Quoted in Michael Duffy and Dan Goodgame, *Marching in Place: The Status Quo Presidency of George Bush* (New York: Simon and Schuster, 1992), 24.

8. Bob Woodward, "Origin of the Tax Pledge: In '88 Campaign Bush Camp Was Split on 'Read My Lips' Vow," *Washington Post*, October 4, 1992; and Duffy and Goodgame, *Marching in Place*, 233–34.

9. The academic literature that was produced from the late 1980s until 2000 or so is vast. For a variety of perspectives see Richard K. Hermann and Richard Ned Lebow, eds., *Ending the Cold War: Interpretations, Causation, and the Study of International Relations* (New York: Palgrave Macmillan, 2004); and William C. Wohlforth, ed., *Cold War Endgame: Oral History, Analysis, Debates* (University Park, Pa.: Penn State University Press, 2003).

10. George F. Kennan, "The G.O.P Won the Cold War? Ridiculous," *New York Times*, October 28, 1992. Kennan was reacting to the partisan tint of triumphalist arguments. Without directly saying so, Kennan's piece is a reminder of his idea of a long, patient struggle; containment; and the multiple contributions to the success of and costs involved in the various versions of containment, especially in "unreal and exaggerated estimates of the intentions and strengths of the other party."

11. Quoted in Maureen Dowd, "A Sense of Wonder among the Mere Bystanders," *New York Times*, February 8, 1990.

12. In defending his 1991 budget Cheney argued that congressional cuts could under-mine the defense strategy that "has directly contributed to the collapse we see in the Soviet Union." Quoted in "Restructuring the Military," *San Jose Mercury News*, January 30, 1990. Jeane Kirkpatrick offered a more nuanced assessment of the impact of Reagan and the buildup: "One was the confident reaffirmation of the case for free institutions. And two I think that the restoration of military strength, occurring as it did with the stagnation of the Soviet economy, really dramatized and illustrated for Gorbachev the problems in that country of technology and economic base." Quoted in Richard Bernstein, "Ideas & Trends; If They've Won, Can Conservatives Still be Important?" *New York Times*, Janu-ary 14, 1990. For a book-length version of this line of argument, see Jay Winik, *On the Brink: The Dramatic behind the Scenes Saga of the Reagan Era and the Men and Women Who Won the Cold War* (New York: Simon & Schuster, 1996).

13. Quoted in Edwin Meese, "The Man Who Won the Cold War: Ronald Reagan's Strategy for Freedom," *Policy Review* 61 (summer 1992): 39.

14. Meese, "Man Who Won the Cold War," 36–39.

15. Ibid., 37.

16. Charles Krauthammer, "Reagan Revisionism," *Washington Post*, June 11, 2004.

17. The closest thing I have found to a public articulation of this effect of the proposed buildup was during an interview Reagan gave as a presidential candidate. He said, "The very fact that we would start [a buildup] would serve a notice on the Soviet Union. . . . I think there's every indication and every reason to believe that the Soviet Union cannot increase its production of arms." Lou Cannon, "Arms Boost Seen as Strain on Soviets," *Washington Post*, June 19, 1980, 3.

18. For an excellent and balanced review and critique of the variety of pro-Reagan arguments see Jeffrey W. Knopf, "Did Reagan Win the Cold War?" *Strategic Insights* (August 2004), www.ccc.nps.navy.mil/si/2004/aug/knopfAUG04.asp.; also Richard Ned Lebow and Janice Gross Stein, "Reagan and the Russians," *Atlantic Monthly*, February 1994, www.theatlantic.com/politics/foreign/reagrus.htm.

19. All quotations from the Republican Party Platform of 1980, www.presidency.ucsb .edu/showplatforms.php?platindex=R1980.

20. Daniel Wirls, *Buildup: The Politics of Defense in the Reagan Era* (Ithaca, N.Y.: Cornell University Press, 1992), 112–18.

21. "Rating Reagan: A Bogus Legacy," www.consortiumnews.com/Print/2004/060 704.html.

22. In another of the more nuanced views following Reagan's death, columnist Jim Hoagland noted that "to one who covered many of the key international events of that day, Reagan seemed in fact to come late to a realistic view of the Soviet Union and the world, and — like most presidents — to have improvised furiously and not always successfully in foreign affairs." See "Assessing Reagan," *Washington Post Weekly Review*, June 2004, 14–20.

For a detailed account of the complexity of Reagan's contribution (as well as Gorbachev's) to the end of the Cold War, see James Mann, *The Rebellion of Ronald Reagan* (New York: Viking, 2009). Martin and Annelise Anderson offer a somewhat strained portrayal of Reagan as a closet nuclear abolitionist fighting the Cold War establishment to save the world from nuclear holocaust. See their *Reagan's Secret War* (New York: Crown, 2009).

23. David Broder, "The Great Persuader," *Washington Post*, June 7, 2004.

24. Jay Ambrose, "Reagan Proved 'em Wrong," *Capitol Hill Blue*, June 7, 2004, www .capi tolhillblue.com/artman/publish/printer _ 4651.shtml.

25. This is from National Public Radio correspondent, John Ydstie, "Reagan's Policies Transformed Economic Debate," *Morning Edition*, June 9, 2004. Ydstie's guest, former Reagan economic advisor William Niskanen, added that the deficit was okay if that was the necessary price to end the Cold War.

26. Klare, *Rogue States*, 14.

27. Lorna S. Jaffe, "The Development of the Base Force, 1989–1992," Joint History Office, Office of the Chairman of the Joint Chiefs of Staff, July 1993, 2–6.

28. For a complete summary of the 1989 defense budget see *CQ Almanac, 1989* (Washington, D.C.: Congressional Quarterly), 423–35.

29. Jaffe, "Base Force" (this is expressed in several places as Powell's paramount concern).

30. Ibid., 11–12; Colin Powell, *My American Journey* (New York: Random House, 1995), 401–3, 435–37.

31. Jaffe, "Base Force," 5, 18, 20. Wolfowitz would, by that spring, be arguing for something quite close to the Base Force.

32. Powell, *Journey*, 403.

33. Jaffe, "Base Force," 21; see also Powell, *Journey*, 444–45.

34. Jaffe, "Base Force," 36.

35. George H. W. Bush, "Remarks at the Aspen Institute Symposium in Aspen, Colorado," August 2, 1990, http://bushlibrary.tamu.edu/research/public _ papers.php?id=21 28&year=1990&month=8.

36. James J. Tritten, "America Promises to Come Back: Our New National Security Strategy," NPS-NS-91-003C, Naval Postgraduate School, Monterey, California, October 23, 1991, 7.

37. In announcing the new strategy and Base Force concept, President Bush mentioned Panama directly as the kind of contingency for which the United States must be prepared: "As we saw in Panama, the U.S. may be called on to respond to a variety of challenges from various points on the compass. In an era when threats may emerge with little or no warning, our ability to defend our interests will depend on our speed and our agility. And we will need forces that give us a global reach." Bush, "Remarks at the Aspen Institute."

38. See Jaffe, "Base Force," for details on Powell's concern and plans to sell the program; Klare, *Rogue States*, 33.

39. "The cold war," argued NSC 68, "is in fact a real war." The text is reprinted in Ernest R. May, *American Cold War Strategy: Interpreting NSC 68* (New York: Bedford Books, 1993).

40. Dick Cheney, *Annual Report to the President and the Congress* (Washington, D.C.: Government Printing Office, January 1991), 3.

41. Carl E. Vuono, "Desert Storm and the Future of Conventional Forces," *Foreign Affairs* (spring 1991): 49.

42. Just after the Iraq invasion Powell, Cheney, and Wolfowitz introduced the Base Force concept to leaders of the congressional defense committees, "but all we heard was, yeah, sure, right. But what's going on in Kuwait?" (Powell, *Journey*, 463). Tritten also comments on the lack of press attention due to the Gulf in "America Promises to Come Back," 3. *Congressional Quarterly Weekly Report* failed to cover Bush's address or anything about the proposed new strategy in the issues of August 1990 while devoting considerable space to the Gulf crisis.

43. With greater eloquence but no less (in due time) irony, the president also said, "The specter of Vietnam has been buried forever in the desert sands of the Arabian peninsula." Both quoted in Norman Solomon, "Beyond the 'Vietnam Syndrome,'" *In These Times*, September 5, 2005, www.inthesetimes.com/site/main/article/2296/.

44. Klare, *Rogue States*, 68–85 focuses on four other lessons more directly related to military power: (1) high-tech weaponry and warfare works, (2) air power can rule the battlefield, but (3) all four services are needed to win wars, and (4) the United States must have and rely on strategic mobility.

45. Jaffe, "Base Force," 48.

46. Vuono, "Conventional Forces"; William J. Perry, "Desert Storm and Deterrence," *Foreign Affairs* (fall 1991): 66–82; Stephen Biddle, "Victory Misunderstood: What the Gulf War Tells Us about the Future of Conflict," *International Security* (fall 1996): 139–79; Thomas G. Mahnken and Barry D. Watts, "What the Gulf War Can (and Cannot) Tell Us about the Future of Warfare," *International Security* (fall 1997): 151–62.

47. See, among others, Klare, *Rogue States*, 68–75; Theodore A. Postol, "Lessons of the Gulf War Experience with Patriot," *International Security* 16, no. 3 (winter 1991–1992): 119–71.

48. Powell briefly discusses U.S. inaction prior to Iraq's invasion of Kuwait (Powell, *Journey*, 459–62).

49. Andrew Krepinevich cites the point about the JCS endorsement of a two-war scenario. See his "The Bottom-Up Review: An Assessment," *Defense Budget Project* (February 1994): 21. Patrick E. Tyler, "War in 1990's: New Doubts," *New York Times*, February 18, 1992.

50. Quoted in Tyler, "War in 1990's."

51. "Excerpts from Pentagon Plan: Prevent the Re-emergence of a New Rival," *New York Times*, March 8, 1992. This is the same draft defense guidance in which Under Secretary Paul Wolfowitz introduced a tentative version of what would under President George Bush be called preemption — the explicit endorsement of preventative war as U.S. policy, as we will see in chapter 4.

52. Gallup Poll data compiled in Harold W. Stanley and Richard G. Niemi, *Vital Statistics on American Politics, 1999–2000* (CD-ROM) (Washington, D.C.: Congressional Quarterly Press, 2000).

53. Ibid.

54. "Through almost a half century of sacrifice, constancy and strength, the American people advanced democracy's triumph in the Cold War. Only new leadership that restores our nation's greatness at home can successfully draw upon these same strengths of the American people to lead the world into a new era of peace and freedom." Also: "In recent years we have seen brave people abroad face down tanks, defy coups, and risk exodus by boat on the high seas for a chance at freedom and the kind of opportunities we call the American Dream. It is time for Americans to fight against the decline of those same

opportunities here at home." *Democratic Party Platform of 1992*. Archived by The American Presidency Project: www.presidency.ucsb.edu/showplatforms.php?platindex=D1992.

55. Ibid. For the lopsided relationship between domestic politics and national security in the Clinton campaign see also Bill Clinton and Al Gore, *Putting People First: How We Can All Change America* (New York: Times Books, 1992).

56. For an elaboration of this argument see Daniel Wirls, "Busted: Government and Elections in the Era of Deficit Politics," *Do Elections Matter?* ed. Benjamin Ginsberg and Alan Stone, 3d ed. (Armonk, N.Y.: M. E. Sharpe, 1996), 65–85.

57. Phil Duncan and Steve Langdon, "When Congress Had to Choose It Voted to Back Clinton," *Congressional Quarterly Weekly Report*, December 18, 1993, 3427–31.

58. Indeed, the administration's attempt to change the military's policy on homosexuals sparked the first filibuster of the session when some Republican senators sought to attach an amendment on the policy to the Family Leave Act.

59. Quoted in Bob Woodward, *The Agenda: Inside the Clinton White House* (New York: Simon and Schuster, 1994), 227.

60. Chairman of the JCS Colin Powell's characterization. Quoted in John Lancaster, "Pentagon Issues Plan for Future," *Washington Post*, September 2, 1993.

61. Les Aspin, Secretary of Defense, *Report of the Bottom-Up Review*, October 1993, iii (hereafter BUR). During the presidential campaign, as House Armed Services chair, Aspin had released an influential study of options for resizing U.S. military forces in the wake of the end of the Cold War and the results of the Gulf War: Les Aspin, *An Approach to Sizing American Conventional Forces for the Post-Soviet Era: Four Illustrative Options*, House Armed Services Committee white paper, February 25, 1992. Some important aspects of Aspin's thinking reflected in this report found its way into the BUR.

62. BUR, 1.

63. Ibid., 1–2.

64. Lancaster, "Pentagon Plan."

65. BUR, 13.

66. Ibid., 18–19.

67. Krepinevich, "An Assessment," 49.

68. BUR, 18–19.

69. Ibid., 30.

70. Ibid., 15.

71. Ibid., 3–4.

72. Remarks of Anthony Lake, Assistant to the President for National Security Affairs, "From Containment to Enlargement," Johns Hopkins University, School of Advanced International Studies, Washington, D.C., September 21, 1993, www.mtholyoke.edu/acad/intrel/lakedoc.html. For a later articulation see *A National Security Strategy of Engagement and Enlargement*, The White House, February 1995, www.fas.org/spp/military/docops/national/1996stra.htm.

73. Kitty Cunningham, "The Senate's Last Word on Gays," *Congressional Quarterly Weekly Online*, September 11, 1993, 2401, http://library.cqpress.com/cqweekly/WR10 3402320; Pat Towell, "Slightly Revised Ban on Gays Is Codified in Defense Bill," *Congressional Quarterly Weekly Online*, October 2, 1993, 2668–69, http://library.cqpress.com/cqweekly/WR103402536.

74. Lawrence J. Korb, "Shock Therapy for the Pentagon," *New York Times*, February 15, 1994; Krepinevich, "An Assessment"; Carl J. Conetta, "Mismatch: The 'Bottom

Up Review' and America's Security Requirements in the New Era," Project on Defense Alternatives, Testimony before the Committee on Armed Services, U.S. House of Representatives, March 10, 1994, www.comw.org/pda/congress.htm; David Isenberg, "The Pentagon's Fraudulent Bottom-Up Review," Policy Analysis no. 206, Cato Institute, April 21, 1994, www.cato.org/pub_display.php?pub_id=1065; Robert L. Borosage, "Disinvesting in America," Michael L. Klare, "The Two War Strategy," and Colleen O'Connor, "The Waste Goes On — & On & On," all in *The Nation*, October 4, 1993, 346–51.

75. Aspin quoted in John M. Collins, "Military Preparedness: Principles Compared with U.S. Practices," CRS Report for Congress, 94-48 S, January 21, 1994, 8. See also Barton Gellman, "Defense Program Exceeds Budget Target, Aspin Says," *Washington Post*, September 15, 1993.

76. Larence T. DiRita, Baker Spring, and John Luddy, "Thumbs Down to the Bottom-Up Review," Backgrounder #957, Heritage Foundation, September 24, 1993, www.heritage.org/Research/NationalSecurity/BG957.cfm.

77. Ibid.

78. "Transcript," *New York Times*, September 26, 1988.

79. "Budget Director Defends Military Spending Plan," *New York Times*, January 29, 1990.

80. "President Urges Caution in Reacting to East Bloc," *San Jose Mercury News*, February 8, 1990.

81. Bush, "Remarks at the Aspen Institute."

82. Cheney, *Annual Report*, 59.

83. Ibid., 66.

84. BUR, 43

85. Ibid., 47.

CHAPTER 3 : What Comes Down Must Go Up

1. *Democratic Party Platform of 1992*. Archived by The American Presidency Project: www.presidency.ucsb.edu/showplatforms.php?platindex=D1992.

2. "Excerpts from President-Elect's News Conference in Arkansas," *New York Times*, November 13, 1992; Eric Schmitt, "The Transition: Challenging the Military; In Promising to End Ban on Homosexuals, Clinton Is Confronting a Wall of Tradition," *New York Times*, November 12, 1992; John H. Cushman Jr., "Gay Rights; Top Military Officers Object to Lifting Homosexual Ban," *New York Times*, November 14, 1992; "Excerpts from Clinton News Conference after Meeting with Lawmakers," *New York Times*, November 17, 1992; John F. Harris, *The Survivor: Bill Clinton in the White House* (New York: Random House, 2005), xxvii.

3. Bob Woodward, *The Agenda: Inside the Clinton White House* (New York: Simon and Schuster, 1994), 111–12. Zoë Baird was Clinton's nominee for attorney general; her nomination would soon be withdrawn.

4. Pat Towell, "Campaign Promise, Social Debate Collide on Military Battlefield," *Congressional Quarterly Weekly Report*, January 30, 1993, 226–29; Harris, *Survivor*, 16–17; "Clinton Announces Compromise on Gays in Military," *Congressional Quarterly Weekly Report*, July 24, 1993, 1975–76.

5. Pulitzer Prize–winning reporting by Eileen Welsome pushed this issue before the public; see her *The Plutonium Files: America's Secret Medical Experiments in the Cold War*

(New York: Dial, 1999). The Final Report of the Advisory Committee on Human Radiation Experiments, which does not seem to be available through the DOE website any longer, is available at: http://biotech.law.lsu.edu/research/reports/ACHRE/report.html.

6. For official assessments of the cleanup project early in the Clinton administration see U.S. Congress, Office of Technology Assessment, "Dismantling the Bomb and Managing Nuclear Materials" (September 1993); Congressional Budget Office, "Cleaning Up the Department of Energy's Nuclear Weapons Complex" (May 1994); U.S. Department of Energy, "Closing the Circle on the Splitting of the Atom: The Environmental Legacy of Nuclear Weapons Production in the United States and What the Department of Energy Is Doing about It" (January 1996).

7. In 1997 the midrange estimate by DOE was $227 billion (in 1996 dollars) over seventy-five years. Mark Holt, "Nuclear Weapons Production Complex: Environmental Compliance and Waste Management," Congressional Research Service, *CRS Issue Brief for Congress*, January 17, 1997.

8. For a history and analysis of how Congress did this, see Charlotte Twight, "Department of Defense Attempts to Close Military Bases: The Political Economy of Congressional Resistance," in Robert Higgs, ed., *Arms, Politics, and the Economy: Historical and Contemporary Perspectives* (New York: Holmes and Meier, 1990); Kenneth R. Mayer, "Closing Military Bases (Finally): Solving Collective Action Problems through Delegation," *Legislative Studies Quarterly* (August 1995): 393–413.

9. General Accounting Office, "Military Bases: Analysis of the DoD's 2005 Selection Process for Base Closures and Realignments," GAO-05-785, July 2005, 18.

10. Statement of Neil M. Singer, Acting Assistant Director, National Security Division, Congressional Budget Office on DoD's Environmental Cleanup before the Subcommittee on Military Readiness and Defense Infrastructure Committee on Armed Services United States Senate, May 4, 1994, www.cbo.gov/doc.cfm?index=4905&type=0.

11. Near the end of the 1990s, the fiscal corner had been turned. By 2001, the GAO estimated that closing and realigning these installations had saved taxpayers around $15.5 billion through fiscal 2001 even taking cleanup costs into account. General Accounting Office, "Military Base Closures: DoD's Updated Net Savings Estimate Remains Substantial," GAO-01-971, July 2001. Even so, the 2005 round of BRAC closures and realignments, by some measures the biggest and most complex yet, was projected to have greater costs than savings for at least twelve years; see Suzanne Gamboa, "GAO: Base Closings to Cost More, Save Less," Associated Press, December 13, 2007, www.armytimes.com/news/2007/12/ap_gaobaseclosings_071212/; General Accounting Office, "Military Bases," July 2005.

12. One study that documents governmental attention to the economic effects and reviews earlier postwar downturns in military spending is U.S. Congress, Office of Technology Assessment, *After the Cold War: Living with Lower Defense Spending*, OTA-ITE-524 (Washington, D.C.: Government Printing Office, February 1992).

13. Leslie Wayne, "The Shrinking Military Complex; After the Cold War, the Pentagon Is Just Another Customer," *New York Times*, February 27, 1998; Norman R. Augustine, "The Last Supper, Revisited,"*Defense News* 26 (June 2006), http://integrator.hanscom.af.mil/2006/June/06292006/06292006-13.htm.

14. Jack Egan and Dana Coleman, "Get Bigger or Get Out," *U.S. News and World Report*, November 24, 1996; Ann R. Markusen and Sean S. Costigan, "The Military Industrial Challenge," in *Arming the Future: A Defense Industry for the 21st Century*, ed. Ann R.

Markusen and Sean S. Costigan (New York: Council on Foreign Relations Press, 1999), 13–14; John J. Dowdy, "Winners and Losers in the Arms Industry Downturn," *Foreign Policy* (summer 1997): 88–101. On this process generally and for a closer look at General Dynamics, see Rachel Weber, *Swords into Dowshares* (Boulder, Col.: Westview Press, 2001).

15. General Accounting Office, "Defense Industry: Consolidation and Options for Preserving Competition" (GAO/NSIAD-98-141), April 1998; William Greider, *Fortress America* (New York: Public Affairs, 1999), 81–83.

16. General Accounting Office, "Defense Industry Restructuring: Cost and Savings Issues" (GAO/T-NSIAD-97-141), April 15, 1997; Weber, *Dowshares*, 91–92; Sanford Gottlieb, *Defense Addiction* (Boulder, Col.: Westview Press, 1997), 24–26.

17. Greg Bischak, "Defense Conversion," *Foreign Policy in Focus* (January 1997), www .fpif.org/briefs/vol2/v2n5def.html; Douglas Jehl, "Clinton Preaches Military Conversion to an Area Hit Hard by Cuts," *New York Times*, August 14, 1993.

18. Les Aspin, Secretary of Defense, "Report of the Bottom-Up Review," October 1993, 34, 57.

19. Ronald O'Rourke, "Navy Attack Submarine Force-Level Goal and Procurement Rate: Background and Issues for Congress," Congressional Research Service, June 2, 2004, www.fas.org/man/crs/RL32418.pdf.

20. *Congressional Quarterly Weekly Report*, August 6, 1994 (Bell Boeing). Among others, see *Congressional Quarterly Weekly Report*, June 20, 1992 (McDonnell Douglas, F/A 18 fighter); October 24, 1994 (General Dynamics, M1A2 tank); June 3, 1995 (Newport News Shipbuilding, New Attack submarine); June 10, 1995 (General Dynamics, Seawolf submarine); June 24, 1995 (General Dynamics, M1A2 tank); August 5, 1995 (Lockheed, Boeing, Pratt & Whitney, F-22 fighter); n.d., about 1995 (American Eurocopter, training helicopter, author copy).

21. Author witnessed. As mentioned in the acknowledgements, the author was an APSA congressional fellow from September 1993 through July 1994 and witnessed many examples of the power of purely economic arguments during this period.

22. From an average of nearly $60 billion in deliveries during 1986–1989 to an average of $41 billion during 1991–1994. State Department, WMEAT 1997, www.fas.org/pro grams/ssp/asmp/factsandfigures/government _ data _ index.html.

23. David Mussington, *Understanding Contemporary International Arms Transfer* (London: Brassey's, 1994), 11.

24. Ethan B. Kapstein, "America's Arms-Trade Monopoly," *Foreign Affairs* (May/June 1994): 16; see also Norman Graham, *Seeking Security and Development* (Boulder, Col.: Lynne Rienner, 1994), 55.

25. U.S. Congress, Joint Economic Committee, Subcommittee on Technology and National Security, "Arms Trade and Nonproliferation" (Washington, D.C.: U.S. Government Printing Office, 1992), 12; William Keller, *Arm in Arm: The Political Economy of the Global Arms Trade* (New York: Basic Books, 1995), 65.

26. Keller, *Arm in Arm*, 68.

27. Ibid., 69.

28. "After the War: The President; Transcript of President Bush's Address on End of the Gulf War," *New York Times*, March 7, 1991; Andrew Rosenthal, "Bush Unveils Plan for Arms Control in the Middle East," *New York Times*, May 30, 1991; Mark Thompson, "Mideast Trade Called Crucial to Jobs in U.S.," *San Jose Mercury News*, April 19, 1992;

Andrew Rosenthal, "The 1992 Campaign: Republicans; Jet Sale to Saudis Approved by Bush, Saving Jobs in U.S.," *New York Times*, September 12, 1992; George Bush, "Remarks to McDonnell Aircraft Employees in St. Louis, Missouri," September 11, 1992, http://bushlibrary.tamu.edu/research/public_papers.php?id=4787&year=1992&month=9.

29. William D. Hartung, *And Weapons for All* (New York: Harper Perennial, 1995), 276–77.

30. Lee Feinstein, "Bush Approves Arms Sales to China, Kuwait in Final Weeks," *Arms Control Today* (January/February 1998): 23.

31. Hartung, *Weapons for All*, 154.

32. Lora Lumpe, "The Administration's Non-Proliferation and Export Control Policy," *Arms Control Today* (November 1993): 9.

33. William Hartung, "Nixon's Children," *World Policy Journal* (summer 1995): 25.

34. Mark Thompson, "Going Up, Up in Arms," *Time*, December 12, 1994, 47–48.

35. Sarah Walkling, "Clinton Signs Sales Directive," *Arms Control Today* (March 1995): 29.

36. White House, Office of the Press Secretary, "Fact Sheet: Conventional Arms Transfer Policy," February 17, 1995; Lora Lumpe, "Bill Clinton's America: Arms Merchant to the World," www.fas.org.asmp/library/articles/tnva595.htm.

37. General Dynamics advertisement from *Congressional Quarterly Weekly Report*, author's copy.

38. Peter Cary, "Weapons Bazaar," *U.S. News and World Report*, December 9, 1996, 27–38. Apparently this scandal did only so much to solve the problem. In 2007 it was revealed that the Pentagon's surplus program had sold important F-14 parts, some of which ended up in the hands of an Iranian agent (who was caught). This is significant because in 2007 Iran was the only country flying the F-14 and it was in need of parts to keep them in the air. Sharon Theimer, "GAO: Pentagon Improperly Sold F-14 Parts," *San Francisco Chronicle*, August 1, 2007.

39. Mary H. Cooper, "Privatizing the Military," *CQ Researcher*, June 25, 2004, 578.

40. Department of the Army, "Logistics Civil Augmentation Program (LOGCAP)," 1985, Army Regulation 700-137, www.aschq.army.mil/supportingdocs/AR700_137.pdf

41. Cooper, "Privatizing"; P. W. Singer, *Corporate Warriors: The Rise of the Privatized Military Industry*, updated edition (Ithaca, N.Y.: Cornell University Press, 2008), 15–17. One calculation put the value of Pentagon contracts with service-providing private military firms at more than $300 billion from 1994 to 2002, before the dramatic expansion with the Iraq war. See Center for Public Integrity, "Making a Killing: The Business of War," October 28, 2002, http://projects.publicintegrity.org/bow/.

42. It is worth emphasizing that the assumption of cost savings relies largely on the existence of competition rather than on privatization itself; see Deborah D. Avant, *The Market for Force: The Consequences of Privatizing Security* (New York: Cambridge University Press, 2005), chap. 3.

43. Vago Muradian, "DoD Can Save Billions by Outsourcing Work, DSB Says," *Defense Daily*, October 1, 1996.

44. Singer, *Corporate Warriors*, 49.

45. Ibid., 142, emphasis added.

46. GAO, "Contingency Operations: Army Should Do More to Control Contract Cost in the Balkans," GAO/NSIAD-00-225, September 2000, www.gao.gov/archive/2000/ns00225.pdf.

47. Jane Mayer, "Contract Sport: What Did the Vice-President Do for Halliburton?" *New Yorker*, February 16, 2004.

48. Roles and Missions Commission of the Armed Forces, "Directions for Defense," Report to Congress, the Secretary of Defense, and the Chairman of the Joint Chiefs of Staff, May 24, 1995, www.fas.org/man/docs/corm95/di1062.html; Bradley Graham, "Consensus Is Building to Privatize Defense Functions," *Washington Post*, March 20, 1995.

49. Larry Lock, "Is Military Outsourcing Out of Control?" USAWC Strategy Research Project, U.S. Army War College, March 15, 2006, 3, www.dtic.mil/cgi-bin/Get TRDoc?AD=ADA449219&Location=U2&doc=GetTRDoc.pdf. See also Albert A. Robbert, Susan M. Gates, and Marc N. Elliot, "Outsourcing of DoD Commercial Activities: Impacts on Civil Service Employees," RAND National Defense Research Institute, 1997, www.rand.org/pubs/monograph _ reports/MR866/.

50. Ann R. Markusen, "The Case against Privatizing National Security," *Governance: An International Journal of Policy, Administration, and Institutions* 16, no. 4 (October 2003): 480–81; citations omitted. See also Report of the Quadrennial Defense Review, May 1997, section VIII, www.defenselink.mil/qdr/archive/sec8.html.

51. Foremost among these is Singer, *Corporate Warriors*, first published in 2003. Singer also published an earlier article that focused on potential problems. See P. W. Singer, "Corporate Warriors: The Rise of the Privatized Military Industry and Its Ramifications for International Security," *International Security* 26, no. 3 (winter 2001–2002): 186–220.

52. Mary Peterson, "Making a Killing: Privatizing Combat, the New World Order," *Center for Public Integrity*, October 22, 2002, http://projects .publicintegrity.org/bow/re port.aspx?aid=148.

53. Singer, *Corporate Warriors*, 123–29.

54. John McCain, "Going Hollow: The Warnings of Our Chiefs of Staff," July 1993 (author's copy).

55. *Congressional Record*, February 10, 1994, S 1331. This came during debate on the Emergency Supplemental Appropriations Act for FY 1994 when Senator John Kerry offered an amendment that would have reduced 1994 defense appropriations by about $4 billion to pay for the Emergency Supplemental. Inouye's comments were about the quality of naval recruits — about 35% apparently were category 4, that is, with IQs under 100 and usually not high school graduates — not the age and condition of the fleet.

56. *Congressional Record*, February 10, 1994, H 239.

57. Media coverage showing congressional involvement: Pat Towell, "Keeping the Fighting Edge: Monitoring Vital Signs," *Congressional Quarterly Weekly Report*, July 23, 1994, 1996; David C. Morrison, "Ringing Hollow," *National Journal*, September 18, 1993, 2242–44; David C. Morrison, "Modernization Morass," *National Journal*, March 26, 1994, 721–24; Eric Schmitt, "Military Making Less into More, but Some Say Readiness Suffers," *New York Times*, July 5, 1994; Eric Schmitt, "G.O.P. Military Overseer Assails Troop Readiness," *New York Times*, November 17, 1994; Pat Towell, "Concerns about Readiness Fuel Battle over Budget," *Congressional Quarterly Weekly Report*, December 31, 1994, 3614–17.

58. Morrison, "Ringing Hollow," 2243.

59. All quotations in this paragraph from *Congressional Record*, February 10, 1994, H 238–42.

60. For a discussion of various issues involved in measuring and things affecting readi-

ness at the time, see John M. Collins, "Military Preparedness: Principles Compared with U.S. Practices," Congressional Research Service, CRS 94-48 S, January 21, 1994.

61. Pat Towell, "The Meaning of 'Readiness,'" *Congressional Quarterly Weekly Report*, February 12, 1994, 336.

62. Don Fierce, then director of strategic planning at the Republican National Committee, quoted in Dan Balz and Ronald Brownstein, *Storming the Gates: Protest Politics and the Republican Revival* (Boston: Little, Brown, 1996), 15.

63. Morris Dees, *Gathering Storm: America's Militia Threat* (New York: Harper Perennial, 1997); Catherine Stock, *Rural Radicals: Righteous Rage in the American Grain* (New York: Penguin, 1997); Kenneth S. Stern, *A Force upon the Plain: The American Militia Movement and the Politics of Hate* (Norman: University of Oklahoma Press, 1997); Joel Dye, *Harvest of Rage: Why Oklahoma City Is Only the Beginning* (New York: Basic Books, 1998).

64. Jim Keith, *Black Helicopters over America: Strikeforce for the New World Order* (Lilburn, Ga.: IllumiNet Press, 1995).

65. Among the many detailed accounts of the early Clinton presidency are Woodward, *The Agenda*, and Harris, *Survivor*. The best account of the health care reform plan, one that puts the story in its larger political context, is Theda Skocpol, *Boomerang: Health Care Reform and the Turn against Government* (New York: W. W. Norton, 1996).

66. www.house.gov/house/Contract/CONTRACT.html.

67. For a history of the development of the Contract, John B. Bader, *Taking the Initiative: Leadership Agendas in Congress and the "Contract with America"* (Washington, D.C.: Georgetown University Press, 1996).

68. David S. Cloud, "Senate May Be the Middle Ground in GOP Conflicts with Clinton," *Congressional Quarterly Weekly Report*, November 12, 1994, 3225.

69. Pat Towell and Carroll J. Doherty, "Republican Agenda: GOP Strikes at Cutbacks, Peacekeeping Missions," *Congressional Quarterly Weekly Report*, November 19, 1994, 3339–40.

70. The debate over the effect of the Contract is mostly between those who cite direct poll numbers that show little voter knowledge of the Contract and those who argue that it was crucial in nationalizing the campaign around a consistent set of themes. Skeptics include Gary Jacobson, "The 1994 House Elections in Perspective," *Political Science Quarterly* 111 (summer 1996): 203–23. Among those who argue it probably had a broader impact are Alan Abramowitz, "The End of the Democratic Era? 1994 and the Future of Congressional Election Research," *Political Research Quarterly* 48, no. 4 (December 1995): 873–89. A postelection Gallup survey showed considerable knowledge of and support for the Contract, and especially its central individual proposals, among the crucial constituents of the Republican majority in 1994, including men, Perot voters, and suburbanites; see "Contract with America: A Gallup Poll Special Report," *Gallup Poll Monthly*, November 1994, 19–34. For a discussion of arguments about how the Contract helped some candidates and hurt others, see Juliana Gruenwald, "Shallow Tactics or Deep Issues: Fathoming the GOP 'Contract,'" *Congressional Quarterly Weekly Report*, November 19, 1994, 3361–62.

71. It is instructive to compare the quotations of Republicans in defense of antigovernment militia groups made before and even after the Oklahoma bombing to the kind of statements made in the wake of the events of September 11, 2001. In May 1995 at a committee hearing, Representative Helen Chenoweth (R-ID) said, "The most peaceful

and responsible thing this body could do is listen to the complaints of people who have resorted to violent action"; quoted in Alan Greenblatt, "Worth Watching: Helen Chenoweth," *Congressional Quarterly Weekly Report*, October 28, 1995, 3266. Also, after resisting hearings on militias, but still eager to probe governmental actions in Ruby Ridge and Waco, tightly scripted hearings were held by the Republican majority after Oklahoma. Opening the hearing in the House, Judiciary Subcommittee Chair Bill McCullom of Florida opined that "the probability that violent anti-government groups will emerge in any given social setting is directly related to the level of discontent within society. Consequently, levels of anti-government violence or domestic terrorism can be used as a rough gauge of the political instability within any particular social system. There is some truth to the notion that domestic terrorism is or may be the tip of an iceberg, and as such, changes in levels of violent anti-government behavior should be given careful consideration instead of merely thinking of it as the ravings of a few deranged madmen" (U.S. Congress, Hearing of the Crime Subcommittee of the House Judiciary Committee, November 2, 1995). Conservative commentators did not have to be as careful, even after September 11, 2001. A year after the attacks author Ann Coulter told a reporter, "My only regret with Timothy McVeigh is he did not go to the New York Times Building." George Gurley, "Coultergeist," *New York Observer*, August 20, 2002, www.observer.com/node/37827?page=all#.

72. David Maraniss and Michael Weisskopf, *"Tell Newt to Shut Up!"* (New York: Touchstone, 1996); Elizabeth Drew, *Showdown: The Struggle between the Gingrich Congress and the Clinton White House* (New York: Simon and Schuster, 1996); Harris, *Survivor*, 151–219.

73. William S. Cohen, Secretary of Defense, Report of the Quadrennial Defense Review, May 1997 (hereinafter QDR 1997).

74. QDR 1997, v, 60.

75. Ibid., 59.

76. "Clinton Says U.S. Won't Sign Land Mine Treaty," *Congressional Quarterly Weekly Report*, September 20, 1997, 2241; Raymond Bonner, "Land Mine Treaty Takes Final Form over U.S. Dissent," *New York Times*, September 19, 1997.

77. In real dollars (FY 2000) the 1994 national defense budget in outlays was $323 billion and in 1998 $282 billion.

78. For a detailed analysis of spending per active duty personnel through the mid-1990s, see Stephen Daggett, "Defense Spending: Does the Size of the Budget Fit the Size of the Force?" Congressional Research Service, February 28, 1994.

79. There were many reasons why the United States was spending more per personnel than in 1980, including increased pay, training, R&D, and more expensive weapons. These are the improvements that everyone argues ended the "hollow force." Whether all this added up to a nearly 50% increase in spending per personnel was difficult to judge.

80. The initial surpluses depended on counting the excess from Social Security revenues. Without that the 1998 budget was still in deficit and in 1999 was nearly dead even.

81. Frances Fitzgerald provides a summary of ballistic missile defense under Clinton in her *Way Out There in the Blue: Reagan, Star Wars, and the End of the Cold War* (New York: Simon and Schuster, 2000), 490–99.

82. Text of the Act is available at www.fas.org/spp/starwars/congress/1996/s960321a.htm.

83. Online NewsHour, PBS, "Star Wars — The Sequel" (transcript), June 4, 1996, www.pbs.org/newshour/bb/military/star _ wars _ 6-4.html.

84. This was later changed to 3+5 with 2005 the target date for completion of deployment.

85. One of the best backgrounds on the Rumsfeld Commission is "Missile Wars," *Frontline*, October 10, 2002, www.pbs.org/wgbh/pages/frontline/shows/missile/.

86. A detailed account of the Team B episode is offered in John Prados, *The Soviet Estimate: U.S. Intelligence and Russian Military Strength* (New York: Dial, 1982).

87. Report of the Commission to Assess the Ballistic Missile Threat to the United States, July 15, 1998, www.fas.org/irp/threat/missile/rumsfeld/toc.htm.

88. "Statement on Signing the National Missile Defense Act of 1999," July 22, 1999, www.presidency.ucsb.edu/ws/index.php?pid=57940.

89. Quoted in Steven A. Hildreth, "Ballistic Missile Defense: Historical Overview," Congressional Research Service, *CRS Report to Congress*, July 9, 2007, 5; Fitzgerald, *Way Out There*, 498–99.

90. "George W. Bush Holds Campaign Rally in Grand Rapids, Michigan," CNN .com, November 3, 2000, http://transcripts.cnn.com/TRANSCRIPTS/0011/03/se.04 .html.

CHAPTER 4: From Ambition to Empire

1. *Republican Party Platform of 2000*, www.presidency.ucsb.edu/ws/index.php?pid =25849.

2. Ibid.

3. George W. Bush, "A Period of Consequences," speech delivered at the Citadel, September 23, 1999, www.citadel.edu/pao/addresses/pres _ bush.html.

4. From the first presidential debate. Commission on Presidential Debates, www.de bates.org/pages/trans2000a.html. Extended comments during the same debate only reinforced the same rather lukewarm themes and ideas. Bush responded to this question — "How would you go about as president deciding when it was in the national interest to use U.S. force, generally?" — in part as follows: "I think we've got to be very careful when we commit our troops. The vice president and I have a disagreement about the use of troops. He believes in nation building. I would be very careful about using our troops as nation builders. I believe the role of the military is to fight and win war and therefore prevent war from happening in the first place. So I would take my responsibility seriously. And it starts with making sure we rebuild our military power. Morale in today's military is too low. We're having trouble meeting recruiting goals. We met the goals this year, but in the previous years we have not met recruiting goals. Some of our troops are not well-equipped. I believe we're overextended in too many places. And therefore I want to rebuild the military power. It starts with a billion dollar pay raise for the men and women who wear the uniform. A billion dollars more than the president recently signed into law. It's to make sure our troops are well-housed and well-equipped. Bonus plans to keep some of our high-skilled folks in the services and a commander in chief that sets the mission to fight and win war and prevent war from happening in the first place."

5. "George W. Bush holds campaign rally in Grand Rapids, Michigan," CNN.com, November 3, 2000, http://transcripts.cnn.com/TRANSCRIPTS/0011/03/se.04.html.

6. Based on word counts from official transcripts. Commission on Presidential Debates, www.debates.org/pages/trans2000a.html.

7. Ibid.

8. Gerald M. Pomper, ed., *The Election of 2000* (New York: Chatham House, 2001), 145–46; Michael Nelson, ed., *The Elections of 2000* (Washington, D.C.: Congressional Quarterly, 2001); Richard Johnston, Michael G. Hagen, and Kathleen Hall Jamieson, *The 2000 Presidential Election and the Foundations of Party Politics* (New York: Cambridge University Press, 2004).

9. www.cnn.com/ELECTION/2000/results/index.epolls.html.

10. Ibid.

11. Furthermore: "We will confront weapons of mass destruction, so that a new century is spared new horrors." Inaugural Address, January 20, 2001. Reprinted in Pomper, *Election of 2000*, 202–5.

12. "Address before a Joint Session of the Congress on Administration Goals," February 27, 2001, American Presidency Project, www.presidency.ucsb.edu/ws/index.php?pid =29643.

13. Carl Conetta, "9/11 and the Meanings of Military Transformation," Project on Defense Alternatives, February 6, 2003, www.comw.org/pda/0302conetta.html.

14. Bush, "Period of Consequences."

15. Ibid.

16. See, e.g., the website for the Association of the U.S. Army for a rather pointed July 2001 commentary on the deleterious effects such a skip would have on the army, www.ausa.org/PDFdocs/issue2.pdf.

17. "The Budget and Economic Outlook: Fiscal Years 2002–2011; Statement of Barry Anderson, Deputy Director, before the Committee on the Budget, U.S. Senate," Congressional Budget Office, January 31, 2001, www.cbo.gov/ftpdocs/27xx/doc2728/Entire -Testimony.pdf.

18. "On the Stump," *PBS News Hour*, November 1, 2000, www.pbs.org/newshour/ bb/politics/july-dec00/stump_11-01.html.

19. "Address of the President to the Joint Session of Congress," February 27, 2007, www.whitehouse.gov/news/releases/2001/02/20010228.html.

20. The White House, "The President's Agenda for Tax Relief," www.whitehouse .gov/news/reports/taxplan.html; Steve Liesman, "Bush's $1.6 Trillion Tax Cut May Not Deliver Right Fix—Some Economists Dislike Using Fiscal Measures to Prop Up Economy," *Wall Street Journal*, January 8, 2001.

21. Liesman, "$1.6 Trillion Tax Cut."

22. For example, see "Press Briefing by Ari Fleisher," Office of the Press Secretary, www.whitehouse.gov, February 27, 2001, www.whitehouse.gov/news/briefings/200102 27.html.

23. Congressional Budget Office, *Pay as You Go Estimate*, June 4, 2001, www.cbo.gov/ ftpdoc.cfm?index=2867&type=0&sequence=0.

24. For a comprehensive analysis of the attack on the estate tax as part of the broader conservative agenda see Michael J. Graetz and Ian Shapiro, *Death by a Thousand Cuts: The Fight over Taxing Inherited Wealth* (Princeton, N.J.: Princeton University Press, 2005).

25. Refers to Revenue Act of 1964 and Economic Recovery Tax Act of 1981. William Ahern, "Comparing the Kennedy, Reagan and Bush Tax Cuts," Tax Foundation, August 24, 2004, www.taxfoundation.org/news/show/323.html.

26. www.whitehouse.gov/news/releases/2001/08/print/20010824.html. See also David E. Sanger, "President Asserts Shrunken Surplus May Curb Congress," *New York Times*, August 25, 2001.

27. "Remarks by Office of Management and Budget Director Mitchell E. Daniels Jr. at Conference Board Annual Meeting," October 16, 2001, www.whitehouse.gov/omb/pubpress/daniels _ conference _ board _ speech10-16-01.html.

28. "A Blueprint for New Beginnings: A Responsible Budget for America's Priorities," www.whitehouse.gov/news/usbudget/blueprint/budtoc.html.

29. For example, compare the histories of his job approval ratings at the Polling Report: www.pollingreport.com/bushjob2.htm; http://abcnews.go.com/images/Politics/Bush _ Retrospective _ Charts.pdf.

30. One survey taken on September 9, 2001 showed only 48% of Americans approving of the president's handling of the economy versus 72% in early November, Washington Post–ABC News Polls, www.washingtonpost.com/wp-srv/politics/documents/postpoll _ 041408.html?sid=ST2008041403445.

31. Passed on September 14 by votes of 98–0 in the Senate and then 420–1 in the House, the Authorization for Use of Military Force was signed by the president on September 18. See Richard F. Grimmett, "Authorization for Use of Military Force in Response to the 9/11 Attacks (P.L. 107-40): Legislative History," Congressional Research Service, January 16, 2007.

32. I discuss the role of the Project for a New American Century briefly near the end of this chapter, but there is a substantial literature documenting the very public campaign in the 1990s to push for greater military power and use it to unilaterally change the world, starting with Iraq, a campaign led by key actors who would become part of the Bush national security and foreign policy team: James Mann, *Rise of the Vulcans: The History of Bush's War Cabinet* (New York: Penguin, 2004); George Packer, *The Assassins' Gate: America in Iraq* (New York: Farrar, Straus, and Giroux, 2005); Andrew Bacevich, *The New American Militarism* (New York: Oxford University Press, 2005); Thomas Ricks, *Fiasco: The American Military Adventure in Iraq* (New York: Penguin, 2006).

33. Donald Rumsfeld, "Testimony before the Senate Armed Services Committee: Defense Review Strategy," June 21, 2001, www.defenselink.mil/Speeches/Speech.aspx?SpeechID=377.

34. Quadrennial Defense Review Report, Department of Defense, September 30, 2001, v (hereinafter QDR 2001).

35. Ibid., iii, 11.

36. Rumsfeld, "Testimony."

37. QDR 2001, iv.

38. The closest thing to such a statement found by the author came from Les Aspin in 1992 while he was still chair of the House Armed Services Committee, several months before becoming Clinton's first and ill-fated Secretary of Defense: "There is no alternative to a threat-based force structure . . . sized and shaped to cope with the 'things' that threaten Americans." Quoted in *Congressional Quarterly Weekly Report*, January 9, 1993, 82.

39. Michael E. O'Hanlon, *Defense Policy Choices for the Bush Administration*, 2d ed. (Washington, D.C.: Brookings Institution, 2002), 13.

40. Ibid., 10.

41. QDR 2001, 13–14 (emphasis added).

42. Richard A. Clarke, *Against All Enemies* (New York: Free Press, 2004); National Commission on Terrorist Attacks upon the United States, *The 9/11 Report* (New York: St. Martin's Press, 2004), chaps. 6–8.

43. J. D. Crouch, Assistant Secretary of Defense for International Security Policy, Special Briefing on the Nuclear Posture Review, January 9, 2002, www.defenselink.mil/transcripts/2002/t01092002 _ t0109npr.html.

44. *National Security Strategy of the United States of America*, The White House, September 2002, 30 (hereinafter NSS 2002).

45. QDR 2001, 12.

46. Ibid., 62.

47. Ibid., 36.

48. Ibid., 11.

49. Ibid., 21.

50. Ibid., 18.

51. Ibid., 17 (emphasis added).

52. Ibid., 3 and 6.

53. Ibid., 32.

54. Ibid.

55. Ibid., 47–48.

56. Bob Woodward, *Bush at War* (New York: Simon and Schuster, 2002); Michael R. Gordon and Bernard E. Trainor, *Cobra II: The Inside Story of the Invasion and Occupation of Iraq* (New York: Pantheon, 2006); Ricks, *Fiasco*.

57. Woodward, *Bush at War*, 60.

58. "Address to a Joint Session of Congress and the American People," September 20, 2001, www.whitehouse.gov/news/releases/2001/09/20010920-8.html.

59. 2002 State of the Union Address, www.whitehouse.gov/news/releases/2002/01/20020129-11.html.

60. "President Bush Delivers Graduation Speech at West Point" (text of address), www.whitehouse.gov/news/releases/2002/06/20020601-3.html.

61. NSS 2002, 15.

62. Ibid.

63. Winslow Wheeler, "The Week of Shame: Congress Wilts as the President Demands an Unclogged Road to War," *Center for Defense Information*, January 2003, 5.

64. NSS 2002, 15.

65. Carl Kaysen, John D. Steinbruner, and Martin B. Malin, "Behind the Prospect of War with Iraq: The New U.S. National Security Strategy," *FAS Public Interest Report*, September/October 2002, www.fas.org/faspir/2002/v55n5/war.htm. See also Michael O'Hanlon, *Defense Strategy for the Post-Saddam Era* (Washington, D.C.: Brookings Institution, 2005), 8–9; Volker Kroening, "Prevention or Preemption? Towards a Clarification of Terminology," www.comw.org/pda/0303kroening.html.

66. NSS 2002, 25, 27, 15.

67. Jeffrey W. Knopf, "Wrestling with Deterrence: Bush Administration Strategy after 9/11," *Contemporary Security Policy* 29, no. 2 (August 2008): 229–65.

68. As Bush put it in his 2002 West Point commencement address: "For much of the last century, America's defense relied on the Cold War doctrines of deterrence and containment. In some cases, those strategies still apply. But new threats also require new thinking. Deterrence—the promise of massive retaliation against nations—means nothing against shadowy terrorist networks with no nation or citizens to defend. Containment is not possible when unbalanced dictators with weapons of mass destruction can deliver those weapons on missiles or secretly provide them to terrorist allies."

69. Michael T. Klare, "The Clinton Doctrine," *The Nation*, April 19, 1999, www.the
nation.com/doc/19990419/klare.

70. "Excerpts from Pentagon Plan: Prevent the Re-emergence of a New Rival," *New
York Times*, March 8, 1992; Patrick E. Tyler, "U.S. Strategy Plan Calls for Insuring No
Rivals Develop a One-Superpower World," *New York Times*, March 8, 1992; and "Pen-
tagon Drops Goal of Blocking New Superpowers," *New York Times*, May 24, 1992.

71. All quotations drawn from the PNAC website, www.newamericancentury.org/
index.html.

72. Rumsfeld, Cheney, and Wolfowitz, all charter members of PNAC, were also par-
tisans and architects of transformation, as we've seen with the QDR and NSS. Some of the
connections have a long history, including Paul Wolfowitz's graduate training at the University of Chicago with Albert Wohlstetter, one of the earliest theorists of the revolution in
military affairs. On this last point, see Andrew Bacevich, *The New American Militarism*
(New York: Oxford University Press, 2005), 158–63.

73. In addition to Ricks, *Fiasco*, see James Fallows, "Blind into Baghdad," *Atlantic
Monthly*, January/February 2004; and "Rumsfeld's War," *Frontline*, PBS, 2004, www.pbs
.org/wgbh/pages/frontline/shows/pentagon/.

74. NSS 2002, prefatory letter.

75. NSS 2002, 13 and 14.

76. Special Briefing on the Nuclear Posture Review, January 9, 2002, www.defense
link.mil/transcripts/2002/t01092002_t0109npr.html; Michael R. Gordon, "U.S. Nuclear Plan Sees New Targets and New Weapons," *New York Times*, March 10, 2002.

77. Nuclear Posture Review, www.globalsecurity.org/wmd/library/policy/dod/npr
.htm (excerpts quoted; hereinafter NPR).

78. QDR 2001, 12.

79. One very direct prequel to the NPR is a January 2001 report by Keith Payne and
the National Institute for Public Policy: "Rationale and Requirements for U.S. Nuclear
Forces and Arms Control," www.ceip.org/files/projects/npp/pdf/nippnukes.pdf. The
participants in the study included Cold War hawks such as Max Kampelman, Colin
Gray, and Fred Ikle, who also signed on to the Project for a New American Century, and
Stephen Cambone, who was staff director of the Rumsfeld commission on BMD in the
late 1990s and who would serve in several positions in the Rumsfeld Pentagon under
President Bush.

80. NPR.

81. Ibid.

82. Ibid.

83. Dan Stober, "Nuclear 'Bunker Busters' Sought," *San Jose Mercury News*, April 23,
2003.

84. For one discussion of the likelihood of significant nuclear fallout with the use
of nuclear bunker-busters: Robert W. Nelson, "Low-Yield Earth-Penetrating Nuclear
Weapons," *FAS Public Interest Report*, January/February 2001, www.fas.org/faspir/2001/
v54n1/weapons.htm.

85. The exact fate of the RNEP program was uncertain. For FY 2006 the House did
not include money for the program and the Senate agreed to take out its line-item at
the request of the DOE. But relevant research continued. Matthew L. Wald, "Nuclear
Weapons Money Is Cut from Spending Bill," *New York Times*, November 23, 2004; "US
Dumps Bunker-Buster—or Not?" *Jane's*, November 17, 2005, www.janes.com/defence/

news/jid/jido511117 _ 1 _ n.shtml; James Sterngold, "Failure to Launch," *Mother Jones*, January/February 2008, 59–63.

86. NPR, 30.

87. "Complex 2030: DOE's Misguided Plan to Rebuild the U.S. Nuclear Weapons Complex," www.ucsusa.org/global _ security/nuclear _ weapons/complex-2030-does -misguided.html. For a detailed summary of how the Complex 2030 plan evolved during the Bush administration, see *Report on the Plan for Transformation of the National Nuclear Security Administration Nuclear Weapons Complex*, Office of Defense Programs, National Nuclear Security Administration, U.S. Department of Energy, January 31, 2007, http:// www.nnsa.energy.gov/news/documents/Trans _ of _ NNSA _ WC _ 2007-31-07.pdf.

88. All quotations in this paragraph are from the NPR.

89. Jane Wales, "US Nuclear Plan Signals a Policy Revolution," www.clw.org/con trol/nprwales.html. For other critiques, see "America as Nuclear Rogue," *New York Times*, March 12, 2002.

90. Richard Sokolsky and Eugene B. Rumer, "Nuclear Alarmists," *Washington Post National Weekly Edition*, March 25–31, 2002; Andrew Krepinevich, "The Real Problem with Our Nuclear Posture," *New York Times*, March 14, 2002.

91. Charlie Savage, *Takeover: The Return of the Imperial Presidency and the Subversion of American Democracy* (New York: Little, Brown, 2007).

92. Among many, two of the best are: Savage, *Takeover*; and Jane Mayer, *The Dark Side: The Inside Story of How the War on Terror Turned into a War on American Ideals* (New York: Doubleday, 2008). For a succinct account, see Elizabeth Drew, "Power Grab," *New York Review of Books*, June 22, 2006. One that covers some of the impact on domestic policy-making as well is Charles Tiefer, *Veering Right: How the Bush Administration Subverts the Law for Conservative Causes* (Berkeley: University of California Press, 2004).

93. Quoted in Kenneth T. Walsh, "The Cheney Factor," *U.S. News and World Report*, January 23, 2006.

94. Harold Koh, *The National Security Constitution: Sharing Power after the Iran-Contra Affair* (New Haven, Conn.: Yale University Press, 1990); Louis Henkin, *Foreign Affairs and the United States Constitution* (New York: Oxford University Press, 1997).

95. For a few of dozens of works addressing the history and pros and cons of the theory of the unitary executive, see Christopher S. Kelley, "Rethinking Presidential Power — The Unitary Executive and the George W. Bush Presidency," paper prepared for the 63rd Annual Meeting of the Midwest Political Science Association, 2005, www.pegc.us/ar chive/Unitary%20Executive/kelly _ unit _ exec _ and _ bush.pdf; Steven G. Calabresi and Christopher S. Yoo, *The Unitary Executive: Presidential Power from Washington to Bush* (New Haven, Conn.: Yale University Press, 2008); John Dean, *Broken Government: How Republican Rule Destroyed the Legislative, Executive, and Judicial Branches* (New York: Viking, 2007), 102–10; Jennifer Van Bergen, "The Unitary Executive: Is the Doctrine Behind the Bush Presidency Consistent with a Democratic State?" Findlaw, January 9, 2006, http:// writ.news.findlaw.com/commentary/20060109 _ bergen.html.

96. Text of the "Detainee Treatment Act of 2005," http://jurist.law.pitt.edu/gazette/ 2005/12/detainee-treatment-act-of-2005-white.php.

97. President's Statement on Signing of H.R. 2863, the "Department of Defense, Emergency Supplemental Appropriations to Address Hurricanes in the Gulf of Mex-ico, and Pandemic Influenza Act, 2006," www.whitehouse.gov/news/releases/2005/12/ 20051230-8.html.

98. T. J. Halstead, "Presidential Signing Statements: Constitutional and Institutional Implications," *Congressional Research Service*, September 17, 2007, 1; drawing on Philip J. Cooper, "George W. Bush, Edgar Allan Poe and the Use and Abuse of Presidential Signing Statements," *Presidential Studies Quarterly* 35, no. 3 (September 2005): 515–32.

99. Phillip J. Cooper, *By Order of the President: The Use and Abuse of Executive Direct Action* (Lawrence: University of Kansas Press, 2002), chap. 7; Christopher S. Kelley, "A Comparative Look at the Constitutional Signing Statement: The Case of Bush and Clinton," presented at the 61st Annual Meeting of the Midwest Political Science Association, 2003. For a clear and cogent defense of signing statements, see Christopher S. Yoo, Testimony before the Senate Judiciary Committee, June 27, 2006, http://judiciary.senate.gov/testimony.cfm?id=1969&wit_id=5481.

100. Cooper, "George W. Bush," 515–32.

101. Charlie Savage, "Bush Challenges Hundreds of Laws, President Cites Powers of His Office," *Boston Globe*, April 30, 2006.

102. T. J. Halstead, "Presidential Signing Statements: Constitutional and Institutional Implications," *Congressional Research Service*, September 17, 2007, 9.

103. Editorial, "Veto? Who Needs a Veto?" *New York Times*, May 5, 2006.

104. Cooper, "George W. Bush," 516.

CHAPTER 5: Hidden in Plain Sight

1. Quoted in Mary H. Cooper, "Bush's Defense Policy," *CQ Researcher*, September 7, 2001.

2. Quoted in Tim Weiner, "A Vast Arms Buildup, yet Not Enough for War," *New York Times*, October 1, 2004.

3. Ibid.

4. *Congressional Record*, 107th Cong., 1st sess., 2001, 147, no. 162: H 8435, H 8452, H 8454. See also comments by Rep. Blumenaur (D-OR), H 8454–56.

5. Ibid., H 8454, H 8456.

6. Pat Towell, "Defense Bill Wins Solid House Passage; Side Issues Delay Senate Action," *Congressional Quarterly Weekly Report*, September 29, 2001, 2278.

7. The examples from and analysis of the appropriation and authorization bills in this paragraph are from Winslow Wheeler, "Mr. Smith Is Dead," *Center for Defense Information* (October 2002).

8. Towell, "Defense Bill."

9. Quoted in Karen Foerstel and David Nather, "Beneath Capitol's Harmony, Debate Simmers Patiently," *Congressional Quarterly Weekly Report*, September 22, 2001, 2188.

10. www.whitehouse.gov/news/releases/2002/01/20020129-11.html.

11. Weiner, "Arms Buildup." This change can be interpreted as a broader "flow of dollars away from the new and into the old economy, from Hollywood and Silicon Valley toward heavy industry and defense contractors," as investors appeared to be "taking their cues from the White House." Herman Schwartz and Aida A. Hozic, "Who Needs the New Economy?" *Salon*, March 16, 2001, www.salon.com/tech/feature/2001/03/16/Schwartz.

12. Dow Jones Indexes, *Dow Jones Industrials History*, www.djindexes.com/ mdsidx/index.cfm?event=showavgDecades&decade=2000. Stock price histories are from the corporate websites of each military contractor. Of the top six, Boeing was the only exception in the first years of the Bush administration. Boeing is more affected by commercial

markets than the others. But like the others Boeing's stock increased steadily from 2003 to 2008.

13. The figures for the military (050) budget authority come from the OMB, while the supplementals come from the CBO. Official sources (OMB, DOD, GAO, CRS) provide somewhat inconsistent figures for the war supplementals. The numbers for 2001–2007 from each source add up to nearly the same total of between $548 and $560 billion. But there are some discrepancies, including in what fiscal year to count some of the spending. For example, some sources include $25 billion in Title IX "bridge" funding as part of 2004's totals because the money was made available to spend in FY 2004, though it was passed as part of the FY 2005 Defense Appropriations Act.

14. In real (2000) dollars, military spending during the Korean War peaked at $416 billion, during Vietnam at $420 billion, and the Reagan buildup reached $399 billion. By 2005, total military spending reached $420 billion and would continue rising for at least three more years. Budget data from the OMB.

15. This is discussed in greater detail in chapter 6. For one of many examples, see Defense Secretary Gates's testimony before Congress on the 2008 budget: Jim Garamone, "Gates: Historical Context Important When Considering Budget Requests," *Armed Forces Press Service*, February 7, 2007, www.defenselink.mil/news/newsarticle.aspx?id=2966.

16. Weiner, "Arms Buildup."

17. Leslie Wayne, "White House Tries to Trim Military Cost," *New York Times*, December 6, 2005.

18. This calculation includes active guard and reserve. Data from the Department of Defense, OMB, and CBO.

19. Guy Raz, "Air Force Plays Smaller Role in Iraq," *NPR Morning Edition*, October 10, 2007, www.npr.org/templates/story/story.php?storyId=15126640.

20. U.S. war supplementals totaled $169 billion in FY 2007. The combined 2006 military budgets of Great Britain, France, and Japan were about $156 billion.

21. Defense-wide programs include the Missile Defense Agency (MDA), Defense Advanced Research Projects Agency (DARPA), Special Operations Command, Defense Intelligence Agency, and Office of the Secretary of Defense.

22. Kennedy produced a two-year burst in military spending that resulted in a 15% real increase from FY 1961 to 1963, with almost all of the increase coming in 1962, but real decreases in FY 1964 and 1965 reduced military spending to a rather modest 8% increase over five years.

23. Major General Robert Scales, U.S. Army (Ret.), "Transformation," *Armed Forces Journal* (March 2005): 22–27.

24. In fact about the only troops in harm's way were those killed by a suicide car bomb attack while in Lebanon on a peacekeeping mission in 1983. A total of 241 American military personnel died, including 220 Marines, on October 23.

25. For analysis of the nuclear peace movement and the military reform movement, see Daniel Wirls, *Buildup: The Politics of Defense in the Reagan Era* (Ithaca, N.Y.: Cornell University Press, 1992); also Douglas C. Waller, *Congress and the Nuclear Freeze* (Amherst: University of Massachusetts Press, 1987).

26. The author did several versions of this kind of search in the *New York Times* and *Washington Post*. The numbers vary with the search terms and other factors, but the pattern and proportions remain the same.

27. In the 107th Congress (2001–2002) the Republicans had a majority in the House

of 221–212. The Senate was 50–49 in favor of the Democrats with one independent for most of the 107th. The Republican majority increased to 229 and then 232 over the next two congresses. The Senate of the 108th Congress had a 51–48 (1 independent) Republican majority, which increased to 55 in the 109th Congress.

28. Wiener, "Arms Buildup."

29. These cuts were announced as part of the 1997 Quadrennial Defense Review under Secretary of Defense William Cohen.

30. Congressional Budget Office, "A Look at Tomorrow's Tactical Air Forces," January 7, 1997, xii.

31. Leslie Wayne, "Air Force Campaigns to Save Jet Fighter," *New York Times*, January 13, 2005.

32. Pat Towell, "House Puts Pentagon on Notice with Move to Hold Up F-22," *Congressional Quarterly Weekly*, July 24, 1999, 1803–4; Pat Towell, "Defense Bill Conferees Agree to Fund Some F-22 Production but also Require More Testing," *Congressional Quarterly Weekly*, October 9, 1999, 2398–99.

33. The *New York Times* put it charitably: "Responding in part to changing global threats, the F/A-22 was redesigned to allow it to make air-to-ground attacks and not just engage in aerial combat against other fighter jets." Wayne, "Air Force."

34. Ibid.

35. Representative Gingrey, Press Release, January 5, 2005, www.house.gov/apps/list/press/ga11_gingrey/FA22_1_5.html; Wayne, "Air Force."

36. Tim Weiner, "Air Superiority at $258 Million a Pop," *New York Times*, October 27, 2004.

37. Congressional Budget Office, "Budgeting for Naval Forces: Structuring Tomorrow's Navy at Today's Funding Level," October 2000, www.fas.org/man/congress/2000/cbo-n/index.html.

38. Report of the Quadrennial Defense Review, Department of Defense, May 1997, sec. VII. The war games were part of the "Army after Next" project and the army was later embarrassed in the Kosovo conflict when it could not get a force of Apache helicopters to Albania before the fighting ended. Alec Klein, "The Future of Combat," *Washington Post Weekly Edition*, January 7–13, 2008, 6–7.

39. Walter Pincus, "U.S. Strike Kills Six in Al Qaeda," *Washington Post*, November 5, 2002; Dana Priest, "U.S. Citizen among Those Killed in Yemen Predator Missile Strike," *Washington Post*, November 8, 2002.

40. Doug Struck, "Casualties of U.S. Miscalculations: Afghan Victims of CIA Missile Strike Described as Peasants, not Al Qaeda," *Washington Post*, February 11, 2002.

41. Eric Schmitt and Jane Perlez, "Pakistan Says Strikes Worsen Qaeda Threat," *New York Times*, February 25, 2009; Mark Mazzetti, "The Downside of Letting Robots Do the Bombing," *New York Times*, March 22, 2009.

42. P. W. Singer, "Robots at War: The New Battlefield," *Washington Quarterly* (winter 2009), www.wilsoncenter.org/index.cfm?fuseaction=wq.essay&essay_id=496613; and P. W. Singer, *Wired for War: The Robotics Revolution and Conflict in the 21st Century* (New York: Penguin, 2008).

43. Thomas E. Ricks, "Rumsfeld Gets Earful from Troops" *Washington Post*, December 9, 2004.

44. U.S. Senate, Committee on the Armed Services, "National Defense Authorization Act for Fiscal Year 2009, Report," May 12, 2008, 125.

45. John Markoff, "Chief Takes over at Agency to Thwart Attacks on U.S.," *New York Times*, February 13, 2002; Jonathan Riehl, "Lawmakers Likely to Limit New High-Tech Eavesdropping," *Congressional Quarterly Weekly*, February 15, 2003, 406–7; Shane Harris, "TIA Lives On," *National Journal*, February 23, 2006, www.nationaljournal.com/about/njweekly/stories/2006/0223nj1.htm. The OIA logo along with an image of the original website available at The Memory Hole: http://www.thememoryhole.org/policestate/iao.

46. William Arkin, "Not Just a Last Resort? A Global Strike Plan, with a Nuclear Option," *Washington Post*, May 15, 2005; Hans M. Kristensen, "Global Strike a Chronology of the Pentagon's New Offensive Strike Plan," Federation of American Scientists, March 15, 2006, www.fas.org/ssp/docs/GlobalStrikeReport.pdf.

47. Quadrennial Defense Review Report, Department of Defense, February 6, 2006, 31.

48. *Republican Party Platform of 2000*, American Presidency Project, http://www.presidency.ucsb.edu/showplatforms.php?platindex=R2000.

49. President Bush Speech on Missile Defense, May 1, 2001, www.fas.org/nuke/control/abmt/news/010501bush.html.

50. Quadrennial Defense Review Report, Department of Defense, September 30, 2001, 42.

51. Manuel Perez-Rivas, "U.S. Quits ABM Treaty," CNN.com, December 14, 2001, http://archives.cnn.com/2001/ALLPOLITICS/12/13/rec.bush.abm/.

52. White House, National Policy on Ballistic Missile Defense Fact Sheet, www.whitehouse.gov/news/releases/2003/05/20030520-15.html; David E. Sanger, "Bush Issues Directive Describing Policy on Antimissile Defenses," *New York Times*, May 21, 2003.

53. "President Announces Progress in Missile Defense Capabilities," December 17, 2002, www.whitehouse.gov/news/releases/2002/12/20021217.html.

54. Missile Defense Agency, "Fact Sheet: Ballistic Missile Defense Flight Test Record," www.mda.mil/mdalink/pdf/testrecord.pdf. The THAAD experienced six straight failures during one stretch of testing. Even the Patriot battlefield system, though much improved since the Gulf War, would have some problems. It "engaged" a handful of slow, short-range missiles but shot down two allied jets, and an F-16 had to destroy a Patriot battery when its tracking system locked onto the F-16.

55. David Ruppe, "Pentagon Cancels Three More Intercept Tests," *Global Security Newswire*, April 18, 2003, www.nti.org/d_newswire/issues/newswires/2003_4_18.html.

56. David Ruppe, "Pentagon Bid to Study Nuclear-Tipped Missile Interceptors Rejected," *Global Security Newswire*, October 22, 2002; Bradley Graham, "Nuclear-Tipped Interceptors Studied; Rumsfeld Revives Rejected Missile Defense Concept," *Washington Post*, April 11, 2002.

57. Missile Defense Agency, "Fact Sheet: Historical Funding for MDA FY85-08," www.mda.mil/mdalink/pdf/histfunds.pdf.

58. CBO, "The Long-Term Implications of Current Defense Plans: Detailed Update for Fiscal Year 2008," March 2008, www.cbo.gov/ftpdocs/90xx/doc9043/03-20-LTDP2008.htm.

59. The Iraq Study Group Report, 59–60, www.usip.org/isg/iraq_study_group_report/report/1206/index.html; Bryan Bender, "Iraq Panel Assails Bush Use of 'Emergency' War Budgets," *Boston Globe*, December 8, 2006.

60. "President's Statement on H.R. 5122, the 'John Warner National Defense Autho-

rization Act for Fiscal Year 2007,'" www.whitehouse.gov/news/releases/2006/10/2006 1017-9.html. Senator Carl Levin's speech in favor of the amendment summarizes the arguments of its proponents: "Senate Floor Speech on McCain-Byrd Amendment to Require Regular Budgeting for Military Operations in Iraq and Afghanistan," http://levin.senate.gov/newsroom/release.cfm?id=257096.

61. Christian Lowe, " 'Two Sets of Books': U.S. Army, Marines Tap Emergency Funds for Long-Term Changes," *Defense News*, February 14, 2005, www.defensenews.com. See also testimony by Stephen M. Kosiak before Congress: "The Global War on Terror (GWOT): Cost Growth and Estimating Funding Requirements: Hearing before the United States Senate Budget Committee," 110th Congress, February 6, 2007.

62. In the October 25, 2006 memo England wrote: "By this memo, the ground rules for the FY '07 Spring Supplemental are being expanded to include the (Defense) Department's overall efforts related to the Global War on Terror and not strictly to Operation Enduring Freedom and Operation Iraqi Freedom." Memo quoted in James Rosen, "House Committee Prepares to Examine Iraq War Costs," *McClatchy Newspapers*, June 8, 2007, www.mcclatchydc.com/staff/james_rosen/story/15381.html.

63. Gopal Ratnam and William Matthews, "DoD Loosens Supplemental Rules," *Defense News*, November 6, 2006, www.defensenews.com.

64. Julian E. Barnes and Peter Spiegel, "Controversy over Pentagon's War-Spending Plan," *Los Angeles Times*, November 29, 2006.

65. These examples are from Brian Bender, "Weapons That Aren't Ready Dot Bush's War Budget," *Boston Globe*, February 8, 2007.

66. Lowe, "Two Sets of Books."

67. My calculation is based on the $169 billion total of the two FY 2007 supplementals compared to the Defense Department's base budget of $438 billion.

68. For another critical analysis of the use of supplementals see Veronique de Rugy, "The Trillion-Dollar War," *Reason*, May 2008, www.reason.com.

69. Winslow Wheeler ("Mr. Smith") makes a similar argument.

70. Pat Towell, "Afghanistan War Effort to Consume Nearly $50 Million per Day from Requested Emergency Funds," *Congressional Quarterly Weekly*, March 30, 2002, 877.

71. "Senate Panel Grills Rumsfeld over Crusader Cancellation," *Congress Daily*, May 21, 2002.

72. Rowan Scarborough, "Rumsfeld Cancels Army's Crusader 155 mm Howitzer," *Washington Times*, May 9, 2002; Thom Shanker and James Dao, "Army Digs in Its Heels and Saves Howitzer Plan, for Now," *New York Times*, May 2, 2002.

73. For background on the Crusader see Global Security, "Crusader History," www.globalsecurity.org/military/systems/ground/crusader-history3.htm.

74. Scarborough, "Rumsfeld"; Vernon Loeb, "Burying a Cold War Relic," *Washington Post National Weekly Edition*, May 13–19, 2002, 13.

75. Loeb, "Cold War Relic."

76. Pat Towell, "Crusader's Friends on Capitol Hill Keep White House Scrambling," *Congressional Quarterly Weekly*, May 18, 2002, 1326.

77. See for examples the back covers of *Congressional Quarterly Weekly* for May 18 and June 15, 2002, and compare to those (prior to the cancellation decision) of April 6 and 20.

78. Pat Towell and Chuck McCutcheon, "Crusader Down: First Salvo in Cancellation Wars," *Congressional Quarterly Weekly*, May 11, 2002, 1203.

79. Towell, "Crusader's Friends," 1326.

80. Pat Towell, "Appropriators Cut Army's Crusader, but Add Money to Save Local Jobs," *Congressional Quarterly Weekly*, June 29, 2002, 1756. The administration's original FY 2003 request for the Crusader was $476 million. The House and Senate "conferees earmarked $369 million to develop a replacement cannon. That action, combined with changes in other artillery-related programs that were either proposed by the administration or initiated by Congress, brought the total for new artillery programs to $591 million—an increase of $115 million over the administration's original budget request." Not included in this were the contract termination fees (estimated to be around $300 million) to be paid to the contractors. *Congressional Quarterly Weekly*, October 12, 2002, 2681.

81. "Army Cancels Comanche Helicopter," CNN.com, February 23, 2004, www.cnn.com/2004/US/02/23/helicopter.cancel/.

82. Pat Towell, "Hunter Pushes Military Spending Hike as He Prepares for His Ascent to Armed Services Chairmanship," *Congressional Quarterly Weekly*, May 25, 2002, 1410.

83. www.af.mil/factsheets/factsheet.asp?fsID=110.

84. Senator John McCain, "Investigation into Air Force Leasing of Boeing Aerial Refueling Tankers," *Congressional Record*, November 19, 2004, www.fas.org/sgp/congress/2004/s111904.html. See also Colin Clark, "McCain's Nose Out of Joint over Boeing Tanker Deal," *Congressional Quarterly Weekly*, August 2, 2003.

85. Clark, "McCain's Nose."

86. Charles Pope, "Boeing Tanker Deal Faces Inquiry," *Seattle Post-Intelligencer*, September 4, 2003; Niels C. Sorrells, "Air Tanker Deal Turns Spotlight on Murky Procurement Process," *Congressional Quarterly Weekly*, September 6, 2003; "Failed Tanker Deal Described as Boeing 'Bailout,'" *Reuters*, June 7, 2005. In the emails (which are dated after Boeing had won the bid) a Boeing official describes how "Darleen told us several times to keep in mind" that the product from Airbus was $5–17 million "cheaper" than what Boeing had to offer. Another email between two high-ranking Boeing officials "argued that the lease should last for 10 years to provide 'political cover' for Darleen Druyun."

87. John M. Donnelly, "Dispute over Tanker Language Continues even after Defense Authorization Clears," *Congressional Quarterly Weekly*, October 16, 2004.

88. Pope, "Tanker Deal."

89. Ibid.

90. Sorrells, "Air Tanker Deal."

91. Charles Pope, "Pentagon Finalizes Boeing Tanker Deal," *Seattle Post-Intelligencer*, November 7, 2003.

92. Donnelly, "Dispute over Tanker"; also Leslie Wayne, "Boeing Dismisses 2 in Hiring of Official Who Left Pentagon," *New York Times*, November 25, 2003.

93. Leslie Wayne, "Report Faults Air Force on Proposed Boeing Deal," *New York Times*, June 8, 2005.

94. Leslie Wayne, "Pentagon Gives Boeing New Chance at Contract," *New York Times*, July 10, 2008; August Cole and J. Lynn Lunsford, "Boeing Gets Reprieve in Fuel-Tanker Contest," *Wall Street Journal*, September 11, 2008.

95. Jonathan Allen, "Earmark Reform: The First Battle Is to Define the Term," *The Hill*, January 25, 2006, www.hillnews.com/thehill/export/TheHill/News/Frontpage/012506/earmark1.html.

96. The Department of Defense sought to build 8 planes and be finished with the

program. The House and Senate appropriation bills added 4 more, "and in closed con-ference, the leaders of the two appropriations committees decided to add 10, bringing the total to 22." David D. Kirkpatrick, "Earmarks Find Way into Spending Bill," *New York Times*, September 30, 2006; Earmark Watch, http://earmarkwatch.org/2008-house -defense/.

97. Congressional Research Service, "Earmarks in Appropriation Acts: FY 1994, FY 1996, FY 1998, FY 2000, FY 2002, FY 2004," March 17, 2004; and "Earmarks in FY 2006 Appropriations Acts," March 6, 2006.

98. The FY 2006 BMD budget was about $8.8 billion.

99. Diana Evans, *Greasing the Wheels: Using Pork Barrel Projects to Build Majority Coalitions in Congress* (New York: Cambridge University Press, 2004).

100. The details of the CFIUS mandate are detailed by the Treasury Department: www.ustreas.gov/offices/international-affairs/exon-florio/.

101. Tim Starks, "Ports Deal on Hold; Issue Still Hot," *Congressional Quarterly Weekly Report*, February 24, 2006, 550–53; Tim Starks, "Ports Deal Falls to Bipartisan Attack," *Congressional Quarterly Weekly Report*, March 10, 2006, 696–98.

CHAPTER 6: Paying the Price

1. The National Security Strategy of the United States of America, March 2006, www.whitehouse.gov/nsc/nss/2006/nss2006.pdf (hereinafter NSS 2006).

2. NSS 2006, 1.

3. Ibid., 23 and 24.

4. Ibid., introductory letter. False dichotomies were a favorite of Bush and his speech-writers. "You're either with us or against us" and so forth. A twist on this was the use of strawman arguments. As others have pointed out, this typically involved the formulation and invocation of a distorted or exaggerated argument that no one was making or a position no one was taking. The false dichotomy in the 2006 NSS was preceded by a simi-lar formulation in the 2006 State of the Union address in which the president at several points contrasted his policy with the alternative of "isolationism." www.c-span.org/execu tive/stateoftheunion.asp.

5. Quadrennial Defense Review Report, Department of Defense, February 6, 2006 (hereinafter QDR 2006), v; Eric Schmitt and Thom Shanker, "U.S. Officials Retool Slo-gan for Terror War," *New York Times*, July 26, 2005.

6. QDR 2006, vi and 36.

7. NSS 2006, 1.

8. "Rumsfeld Warns on China Military," CNN.com, June 4, 2005, www.cnn.com/ 2005/WORLD/asiapcf/06/04/rumsfeld.asia.ap/; Donna Miles, "Rumsfeld Urges More Transparency from Chinese Military," *American Forces Press Service*, October 20, 2005, www.defenselink.mil/news/Oct2005/20051020_3099.html.

9. Office of the Secretary of Defense, *Annual Report to the Congress: Military Power of the People's Republic of China 2008*, www.defenselink.mil/pubs/china.html.

10. The increases in East Asia and the Middle East are from 2000 to 2006. All changes based on constant dollar measures of defense spending provided by the Stockholm Inter-national Peace Research Institute (SIPRI), www.sipri.org/contents/milap/milex/mex_ trends.html.

11. An example of this are the lessons Saddam Hussein seemed to have drawn from the

Gulf War about how to deal with another U.S. invasion; see Michael R. Gordon and Bernard E. Trainor, *Cobra II: The Inside Story of the Invasion and Occupation of Iraq* (New York: Pantheon, 2006).

12. For an analysis of the decrease in coverage of Afghanistan see Sherry Ricchiardi, "The Forgotten War," *American Journalism Review*, August/September 2006, www.ajr .org/Article.asp?id=4162. As a *New York Times* editorial put it in mid-2005, "Afghanistan is out of the headlines, but its war against the Taliban goes on. These days, it is not going well." "Afghanistan's Forgotten War," August 5, 2005.

13. CNN.com, www.cnn.com/ELECTION/2006/special/issues/iraq/. The economy was a close second in preelection polling, but it eclipsed Iraq in some election-day exit polls.

14. Bob Benenson, "Election 2006: Eight Electoral Signposts," *CQ Weekly*, October 30, 2006, 2867. Republican resignations that resulted from scandals and/or legal convictions include Majority Leader Tom Delay and Representatives Randy "Duke" Cunningham, Bob Ney, and Mark Foley.

15. Nita Lowey, a Democrat on the House Appropriations Committee. Lowey and Pelosi quoted in Michael Abramowitz and Lori Montgomery, "Bush to Request Billions for Wars," *Washington Post*, February 3, 2007.

16. Senator Harry Reid, Press Release, February 2, 2007, http://reid.senate.gov/newsroom/record.cfm?id=268452.

17. Robin Wright and Ann Scott Tyson, "Joint Chiefs Advise Change in War Strategy: Leaders Seek No Major Troop Increase, Urge Shift in Focus to Support Iraqi Army," *Washington Post*, December 14, 2006; Robin Wright and Peter Baker, "White House, Joint Chiefs at Odds on Adding Troops," *Washington Post*, December 19, 2006. Michael Gordon and Thom Shanker, "The Struggle for Iraq; Bush to Name a New General to Oversee Iraq," *New York Times*, January 5, 2007.

18. Thom Shanker and Jim Rutenberg, "President Wants to Increase Size of Armed Forces," *New York Times*, December 20, 2006.

19. Thom Shanker and David S. Cloud, "Rumsfeld Shift Lets Army Seek Larger Budget," *New York Times*, October 8, 2006.

20. "Rebuilding the Army," *Washington Post*, February 6, 2005; "The Army We Need," *New York Times*, November 19, 2006. Oddly the *Times* two days later produced another lead editorial opposing Representative Charles Rangel's proposal to revive the draft even as they acknowledged the difficulty the military was having meeting its rather modest recruiting goals. See "Rejecting the Draft," *New York Times*, November 21, 2006.

21. "Letter to Congress on Increasing U.S. Ground Forces," Project for a New American Century, January 28, 2005, www.newamericancentury.org/defense-20050128.htm.

22. www.heritage.org/Research/NationalSecurity/sr18.cfm.

23. James Jay Carafano, Baker Spring, and Mackenzie M. Eaglen, "Four Percent for Freedom: Maintaining Robust National Security Spending," Heritage Foundation, April 10, 2007, www.heritage.org/Research/NationalSecurity/sr18.cfm.

24. Mitt Romney directly endorsed the 4 percent commitment. Others such as McCain used it as the benchmark to argue that we could afford to spend more. Mitt Romney, "Rising to a New Generation of Global Challenges," *Foreign Affairs* (July/August 2007): 23–24; John McCain, "An Enduring Peace Built on Freedom," *Foreign Affairs* (November/December 2007): 24.

25. Otto Kreisher, "Budget Office Reports War Costs Could Reach $2.4 trillion by

2017," *Congress Daily*, October 24, 2007, www.govexec.com/dailyfed/1007/102407cdpm2 .htm.

26. Thom Shanker, "Joint Chiefs Chairman Looks beyond Current Wars," *New York Times*, October 22, 2007.

27. "Remarks by General James T. Conway, Commandant of the Marine Corps," Center for a New American Security, October 15, 2007, www.marines.mil/cmc/ 34cmc .nsf/speeches?readform.

28. Gates from 2007 quoted by National Public Radio: Guy Raz, "Bush Wants $46 Billion More for Iraq, Afghanistan," *Morning Edition*, October 23, 2007, www.npr.org/ templates/story/story.php?storyId=15546017; Gates's press secretary quoted in Thom Shanker, "Proposed Military Spending Is Highest since WWII," *New York Times*, February 4, 2008; see also Jim Garamone, "Gates: Historical Context Important when Considering Budget Requests," Armed Forces Press Service, February 7, 2007, www.defense link.mil/news/newsarticle.aspx?id=2966.

29. Kim Holmes and Mackenzie Eaglen, "Avoiding a Hollow Force," *Washington Times*, December 28, 2007.

30. In addition to other instances cited below, the following article typifies the exclusive emphasis on war spending: John M. Broder, "Views on Money for Iraq War, and What Else Could be Done with It," *New York Times*, April 14, 2008.

31. Interview while Bush was in Tanzania, February 2, 2008; Video: http://today .msnbc.msn.com/id/21134540/vp/23220908#23220908; Transcript: www.democracynow .org/2008/2/29/exclusive _ the _ three _ trillion _ dollar _ war.

32. Broder, "Money."

33. "President Bush Discusses Iraq," April 10, 2008, www.whitehouse.gov/news/re leases/2008/04/20080410-2.html.

34. Joseph E. Stiglitz and Linda J. Bilmes, *The Three Trillion Dollar War: The True Cost of the Iraq Conflict* (New York: W. W. Norton, 2008).

35. OMB Data, FY 2009 Budget. These increases are measured in current dollars of budget authority. On the VA scandal, see Dana Priest and Anne Hull, "Soldiers Face Neglect, Frustration at Army's Top Medical Facility," *Washington Post*, February 18, 2007; Anne Hull and Dana Priest, "The Hotel Aftermath: Inside Mologne House, the Survivors of War Wrestle with Military Bureaucracy and Personal Dilemmas," *Washington Post*, February 19, 2007.

36. Dina Rasor and Robert Bauman, *Betraying Our Troops: The Destructive Results of Privatizing War* (New York: Palgrave Macmillan, 2007); Jeremy Scahill, *Blackwater: The Rise of the World's Most Powerful Mercenary Army* (New York: Nation Books, 2008); James Jay Carafano, *Private Sector, Public Wars: Contractors in Combat — Afghanistan, Iraq, and Future Conflicts* (Westport, Conn.: Praeger, 2008).

37. "Rumsfeld Foresees Swift Iraq War," *BBC News Online*, February 7, 2003, http:// news.bbc.co.uk/2/hi/middle _ east/2738089.stm.

38. Cooper, "Privatizing"; P. W. Singer, *Corporate Warriors: The Rise of the Privatized Military Industry*, updated ed. (Ithaca, N.Y.: Cornell University Press, 2008), 245.

39. T. Christian Miller, "Contractors Outnumber Troops in Iraq," *Los Angeles Times*, July 4, 2007.

40. Congressional Budget Office, "Contractors' Support of U.S. Operations in Iraq," August 2008, http://cbo.gov/ftpdocs/96xx/doc9688/08-12-IraqContractors.pdf.

41. U.S. House of Representatives, Committee on Oversight and Government Re-

form, "More Dollars, Less Sense: Worsening Contracting Trends under the Bush Administration," June 2007, 3, oversight.house.gov/features/moredollars/.

42. Ibid.

43. "Private Warriors: Does Privatization Save Money?" *PBS Frontline*, June 21, 2005, www.pbs.org/wgbh/pages/frontline/shows/warriors/contractors/ceff.html.

44. Rebecca Leung, "All in the Family: Company Official Defends No-Bid Army Contract," *CBS News Online*, September 21, 2003, www.cbsnews.com/stories/2003/04/25/60minutes/main551091.shtml.

45. For example, Max Boot, "Don't Blame Halliburton" (editorial), *Los Angeles Times*, April 22, 2004.

46. "More Dollars, Less Sense," 6. This report examines all government contracts to private companies, not just those to military providers. However, the numbers do offer a clear picture of the overall trend toward outsourcing, of which military contracting was a key part.

47. Federal Acquisition Regulation, www.acquisition.gov/far/current/html/Subpart %2016_3.html.

48. Laura Peterson, "Windfalls of War: Outsourcing Government," Center for Public Integrity, October 30, 2003, http://projects.publicintegrity.org/WOW/report.aspx ?aid=68.

49. Erik Eckholm, "Democrats Step Up Criticism of Halliburton Billing in Iraq," *New York Times*, June 28, 2005. See also Singer, *Corporate Warriors*, postscript.

50. The House Committee on Oversight and Governmental Reform was active in this regard, http://oversight.house.gov/investigations.asp?ID=250.

51. As just one example, a Pentagon audit of $8.2 billion distributed by the army to contractors in Iraq found widespread violation of contracting rules, including inadequate documentation of "what, if anything, was received" for the payments. James Glanz, "Iraq Spending Ignored Rules, Pentagon Says," *New York Times*, May 23, 2008; for another, see Dana Hedgpeth and Amit R. Paley, "U.S. Says Contractors Made Little Progress on Iraq Projects," *Washington Post*, July 28, 2008. The Global Policy Forum provided links to a variety of other reports and stories, www.globalpolicy.org/security/issues/iraq/contract index.htm.

52. "More Dollars, Less Sense," 9; General Accounting Office, "Defense Contracting: Army Case Study Delineates Concerns with Use of Contractors as Contract Specialists," GAO-08-360, March 26, 2008.

53. Rasor and Bauman, *Betraying Our Troops*; Ann Scott Tyson, "U.S. Army Battling to Save Equipment," *Washington Post*, December 5, 2006.

54. The Boeing-tanker scandal, discussed in chapter 5, is the one notable exception. In late 2005 when Republican Representative Randy "Duke" Cunningham pled guilty to charges of conspiracy to commit bribery, among other things, the fact that the main payoffs came from a military contractor was not a central part of the story.

55. One example of a nonwar scandal was the following from the summer of 2008: GAO, "DCAA Audits: Allegations That Certain Audits at Three Locations Did Not Meet Professional Standards Were Substantiated," GAO-08-857, 22July 2008. For more on Operation Ill Wind, see Daniel Wirls, *Buildup: The Politics of Defense in the Reagan Era* (Ithaca, N.Y.: Cornell University Press, 1992), 204–7.

56. Singer, *Corporate Warriors*.

57. Minivans were displaced in the 1990s by SUVs in the popularity contest for larger

family vehicles. As sales of pickups and SUVs skyrocketed so did the percentage of highway miles driven by light trucks. This means that figures for average mileage of vehicles sold would bear little relationship to the amount of gas actually being consumed. From 1990 to 2003, vehicle miles of passenger cars increased about 18% while miles for light trucks increased by 74%. Bureau of Transportation Statistics, www.bts.gov/publications/national _ transportation _ statistics/2004/html/table _ 01 _ 32.html. For a detailed account of the policies and politics that facilitated the rise of the SUV, see Keith Bradsher, *High and Mighty: The Dangerous Rise of the SUV* (New York: Public Affairs, 2002).

58. President Bush urged Americans to go to Disney World, as an example, and asked "your continued participation and confidence in the American economy," www.time.com/time/nation/article/0,8599,175757,00.html. His brother Jeb, governor of Florida, wanted Americans to "consider it their patriotic duty to go shopping, go to a restaurant, take a cruise, travel with their family. . . . Frankly, the terrorists win if Americans don't go back to normalcy," www.seemagazine.com/Issues/2001/1108/front1.htm.

59. Bureau of Economic Analysis, www.bea.gov/national/xls/gap _ hist.xls.

60. For more on the cultural politics of SUVs and their relation to notions of security and masculine identity, albeit pre-9/11, see Bradsher, *High and Mighty*. To the media and advertisers so-called soccer moms became "security moms" and "SUV moms," "Goodbye 'Security Moms,' Hello 'SUV Moms,'" www.greenbergresearch.com/index.php?ID =1814; Susan Faludi, *The Terror Dream: Fear and Fantasy in Post-9/11 America* (New York: Metropolitan, 2007), especially 156–63.

61. Thom Shanker, "Proposed Military Spending Is Highest since WWII," *New York Times*, February 4, 2008; Josh White, "White House Requests $515 Billion for the Pentagon," *Washington Post*, February 5, 2008. As far as budget authority, total military spending reached the highest level since World War II in 2007. Department of Defense, Office of the Undersecretary of Defense (comptroller), *National Defense Estimates for FY 2010*, www.defenselink.mil/comptroller/Budget2010.html.

62. General Accounting Office, "Defense Acquisitions: Assessments of Selected Weapons Programs," GAO-08-467SP, March 2008; Charlie Savage, "Senator Warns of a Crisis in Pentagon Cost Overruns," *New York Times*, June 4, 2008; Walter Pincus, "GAO Cites Spiraling Costs of New Weapons Programs," *Washington Post*, July 7, 2008.

63. Michael Luo, "Romney Says He'll Expand Armed Forces by 100,000," *New York Times*, April 11, 2007; "Policy Briefing: Governor Mitt Romney's Remarks at the George Bush Presidential Library Center," April 10, 2007, www.mittromney.com; Mitt Romney, "Rising to a New Generation of Global Challenges," *Foreign Affairs* (July/August 2007): 23–24.

64. Chris Dixon and Marc Santora, "Giuliani, Speaking at the Citadel, Calls for a Bigger Army," *New York Times*, May 6, 2007.

65. John McCain, "An Enduring Peace Built on Freedom," *Foreign Affairs* (November/December 2007): 23–24.

66. Michael D. Huckabee, "American's Priorities in the War on Terror," *Foreign Affairs* (January/February 2008): 158–59.

67. Hillary Rodham Clinton, "Security and Opportunity for the Twenty-first Century," *Foreign Affairs* (November/December 2007): 7–8.

68. "The fact of the matter is, we are going to need more troops than we currently possess. . . . There's probably going to be a bump in initial military spending just to get back to where we were." David Yepsen, "Can a Candidate Be Too Candid? Obama's Bid May

Provide Answer," *Des Moines Register*, February 12, 2007, desmoinesregister.com; Barack Obama, "Renewing American Leadership," *Foreign Affairs* (July/August 2007): 6–7.

69. John Edwards, "Reengaging with the World: A Return to Moral Leadership," *Foreign Affairs* (September/October 2007): 32.

70. See Obama's speech to the Chicago Council on Global Affairs, April 23, 2007, www.cfr.org/publication/13172/.

71. Commission on Presidential Debates, www.debates.org/pages/debtrans.html. In the first debate, and in reference to the deficit and budget discipline, McCain promoted the idea of a budget freeze except for military and veteran spending. McCain also made a reference to his role in stopping the Boeing tanker deal that was probably incomprehensible to most viewers without greater context and explanation. Obama criticized the war in Iraq and vowed to send more troops to Afghanistan but said nothing about the buildup or military spending.

72. Politicians aside, some articles written by academics echoed these hawkish assumptions and arguments in an often careless and essentially data-free manner. For example, prominent Harvard economist Martin Feldstein, a former chairman of the President's Council of Economic Advisors, argued that the Pentagon is "underfunded" and the defense budget required a "substantial rise" ("The Underfunded Pentagon," *Foreign Affairs* [March/April 2007]: 134–40). Others were more careful, including Charles A. Kupchan and Peter L. Trubowitz ("Grand Strategy for a Divided America," *Foreign Affairs* [July/August 2007]: 71–83), who advocated a "politically solvent" strategy that scales back commitments to balance ends and means but called for the U.S. to "rebuild its hard power" by allocating the money necessary to "redress the devastating effect of the Iraq war."

73. Congressional Budget Office, "A Preliminary Analysis of the President's Budget and an Update of CBO's Budget and Economic Outlook," March 2009, www.cbo.gov/ftpdocs/100xx/doc10014/toc.htm.

74. "Public Support for Stimulus Package Unchanged at 52%, Seven in 10 Favor Some Type of Stimulus Legislation," www.gallup.com/poll/114184/Public-Support-Stimulus-Package-Unchanged.aspx; "Support for Stimulus Plan Slips, but Obama Rides High," http://people-press.org/report/490/obama-stimulus.

75. Thom Shanker, "After Stimulus Package, Pentagon Officials Are Preparing to Pare Back, *New York Times*, February 18, 2009.

76. DoD News Briefing with Secretary Gates from the Pentagon, transcript, April 6, 2009, www.defenselink.mil/transcripts/transcript.aspx?transcriptid=4396.

77. See for example, Kathryn Buschman Vasel, *Fox Business News*, "Gates' Cuts Could Hurt Defense Contractors," April 7, 2009, www.foxbusiness.com/story/markets/industries/government/gates-cuts-hurt-defense-contractors/; CNN.com, "Congress Reacts to Gates' Pentagon Budget Shifts," April 7, 2009, www.cnn.com/2009/POLITICS/04/07/congress.defense/index.html?iref=newssearch; CBS News, "Pentagon Seeks Defense Budget 'Overhaul,'" April 6, 2009, www.cbsnews.com/stories/2009/04/06/politics/main4923173.shtml?source=search_story.

78. DoD News Briefing with Secretary Gates from the Pentagon, Transcript, April 6, 2009, www.defenselink.mil/transcripts/transcript.aspx?transcriptid=4396; Christopher Drew and Elisabeth Bumiller, "Military Budget Reflects a Shift in U.S. Strategy," *New York Times*, April 7, 2009; Greg Jaffe and Shailagh Murray, "Gates Seeks Sharp Turn in Spending, Defense Budget Focuses on Lower-Tech Weapons," *Washington Post*, April 7, 2009.

79. Associated Press, "Obama Seeks $83B for War Spending in Iraq, Afghanistan," April 9, 2009.

80. Dana Milbank, "Pentagon Chief Calls for Cuts; Congress Opens Fire," *Washington Post*, April 7, 2009.

81. Lockheed Martin sponsored, among other things, a web-based petition campaign and designed location-specific ads, www.preserveraptorjobs.com/.

82. Press releases and a copy of the Connecticut delegation letter were available at several members' websites: http://lieberman.senate.gov/newsroom/http//:chrismurphy.house.gov/; http://delauro.house.gov/release.cfm?id=2280.

83. Scott Mayerowitz, "Will New Military Budget Prolong Recession?" ABC News, April 8, 2009, http://Abcnews.Go.Com/Business/Economy/Story?Id=7282659&Page=1.

84. Two Boeing airframe programs, the F-18 and the C-17 transport, were being ended or curtailed, and Boeing was affected by other cuts as well, including in missile defense; "Bond: We Cannot Afford to Sacrifice National Security," April 6, 2009, http://bond.senate.gov/public/index.cfm?FuseAction=PressRoom.NewsReleases.

85. Rosa DeLauro (D-CT), one of the most liberal members of Congress, illustrates how far this could go. In one and the same April 7, 2009 press release, the representative lamented the termination of F-22A production and applauded Gates's toughness elsewhere, including termination of the new presidential helicopter program. But DeLauro added that the original contractor for that program, Lockheed Martin, had no experience with helicopters, whereas Connecticut's "Sikorsky has a strong five-decade record of building these helicopters — on-time and on-budget." Anticipating better luck for her state with the helicopter program, DeLauro pledged that when a new program was put forward she would ensure that taxpayers get the best value; http://delauro.house.gov/release.cfm?id=2280.

86. "Inhofe Says Obama Defense Cuts Will 'Disarm America,'" April 6, 2009, http://inhofe.senate.gov/public/index.cfm?FuseAction=PressRoom.PressReleases.

87. "Bipartisan Group of Senators Oppose Cuts in Missile Defense," April 6, 2009, http://murkowski.senate.gov/public/index.cfm?FuseAction=PressOffice.PressReleases.

88. http://lgraham.senate.gov/public/.

89. http://mccain.senate.gov/public; http://webb.senate.gov/public.

90. Audrey Hudson and Eli Lake, "Federal Agency Warns of Radicals on Right," *Washington Times*, April 14, 2009; Eileen Sullivan, "Report: US Is Ripe for Recruiting by Extremists," Associated Press, April 14, 2009. A report by the Southern Poverty Law Center made a similar argument based on their survey of group membership and activities, www.splcenter.org/intel/intelreport/article.jsp?aid=1027.

91. Elisabeth Bumiller, "Going Slow on Gay Issue," *New York Times*, April 17, 2009.

index

Abercrombie, Neil, 75
Abu Ghraib, 125
Afghanistan, war in, 2, 109, 116, 118, 151,
    185; G. W. Bush and, 132, 160, 168; Cold
    War and, 24, 26, 42; Congress and, 12,
    130; cost of, 157–58, 179–80, 193, 197; as
    "forgotten war," 174; military buildup
    and, 16, 134; Obama and, 17, 191, 193;
    supplemental war appropriations for, 1,
    155–56; transformation and, 148–49
air force, U.S., 158, 161–63; increases in
    funding for, 138; proposed cuts to, 44–45,
    80–81, 137; weapons systems for, 1, 145–
    46, 148, 194
Al Qaeda, 103, 128, 149, 152, 168
Anti-Ballistic Missile Treaty (ABM), 151–53
Armey, Dick, 77
arms sales: G. H. W. Bush and, 65–66; Clin-
    ton and, 66–69; Congress and, 67–68;
    control of, 65; defense industry support
    of, 67–68; Direct Commercial Sales, 68;
    Excess Defense Articles (EDA), 68–69;
    Foreign Military Sales (FMS), 66–68; in-
    crease in, 63–64; of surplus military parts,
    69, 209n38
army, U.S., 29; funding, increases in, 137–
    38, 194–95; increased size of under G. W.
    Bush, 177; increasing size of, calls for,
    191–92; overextension of troops, 149–50;
    privatization and, 70–71, 185; proposed
    cuts to, 44–45; transformation and, 96,
    138, 155–56, 158–60; weapons sales and,
    66, 68; weapons systems for, 1, 145, 147–
    48, 155–56
Aspin, Les, 41, 42, 44, 47, 54, 59
axis of evil. See *under* global war on terror

B-1 Lancer, 45
B-2 Stealth Bomber, 83, 146
B-52 Stratofortress, 35
Bacon, Ken, 67
Baird, Zoë, 53
ballistic missile defense (BMD), 1, 117, 141,
    195, 222n54; G. H. W. Bush and, 48, 94;
    G. W. Bush and, 92–94, 131, 141, 144,
    151–54; Clinton and, 14, 45, 50, 79, 86–
    88; Commission to Assess the Ballistic
    Missile Threat (Rumsfeld Commission),
    87; Congress and, 20, 87, 128, 131, 152,
    153, 164; cost of, 154; deterrence and,
    119–20; Global Protection against Lim-
    ited Strikes (GPALS), 47, 49–50, 152–53;
    Gulf War and, 49; Obama and, 195–96;
    Reagan and, 20–21, 24, 26, 48, 139, 154;
    Republican support of, 14–15, 48, 78, 87–
    89, 92, 151
Base Force, 27, 29–33, 36, 41–42, 44, 49,
    59, 82
bases, military, post–Cold War closures, 61;
    Base Realignment and Closure Commis-
    sion (BRAC), 56–57; clean up, costs of,
    57–58, 207n11; Congress and, 56–57,
    130–31
Begich, Mark, 196
Bereuter, Doug, 130
Black Hawk helicopter, 160
Boeing, 60, 195, 219–20n12; tanker scandal,
    161–63, 224n86
Bond, Chris, 195
Bosnia, war in, 5, 14, 72, 73, 74
Bottom-Up Review (BUR), 13–14, 52, 54,
    62; conservative critique of, 46–47, 80;
    cuts in military personnel, proposed, 44,